I0795638

IMAGES
of America

WILLINGBORO

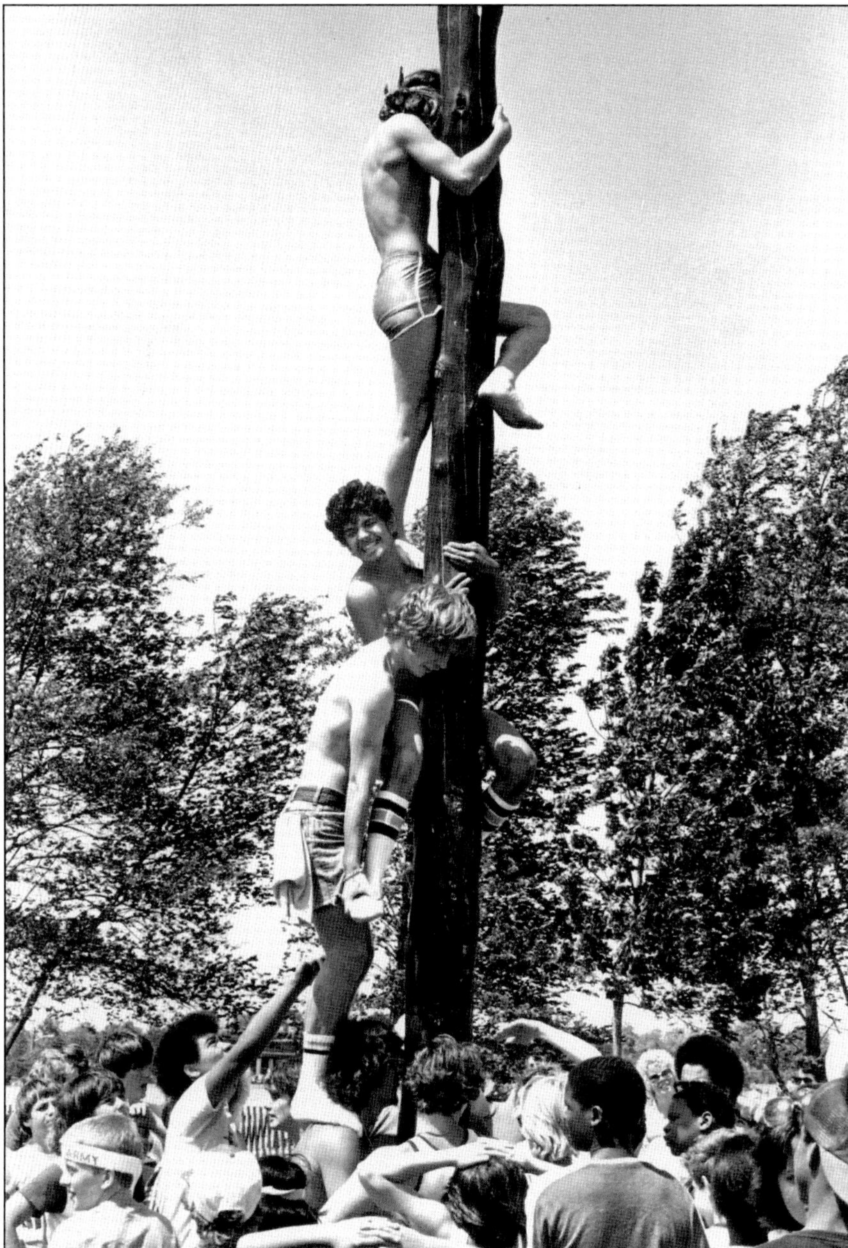

The township's recreation department sponsored the first Fun Day at Mill Creek Park in 1976. At the event in 1980, several shirtless boys attempt to scale a greased pole. They did not make it. (Courtesy Burlington County Times.)

On the cover: Children bicycle down a paved path under the high-tension wires that stretch across the township. In 1960, the Westinghouse Corporation used Willingboro as the backdrop for its "picture of everyday American family life" advertising campaign. (Courtesy Willingboro Township Manager's Office.)

IMAGES
of America

WILLINGBORO

Josh Bernstein

ARCADIA
PUBLISHING

ISBN 978-0-7385-1088-0

Published by Arcadia Publishing
Charleston, South Carolina

Printed in the United States of America

Library of Congress Catalog Card Number: 2002107715

For all general information contact Arcadia Publishing at:
Telephone 843-853-2070
Fax 843-853-0044
E-Mail sales@arcadiapublishing.com
For customer service and orders:
Toll-Free 1-888-313-2665

Visit us on the Internet at www.arcadiapublishing.com

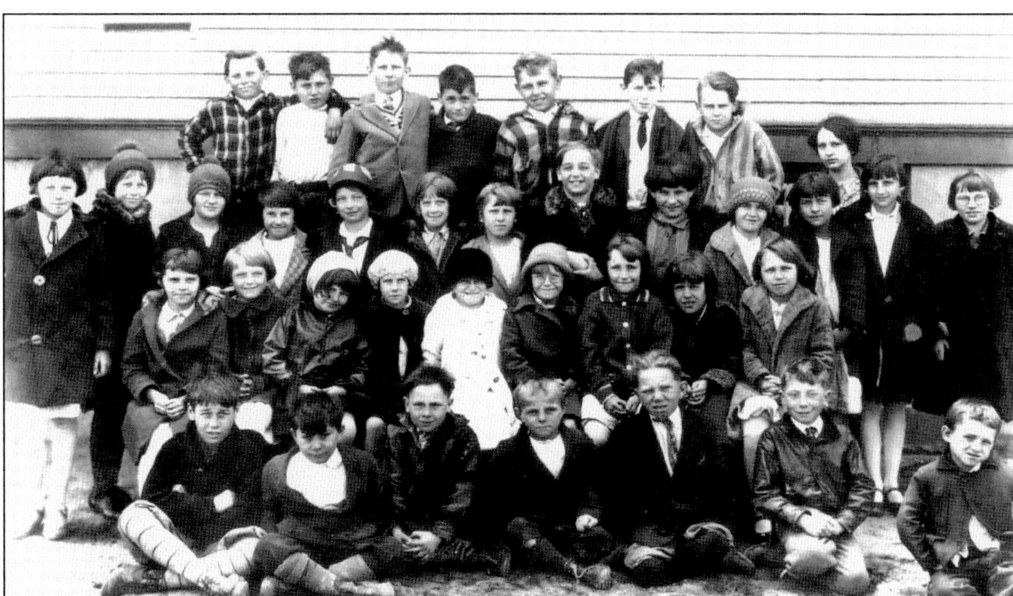

These bundled-up yet well-dressed pupils pose for a class photograph in 1927. During the 1920s, more than 700 people lived in rural Willingboro. (Courtesy Carol J. Suplee.)

Contents

ACKNOWLEDGMENTS

My deepest appreciation goes to my wife, Angie, for all her love and support, and for giving me first shot at the computer for six months. This book would have been impossible without the assistance of the management, staff, and photographers—past and present—of the Burlington County Times, whose existence mirrors Levitt and Sons' development. I also would like to thank the following for their help and contributions to this project: the Willingboro Township Manager's Office, the Willingboro Township Council, the Willingboro Public Library, the Willingboro and Rancocas Historical Societies, the Delanco Township Committee, Betty Sever, Carol Suplee, Dave Retzko, Marion Huddleston, Christopher Bishop, the Corpus Christi Roman Catholic Church, and the Stuart and Cramp families.

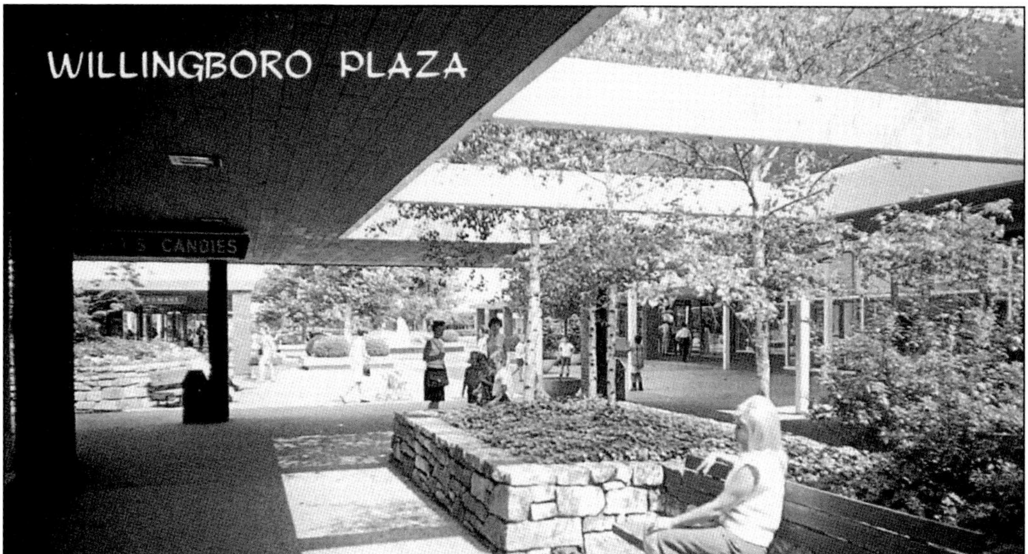

Like many newer towns in the region, Levitt's Willingboro did not have a main street. However, the town did have a gathering place and center of commerce. The Willingboro Plaza, as shown in this postcard, was built on 56 acres along Route 130. It was the area's first large open-air mall and for many years was the premier place to shop. (Courtesy Carol J. Suplee.)

Introduction

For millennia, a stretch of the Rancocas Creek near the Delaware River was a haven for the Lenape Indians. Fish filled the creek, waterfowl thrived, and elk, bear, and deer populated the woods. Early in the 17th century, Dutch and Swedish settlers found the area attractive and traded with the Lenape. In 1677, a group of Quaker commissioners from England purchased the land from the Lenape for the less-than-grandiose price of six match coats, guns, hatchets, and kettles. The region that became known as West Jersey was born.

Among those West Jersey Quakers was a man named Thomas Ollive. Along with several others, Ollive quickly purchased land along the Rancocas Creek and Delaware River. By 1682, Ollive had named his portion of land Wellingborough after his English hometown. Six years later, the Colonial governor established the constabulary of Wellingborrow. Wellingborough became 15 square miles located between Philadelphia and the West Jersey capital of Burlington and was one of Burlington County's 11 original municipalities. The spelling of the town's name varied over the years: Wellingborough, Wellingborrow, and Willingborough. Farms dominated the landscape. There were three villages: Rancocas, Charleston, and Coopertown. Residents traveled by land and by water, but traveling was not free. Burlington County records show that in 1692 the first toll bridge in West Jersey was constructed across Thomas Ollive's Mill Dam.

In the mid-18th century, discontent with British rule—especially with taxes—swept through the colonies. Not far from Philadelphia and New York, Willingboro's farmers were not immune from revolutionary feelings. Although no tea parties occurred here, Willingboro did have a focus for its British hatred.

In 1770, William Franklin, son of Philadelphia statesman Benjamin Franklin and the last royal governor of New Jersey, purchased a Georgian-style country house at what now is the intersection of Beverly-Rancocas Road and John F. Kennedy Way. The 525-acre estate included farmland, English-style gardens, and a forest filled with deer. The simmering rebellion frightened Franklin. Within five years of moving to Willingboro, he fled to a mansion owned by British sympathizers in Perth Amboy, East Jersey. Franklin could not escape, however, and Colonial revolutionaries arrested him in June 1776. Franklin sold the Willingboro estate in 1785. He died in England in 1813. The house burned to the ground in 1839.

No Revolutionary War battles were fought in Willingboro, but its access to the Delaware River and Rancocas Creek made it a convenient corridor for British and Colonial troops marching through the state. Six months after the Colonials deposed Franklin, Gen. George Washington massed his battered army at Valley Forge, Pennsylvania. Gen. George Washington crossed the Delaware River on Christmas day of 1776 and surprised the Hessians camped at Trenton. Many people may be unaware that Washington also planned to send 1,600 men across the river to a wharf in Willingboro known as Dunk's Ferry. The troops were to march through town and attack the British in Mount Holly. Poor weather prevented a large-scale local crossing, but older residents have not forgotten Washington's intentions.

After the war, Willingboro settled into a quiet farming existence. In 1834, the Camden and Amboy Railroad installed tracks through the town. Four years later the first post office opened here.

Willingboro grew throughout the early 19th century. In 1844, some 900 people called the town home. However, many of the newcomers settled in a development on the banks of the Delaware called Beverly. By 1858, the "city" dwellers outnumbered the farmers. The Beverly residents moved the polls into the town and then challenged the credentials of the farmers who came there to vote. Beverly residents also exempted themselves from paying taxes for road maintenance, forcing the farmers to shoulder an increased financial burden. That year, the township committee voted to divide the town. The state legislature made the act final in 1859, setting the boundary at the Burlington-Willingboro Turnpike (Route 130). With a stroke of the pen, Willingboro's population fell to 643.

Life in Willingboro remained fairly stable for the next 90 years, even as its young men left to fight the Civil War, World War I, and World War II. In 1950, the population of the town stood at 852.

In the early 1950s, however, everything began to change. Soldiers returning from World War II created a demand for new housing at affordable prices. One of the first developers to realize this need was New Yorker William Levitt. On Long Island, his company bought adjoining tracts of land in a number of towns and built houses. That development became the nation's first Levittown. A few years later, Levitt purchased land in congruous municipalities in Bucks County, Pennsylvania. This new community became known as Levittown as well. Building a development in different towns was problematic. Each town possessed its own zoning and construction regulations—legal headaches Levitt swore to avoid in his next project. The third Levittown, he determined, would be carved out of one locality.

In 1954, Levitt and Sons began purchasing farms in Willingboro. Within two years, the company spent $8 million on 4,500 acres of land—90 percent of the township. In 1956, the state legislature redrew Willingboro's boundaries, which gave Rancocas Village to Westampton. The new Willingboro had shrunk to seven and a half square miles. Within four years of Levitt's first land purchase, the new community began to take shape. Levitt burned the old buildings—some of them dating to 1790—and replaced them with prefabricated homes that were transported to Willingboro in pieces. Leo Mount and his wife purchased the first new Levittown home on Sussex Drive in 1958. In 1959, the changing community's new residents voted to change the name of the town from Willingboro to Levittown.

This third Levittown became the finest example of post–World War II suburban planning, with affordable homes divided into neighborhoods called parks. Each park had a school and a swimming pool, with winding streets that eventually opened onto broad, landscaped parkways. The first letter of each street was the same as the park name. Therefore, if people said they lived on Pebble Lane, you could tell they lived in Pennypacker Park.

The new Levittown, however, was segregated. Levitt would not sell homes to African Americans, and the deeds he conveyed forbade their sale to minorities. Like many of the potential new residents, Rev. Willie James was a soldier at nearby Fort Dix. After Levitt refused to sell James a house, the soldier sued. The U.S. Supreme Court found in James's favor, forcing Levitt to open Willingboro and his other communities to minorities.

Between 1958 and 1972, Levitt built 11,000 homes in 13 parks. From 1950 to 1970, Levittown's population skyrocketed from 852 to 43,236. In 1960, the Westinghouse Corporation used the town as the backdrop for its "picture of everyday American family life" advertising campaign. Indeed, the residents of Willingboro (voters changed the name back in 1963) possessed many amenities. The town had religious institutions, a hospital, a golf course, the region's premier shopping mall, and a lakefront resort.

Thomas Ollive probably would not recognize today's diverse Willingboro. But the community he founded on the banks of the Rancocas Creek more than 300 years ago has left its mark on the American landscape.

One

West Jersey Farmers

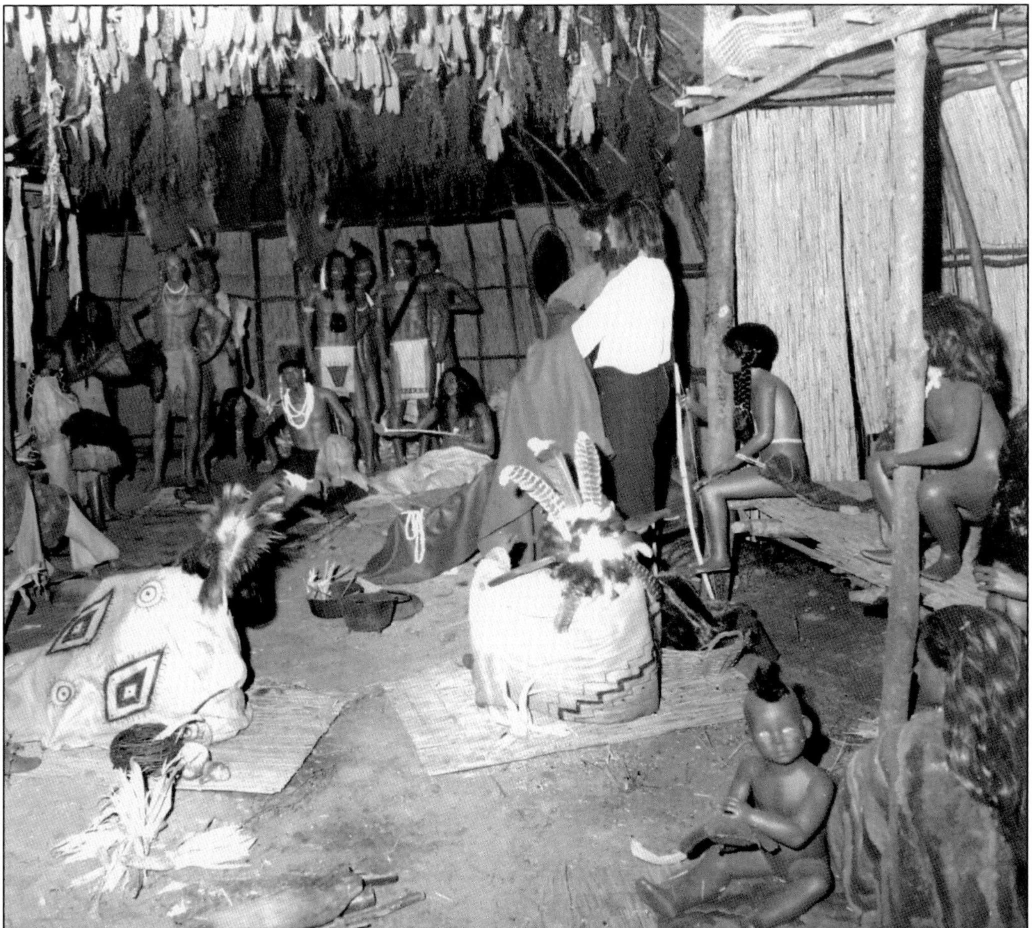

Long before Europeans came to the New World, Native Americans inhabited the land. In New Jersey, they were the Lenape Indians, part of the Algonquin nation. In 1677, a group of Quakers "purchased" from the Lenape the land that came to include Willingboro, reportedly for six match coats, guns, hatchets, hoes, and kettles. Although it is difficult to say just how the Quakers and Lenape interacted, this depiction from Waterloo Village State Park gives us an idea. (Courtesy Carol J. Suplee/Waterloo Village State Park.)

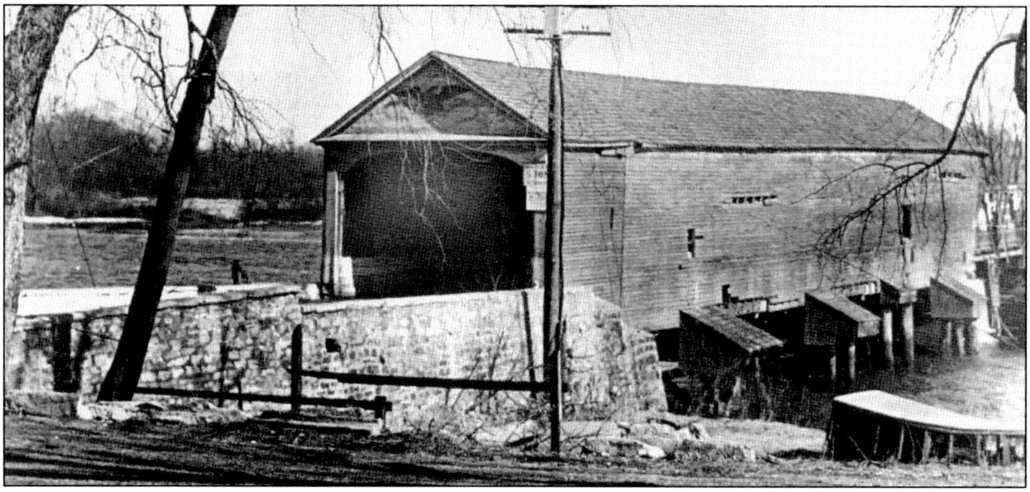

In 1747 and 1748, area residents established a road going from Burlington to Cooper's Ferry in Camden. From 1748 to 1793, the only way to cross the Rancocas Creek at Bridgeboro was by ferry. In 1793, residents constructed a toll bridge across the creek. In 1838, that span was replaced by a wood covered bridge (above) at a cost of $19,537. The floor of the bridge was supported by four massive oak arches—two on each side of a single draw—which slid back over the floor to allow a boat to pass. A wood frame covered the outside of the arches. According to township records, locust wood pins held the structure together. At one end of the bridge, there was a painting of a large American eagle with the motto *E Pluribus Unum*. (Courtesy Burlington County Times/Burlington County Historical Society.)

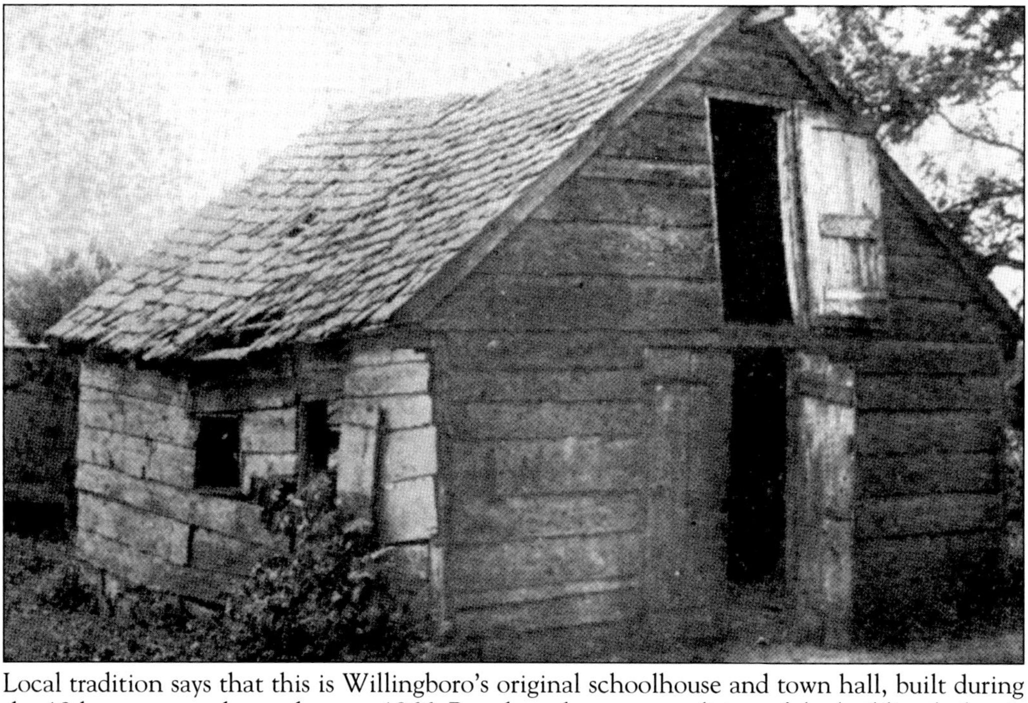

Local tradition says that this is Willingboro's original schoolhouse and town hall, built during the 18th century and torn down c. 1866. Based on the poor condition of the building before it was razed, one can debate when, or whether, it actually was used for classes. (Courtesy Carol J. Suplee/Stuart family.)

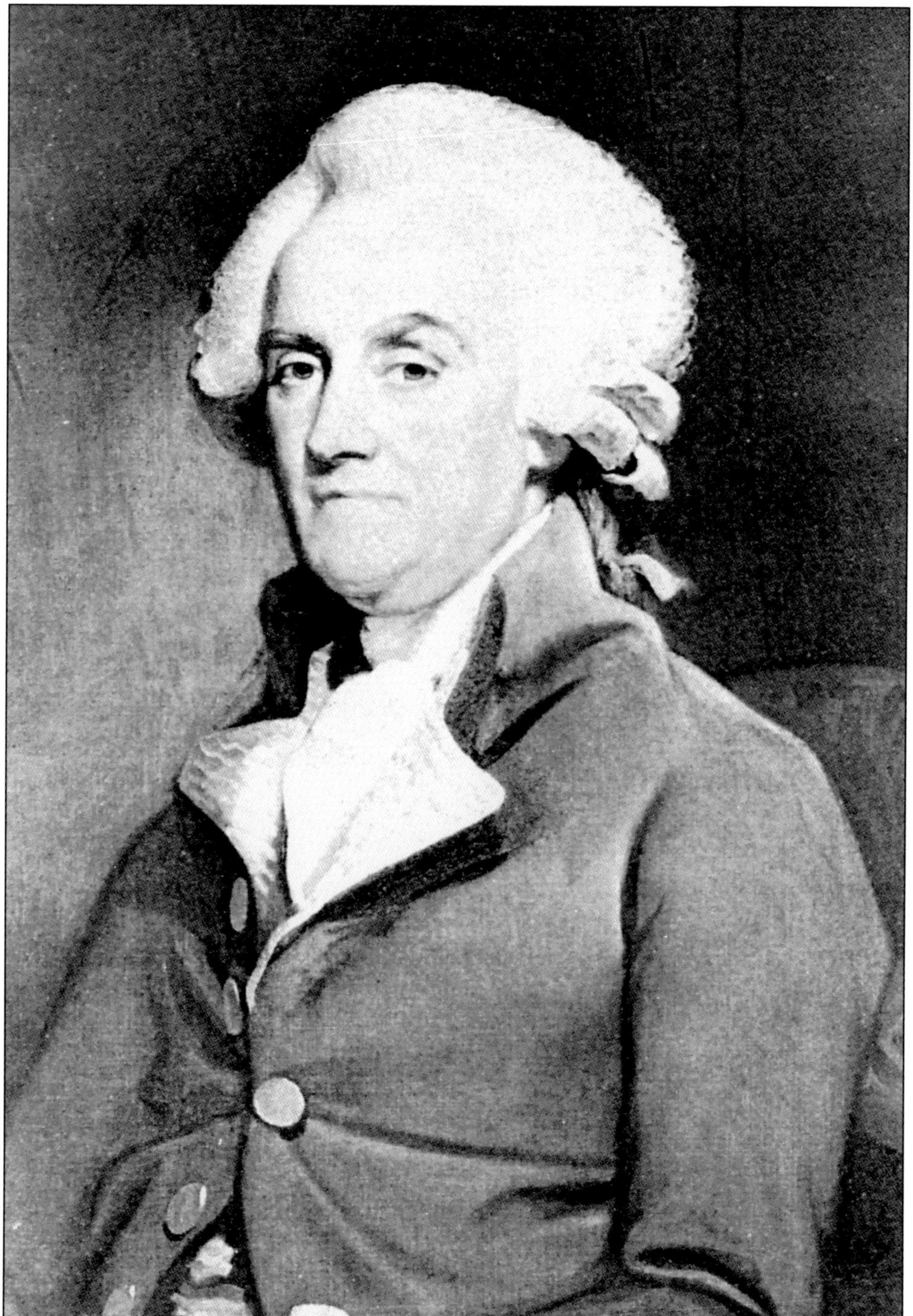

Willingboro's most famous resident was William Franklin, son of Benjamin Franklin and the last royal governor of New Jersey. William Franklin owned a Georgian-style country house and more than 500 acres of farm, gardens, and woods populated with deer from 1770 to 1785. Colonial revolutionaries arrested him in June 1776, and he died in England in 1813. (Courtesy Burlington County Times.)

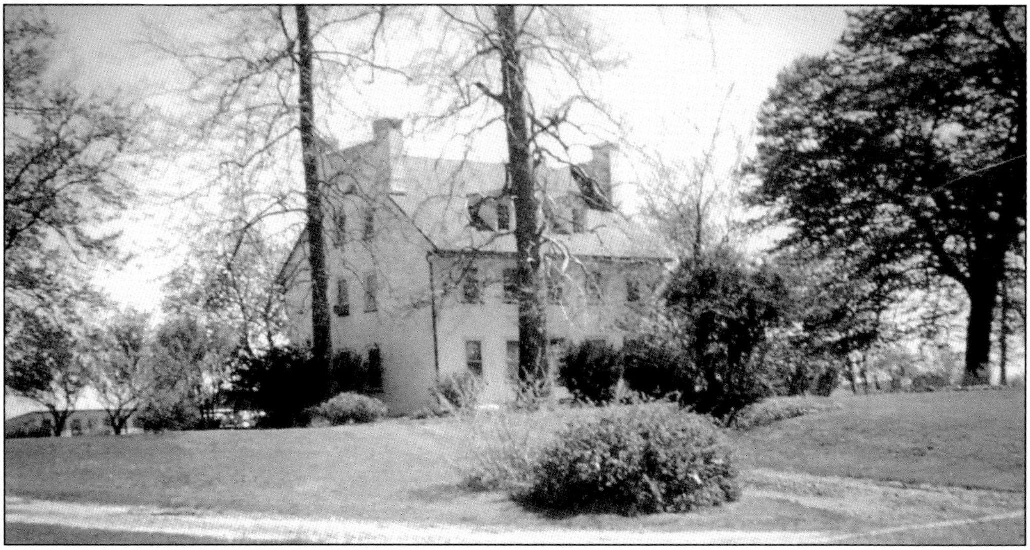

This house at Beverly-Rancocas Road and John F. Kennedy Way stood on the site of the homestead of William Franklin, son of Benjamin and the last royal governor of New Jersey. Franklin owned the 525-acre property from 1770 to 1785. It included English-style gardens and a forested area filled with deer that came to be known as Deer Park. The Franklin home burned down in 1839. The rebuilt home (above) belonged to the Buzby family but fell to the wrecking ball in the later years of the township's development. (Courtesy Carol J. Suplee/Cramp family.)

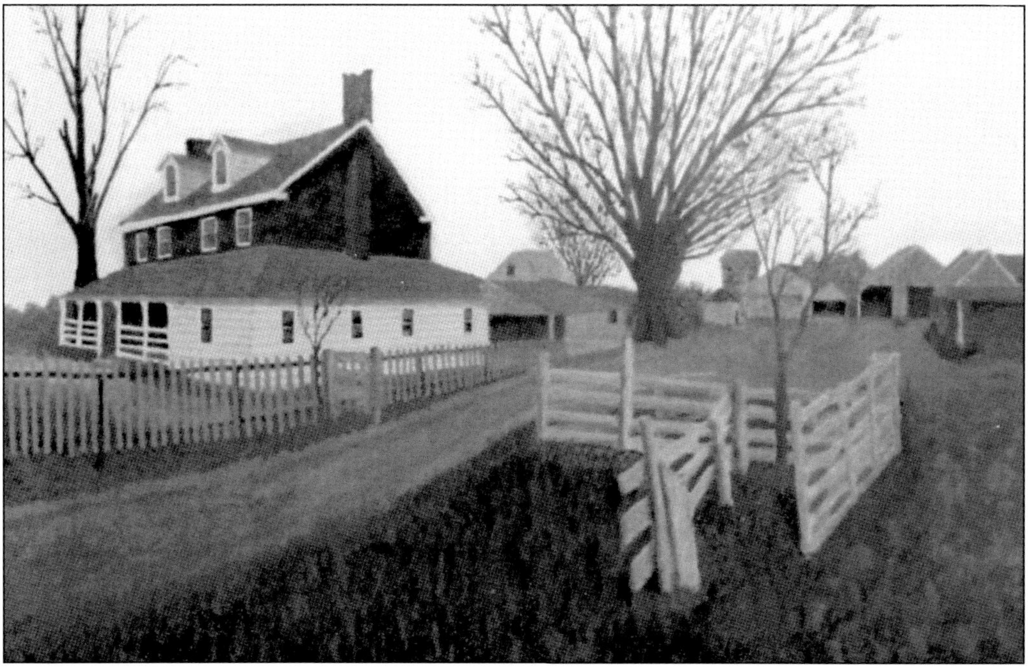

While Quakers opposed slavery, the practice did exist in Burlington County and early Willingboro. Indeed, Thomas Ollive, the town's founder, owned slaves. This is a painting of the Bishop farm where, according to a descendant, slaves lived and worked. (Courtesy Christopher Bishop.)

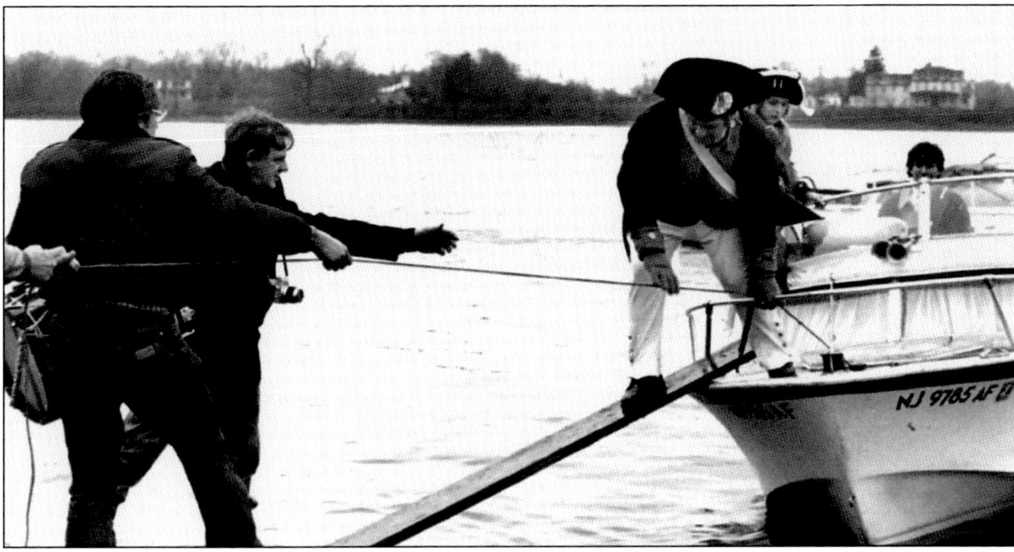

Everyone may know that Gen. George Washington crossed the Delaware River on Christmas 1776 to surprise the Hessians camped at Trenton; however, many people may not be aware that Washington planned to send 1,600 men across the river to a wharf in Wellingborough known as Dunk's Ferry. The troops were to march through town and attack the British in Mount Holly. Poor weather prevented a large-scale local crossing; therefore, the town was not allowed this significant role in the Revolutionary War. Still, these volunteers in December 1975 demonstrate how the crossing would have appeared. (Courtesy Burlington County Times.)

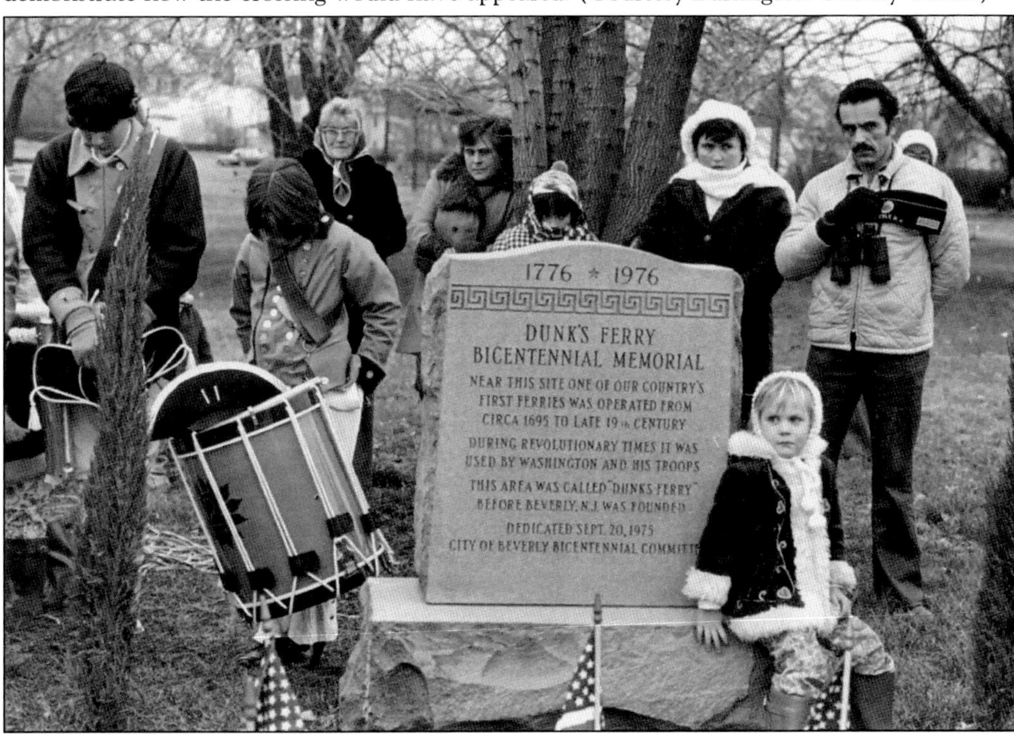

Today, Dunk's Ferry is part of Beverly. In 1975, the city dedicated a monument to the site's history. (Courtesy Burlington County Times.)

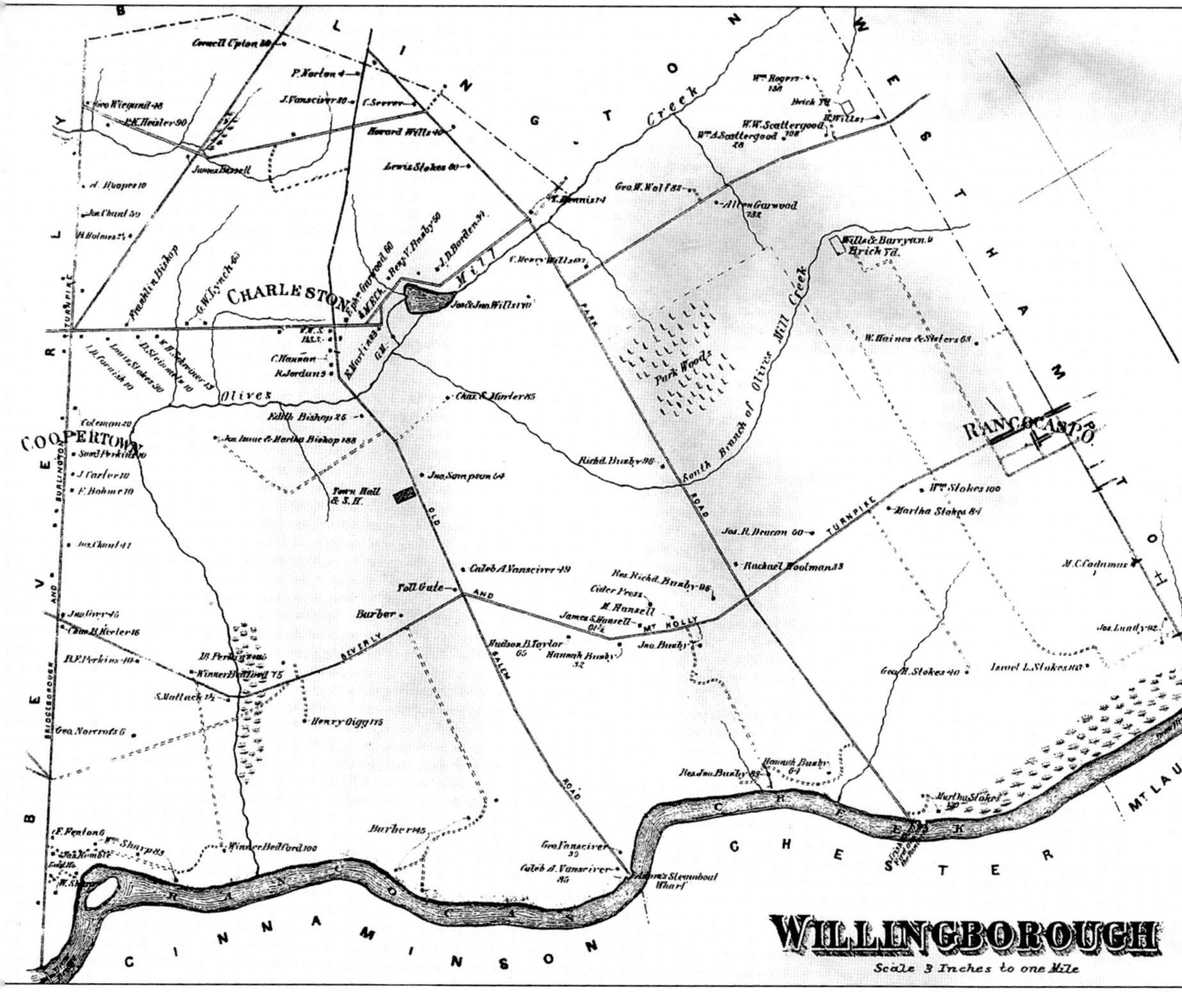

This map by Philadelphia native J.D. Scott depicts Willingboro's villages, streets, and farms in 1876. At the time, the town's name was spelled "Willingborough." Until the early 20th century, the name had several different spellings. (Courtesy *Combination Atlas Map of Burlington County*, republished by the Burlington County Historical Society.)

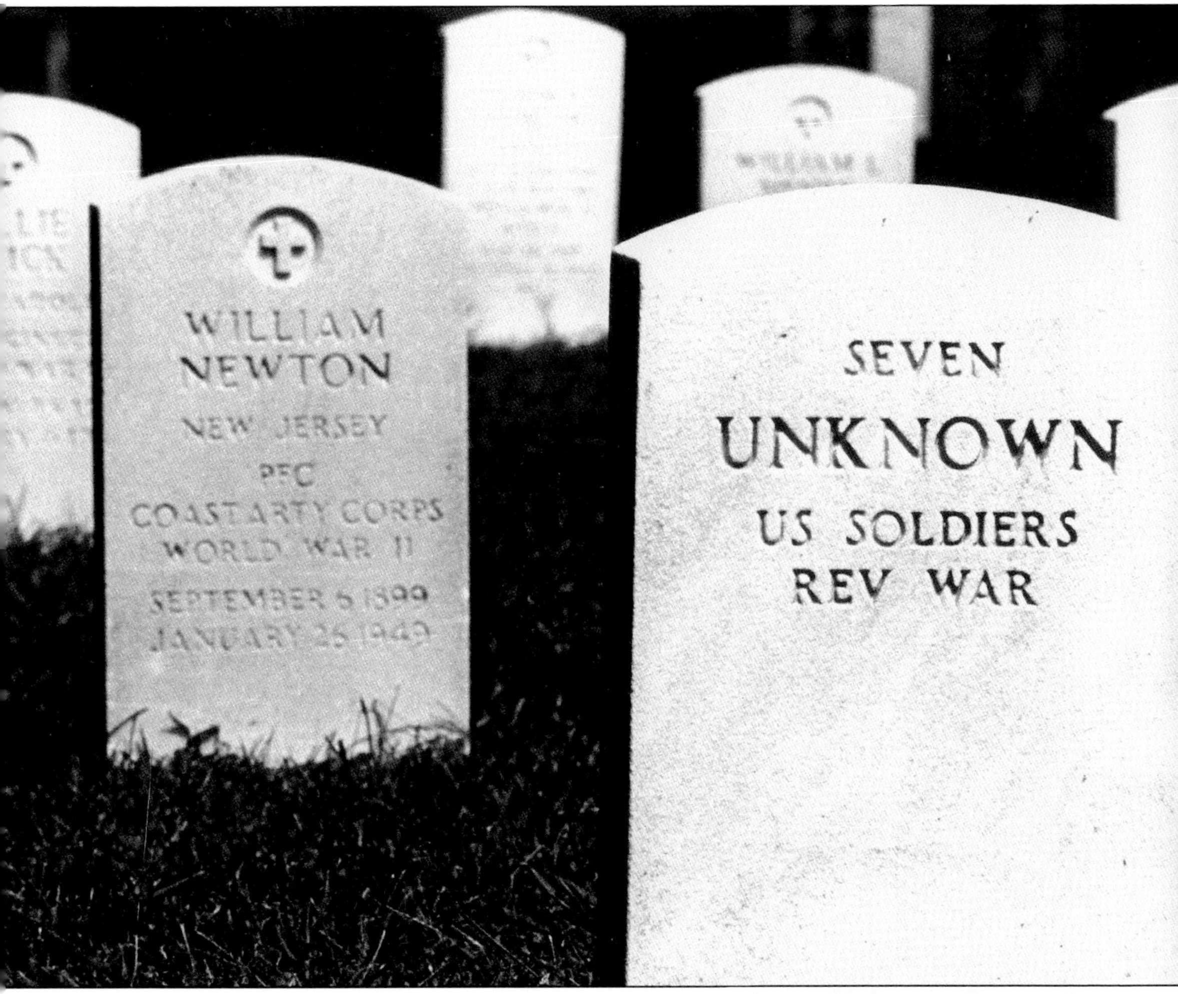

In 1862, Pres. Abraham Lincoln signed an act authorizing the establishment of national cemeteries "for soldiers who shall die in the service of the country." Beverly National Cemetery was established in August 1864 to inter the remains of those killed in the Civil War. Although no battles were fought in Beverly, which until 1859 was part of Willingboro, the area was used to treat wounded soldiers who could not be cared for in the crowded hospitals of Philadelphia. Patients were transported from Philadelphia to Beverly on the river steamer *John A. Warner*. Local residents then used wagons to take the patients to a building on Broad Street. Although the building was officially a "convalescent hospital," operations and amputations were performed there. Amputated limbs and dead soldiers were taken to a 1.2-acre property owned by Christian Weyman, who later conveyed the property to the federal government. Today, the cemetery is part of Edgewater Park and contains the remains of soldiers from the Revolutionary War through the Persian Gulf War. (Courtesy Burlington County Times.)

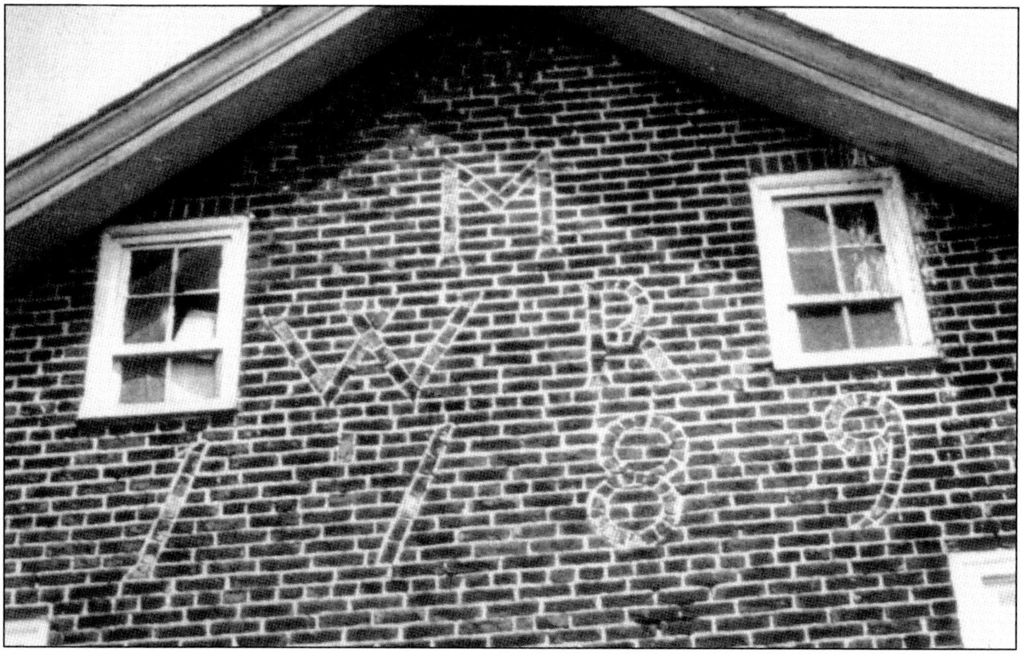

This large brick house bearing the initials MWR was built in 1789, the year the Constitution was ratified. It served as home for Willingboro families for 170 years before being burned to the ground in 1959 to make way for Levitt and Sons' new community. (Courtesy Willingboro Public Library/Stuart family.)

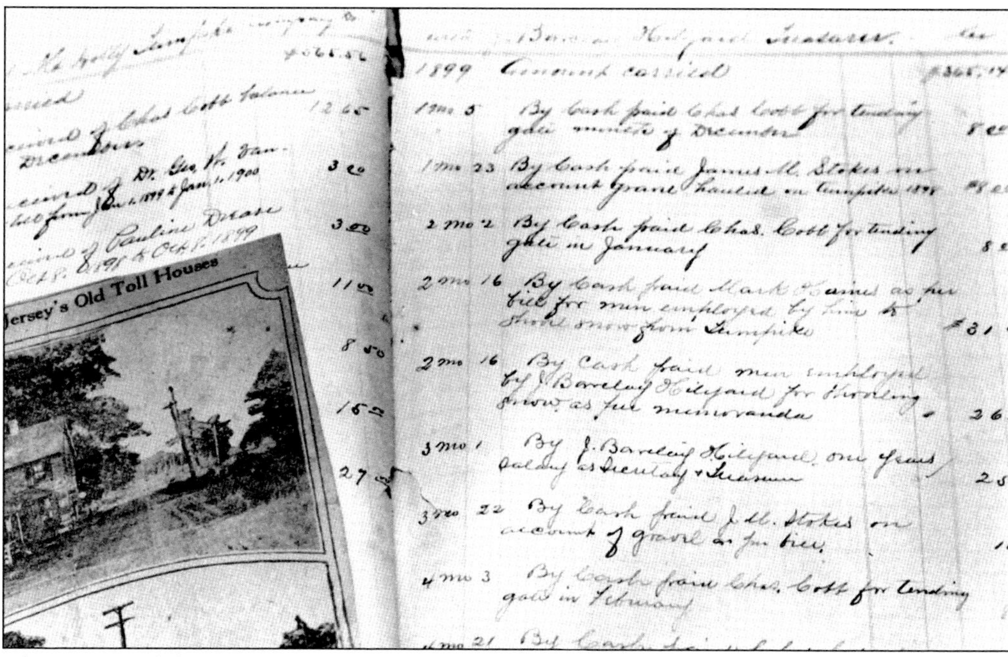

The owners of the Beverly and Mount Holly Turnpike Company kept careful records of who used the road and passed by the tollhouse at Salem Road and Beverly–Mount Holly Road, which was also known as the Oyster Shell Trail and, later, Beverly-Rancocas Road. The above records are from 1899. (Courtesy Burlington County Times.)

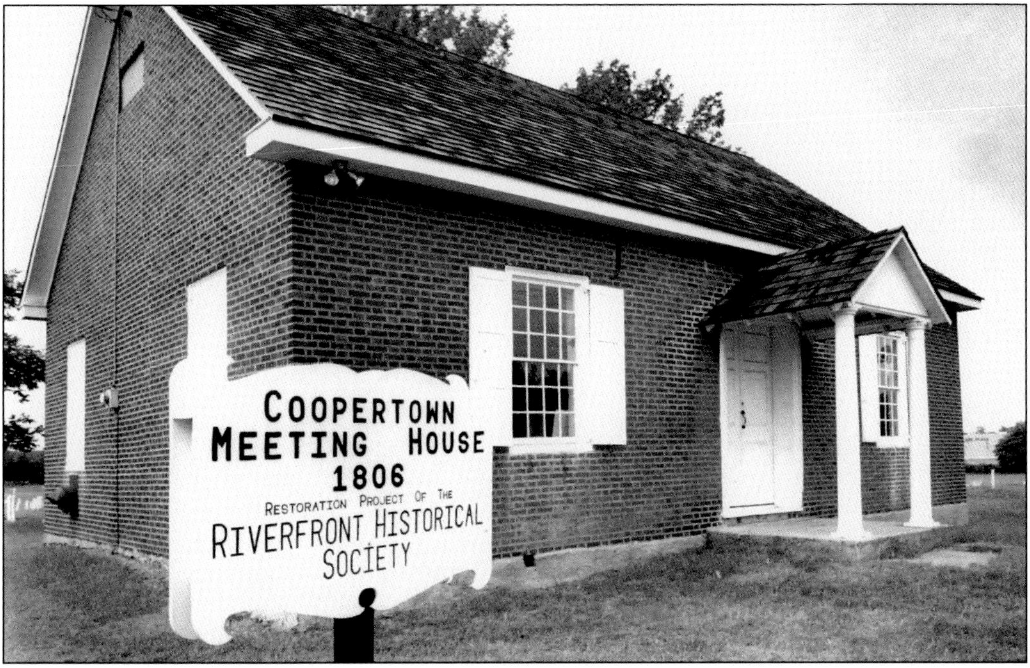

Coopertown was a small village within Willingboro. The village received its name from William Cooper, father of author James Fenimore Cooper. The Quaker meetinghouse was established in 1806. (Courtesy Burlington County Times.)

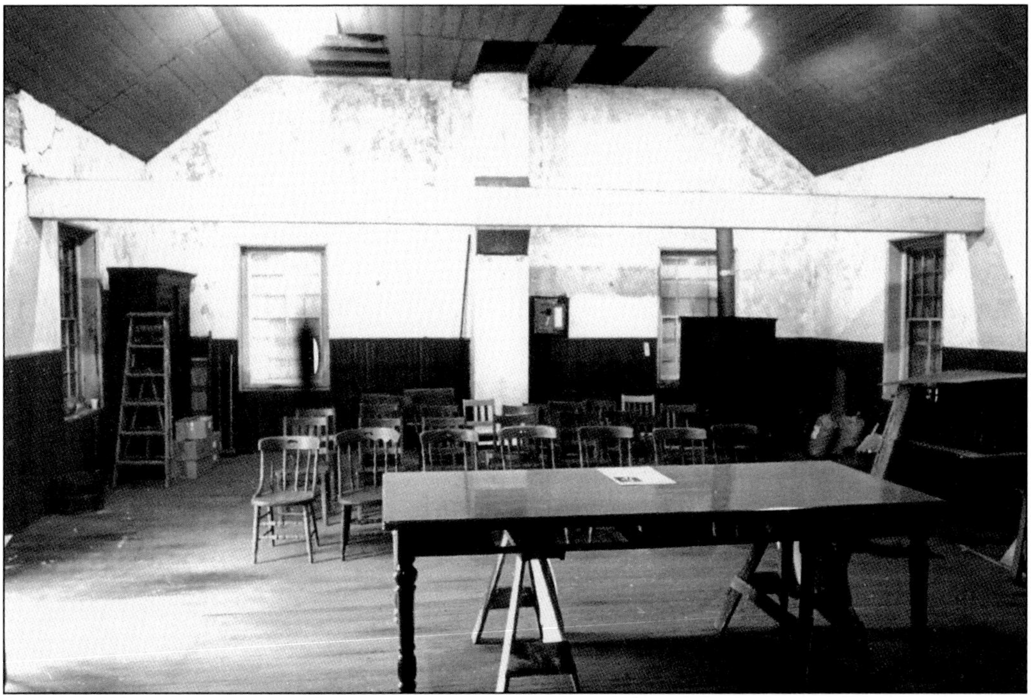

This is an interior view of the Coopertown Meeting House, which also has an adjoining cemetery. The English settlers of West Jersey, including Willingboro, were Quaker, and the area has a number of meetinghouses. (Courtesy Burlington County Times.)

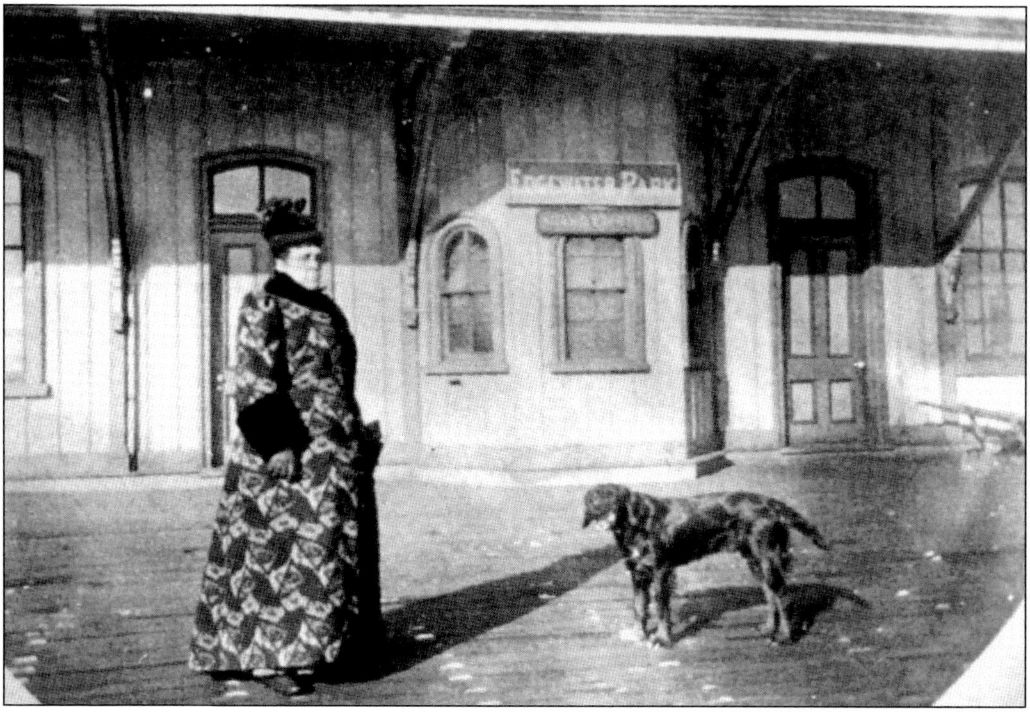

The Camden and Amboy Railroad placed tracks through the township in 1834. Shown above is a well-dressed woman and her canine friend waiting at the Edgewater Park Railroad Station in the 1890s. Below, a train traverses a bridge over the Rancocas Creek in the mid-1800s,. Willingboro included the areas that became Edgewater Park, Beverly, and Delanco until 1859. (Courtesy Burlington County Times and Delanco Bicentennial Committee.)

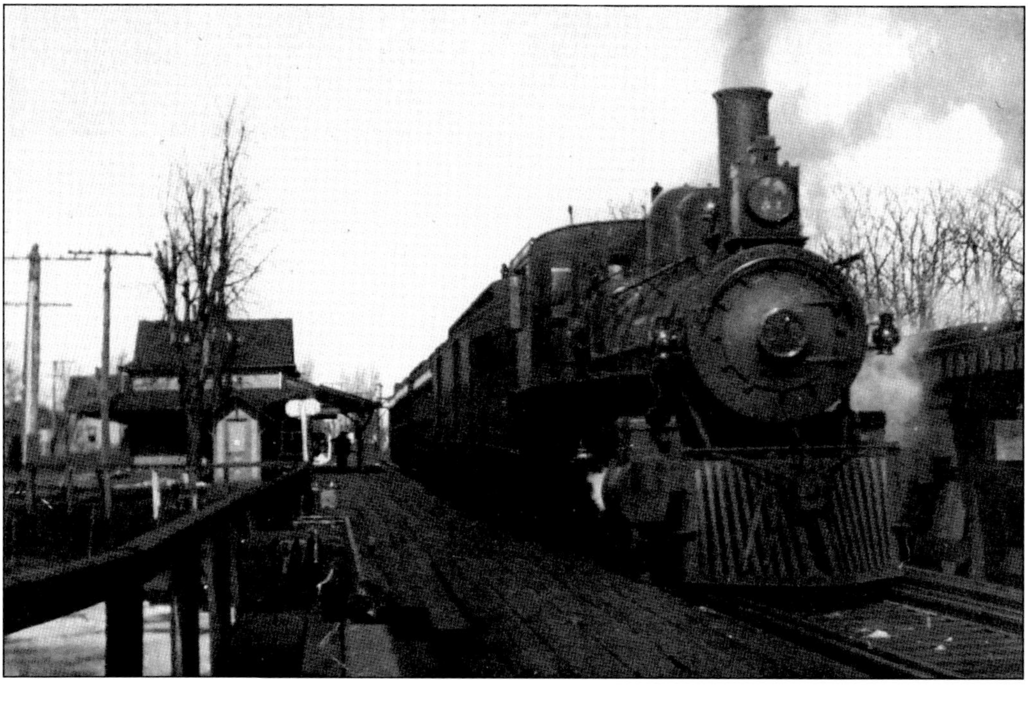

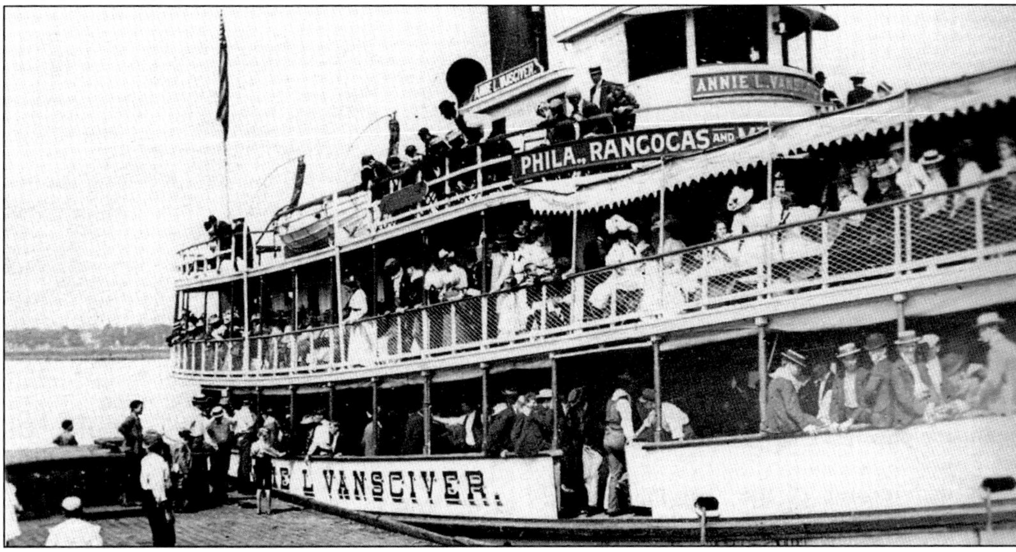

Ferries were common forms of transportation for people living along the Rancocas Creek and Delaware River in the 1800s and early 1900s. In Willingboro, steamboats such as the *Norristown*, *Lafayette*, *Independence*, and *Annie L. Van Sciver* (built in 1902 and shown above) picked up passengers at Adams and Irish Wharves and took them to Philadelphia or Mount Holly. (Courtesy Delanco Bicentennial Committee.)

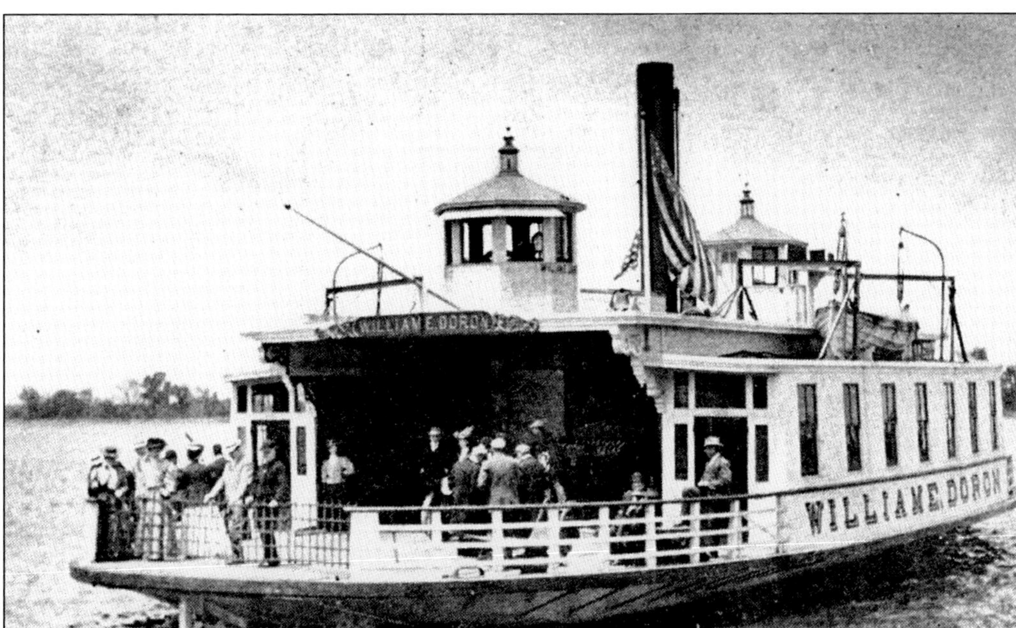

People wishing to travel to Bristol, Pennsylvania, could go north to Burlington City and take the *William E. Doron*. (Courtesy Burlington County Times.)

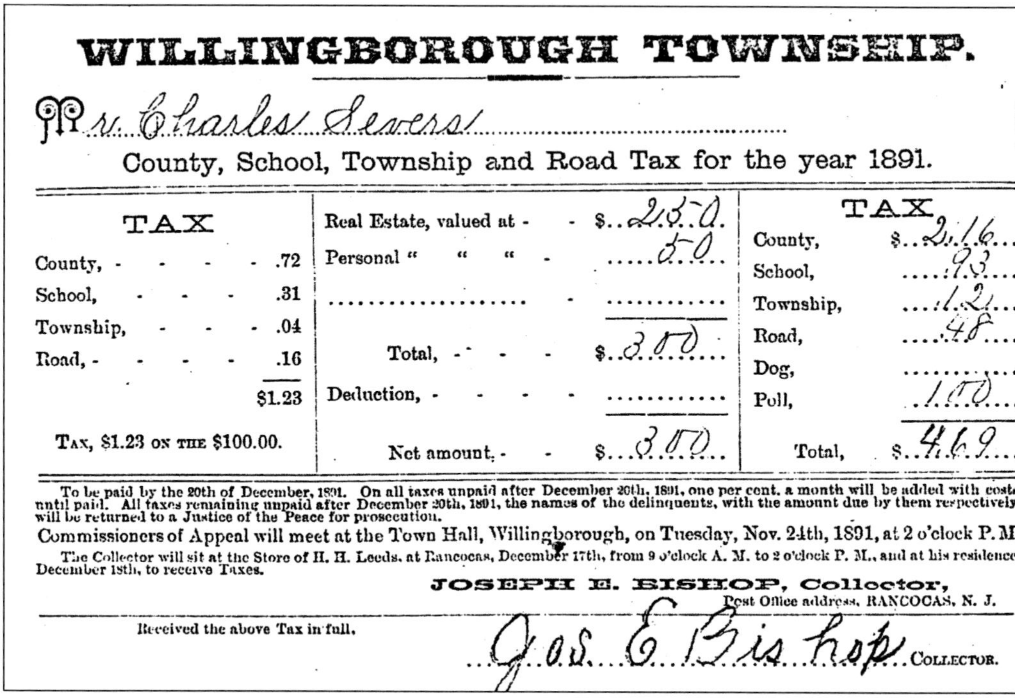

WILLINGBOROUGH TOWNSHIP.

Mr. Charles Severs

County, School, Township and Road Tax for the year 1891.

TAX					TAX	
County,	.72	Real Estate, valued at	$ 250		County,	$ 2.16
School,	.31	Personal " " "	50		School,	.93
Township,	.04				Township,	1.2
Road,	.16	Total,	$ 300		Road,	.48
	$1.23	Deduction,			Dog,	
Tax, $1.23 on the $100.00.		Net amount,	$ 300		Poll,	1.00
					Total,	$ 4.69

To be paid by the 20th of December, 1891. On all taxes unpaid after December 20th, 1891, one per cent. a month will be added with costs until paid. All taxes remaining unpaid after December 20th, 1891, the names of the delinquents, with the amount due by them respectively will be returned to a Justice of the Peace for prosecution.

Commissioners of Appeal will meet at the Town Hall, Willingborough, on Tuesday, Nov. 24th, 1891, at 2 o'clock P.M.

The Collector will sit at the Store of H. H. Leeds, at Rancocas, December 17th, from 9 o'clock A. M. to 2 o'clock P. M., and at his residence, December 18th, to receive Taxes.

JOSEPH E. BISHOP, Collector,
Post Office address, RANCOCAS, N. J.

Received the above Tax in full,
Jos. E Bishop Collector.

This is a copy of an 1891 Willingborough Township tax bill for Charles Severs. According to local tax collector Joseph E. Bishop, Severs owed a whopping $4.69 in taxes to Burlington County, the school district, and the township. There also were separate road and poll taxes. (Courtesy Betty Sever.)

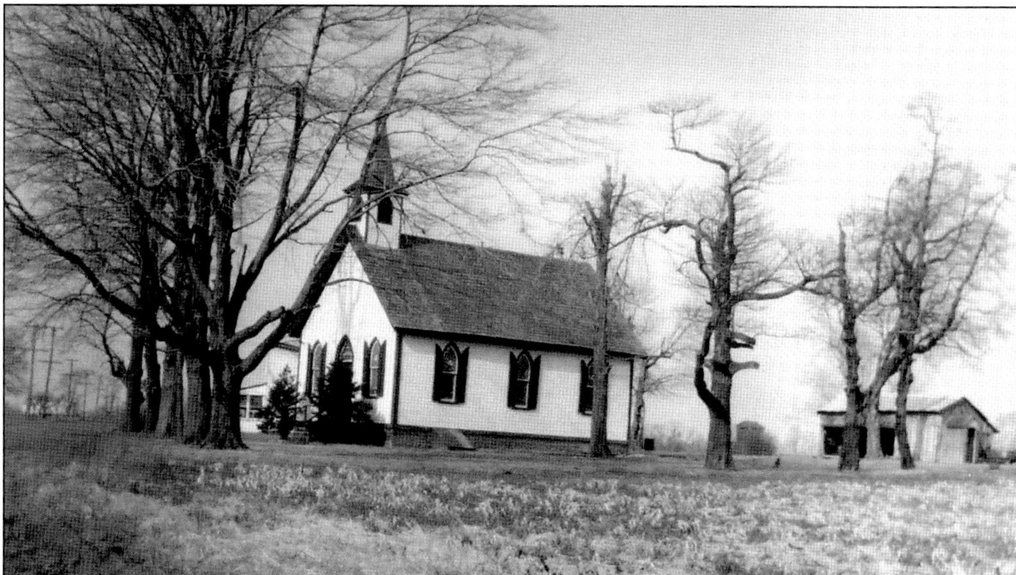

The Charleston Methodist Church served the residents of the villages of Masonville, Charleston, and Rancocas. Members of the congregation purchased stained-glass memorial windows for this tiny church on Charleston Road. It was torn down in 1959 to make way for the St. Paul Methodist Church. (Courtesy Willingboro Public Library/Stuart family.)

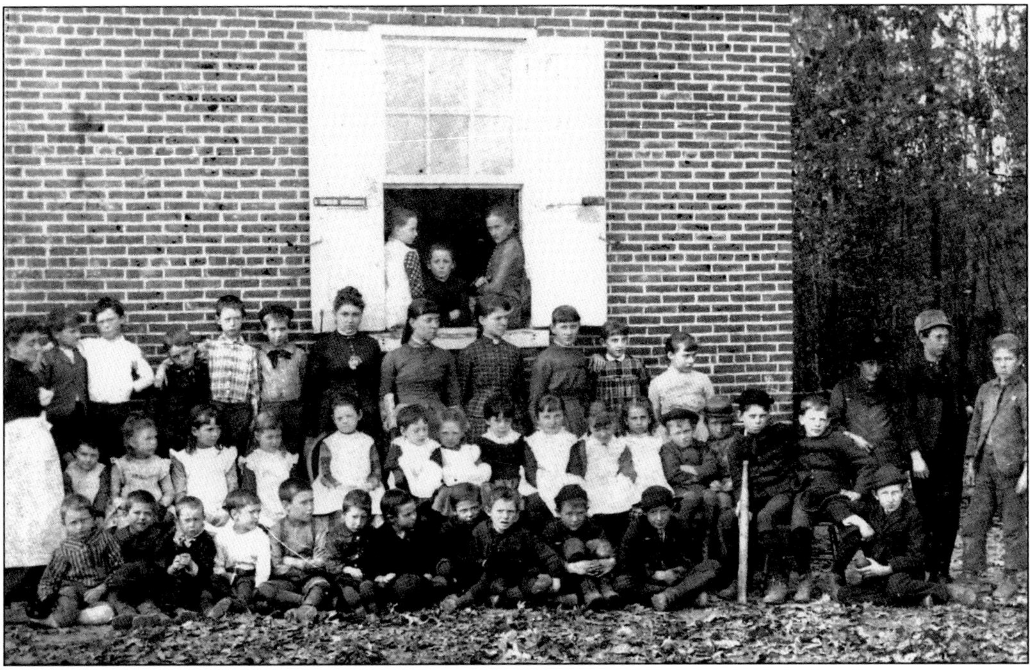

Willingboro students pose for a class photograph behind their one-room schoolhouse on Salem Road in 1900. The building was constructed in 1866 at a cost of $995 and is now a National Historic Landmark. (Courtesy Willingboro Historical Society.)

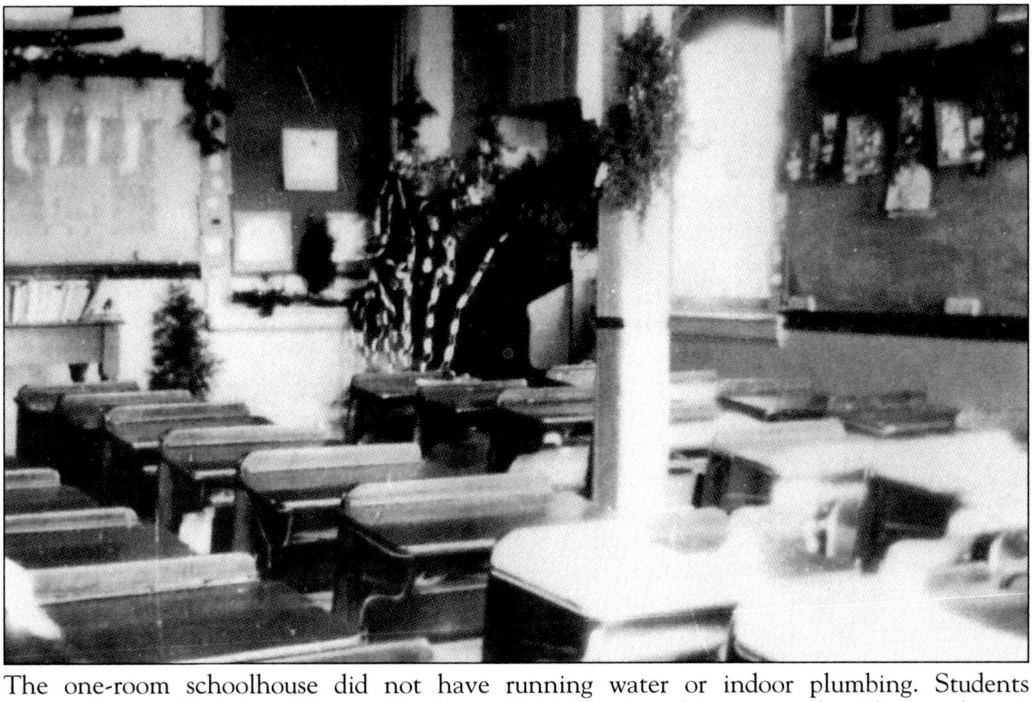

The one-room schoolhouse did not have running water or indoor plumbing. Students retrieved water from a well (owned by James Stuart) across the street and used an outhouse. In this *c.* 1925 photograph, the school is decorated for Christmas. (Courtesy Willingboro Historical Society.)

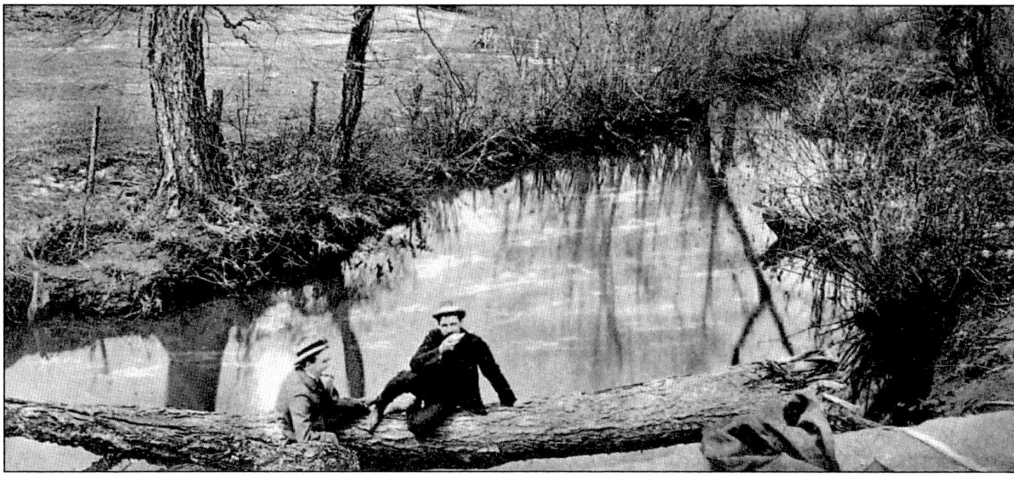

This postcard of two men sitting on a log at "Charleston Meadow near Beverly, N.J." was sent to Rev. Kelsey Walling of Merchantville by his daughter on September 9, 1908. In her message saying she would soon arrive home by boat, the daughter identifies one of the men in the photograph as Mr. Cherry. The postcard carried a one-cent stamp bearing the image of Benjamin Franklin. Beverly refers to the nearest post office. (Courtesy Willingboro Township Manager's Office.)

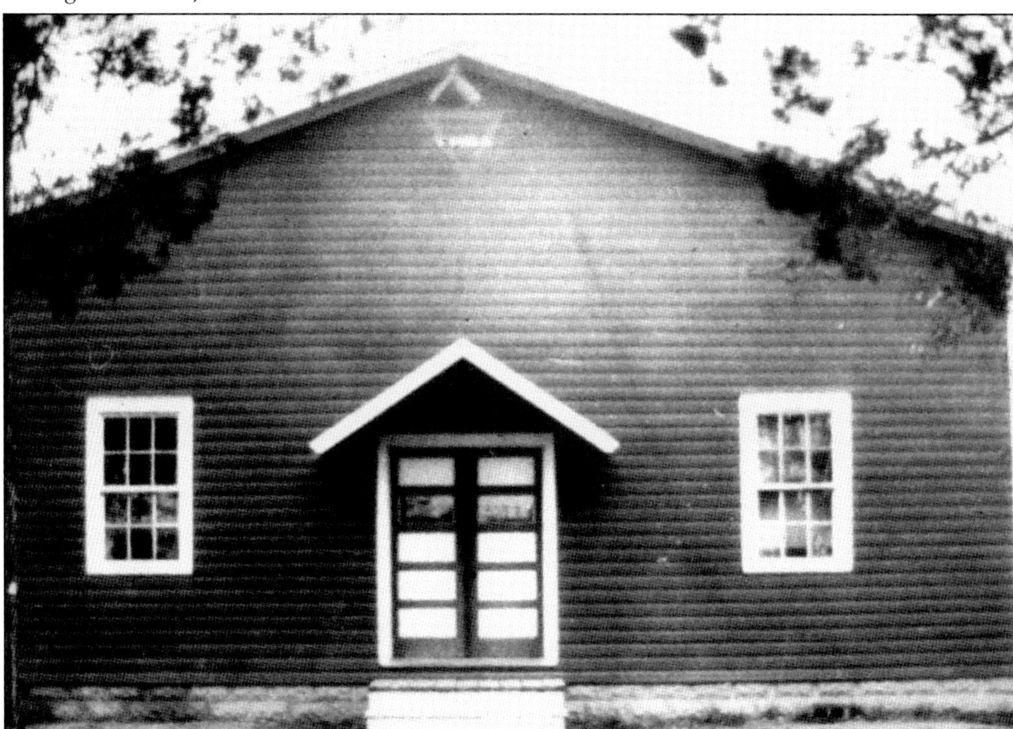

This building, at the intersection of Charleston Road and Sedgwick Lane, served as the Willingboro YMCA from 1922 to 1957. The building was purchased from nearby Fort Dix for $200, dismantled, and erected in Willingboro at a cost of $5,000. Always open, this building served the recreational needs of Willingboro and the surrounding riverfront communities. (Courtesy Willingboro Public Library.)

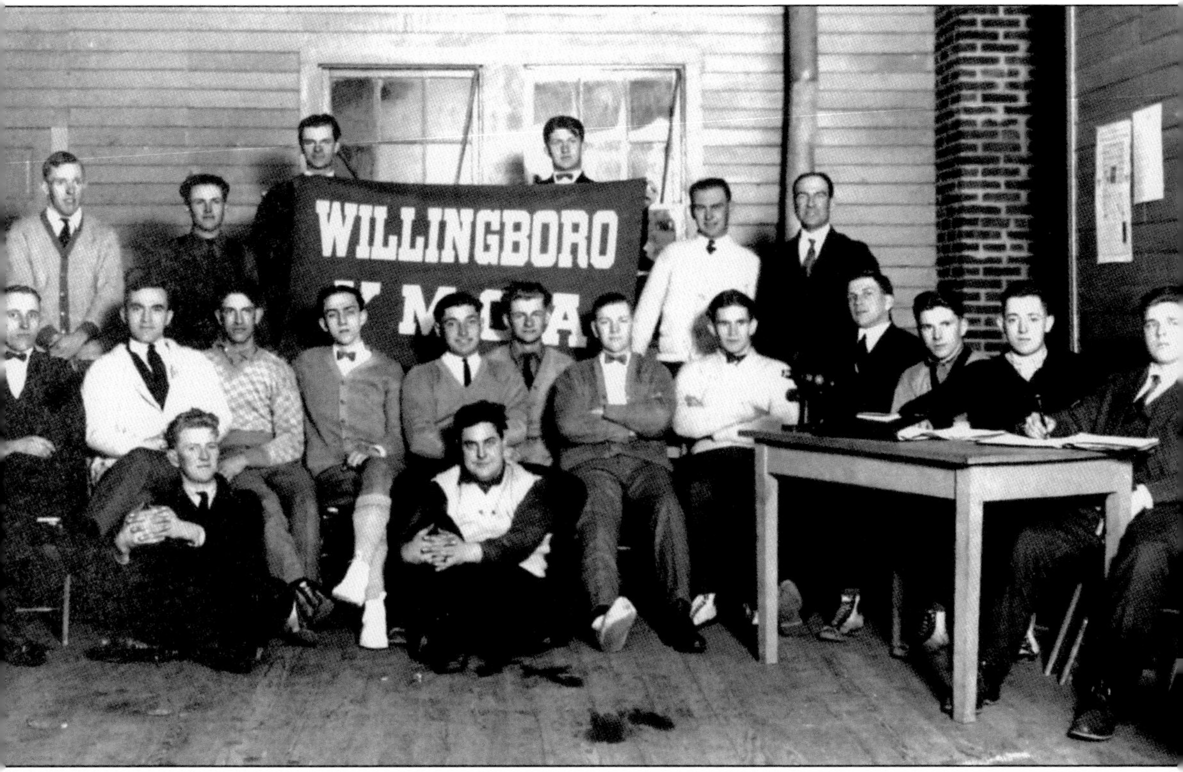

Members of the Willingboro YMCA gather in 1943 to celebrate the organization's 25th anniversary. From left to right are the following: (front row) Wilson Vanalstyne and Daniel Warner; (middle row) Lynton Bell, Arthur Smith, William Walton, Victor Bertrano, Joseph Snyder, Stanley Perkins, Albert Bintliff, unidentified, Ernest Janney, Robert Stuart, Frank Pennington, and John Donaldson; (back row) Jackson Kolster, William Grovatt, Earle Sever, Ed Johnson, and Porter Ashbrook. Ashbrook was the YMCA's assistant coordinator for Burlington County. (Courtesy Carol J. Suplee/Stuart family.)

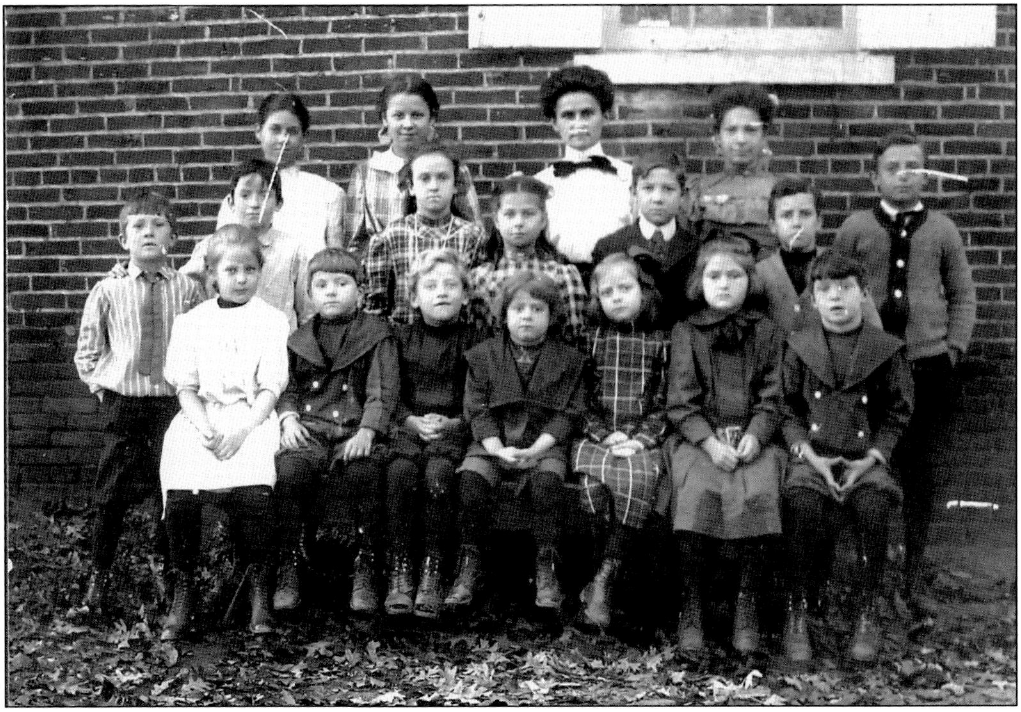

Seventeen Willingboro students pose for a class photograph with their teacher in 1910. According to township records, at that time this farming community had a population of 562. Within 60 years, the number of people calling Willingboro home would swell to more than 43,000. (Courtesy Willingboro Historical Society.)

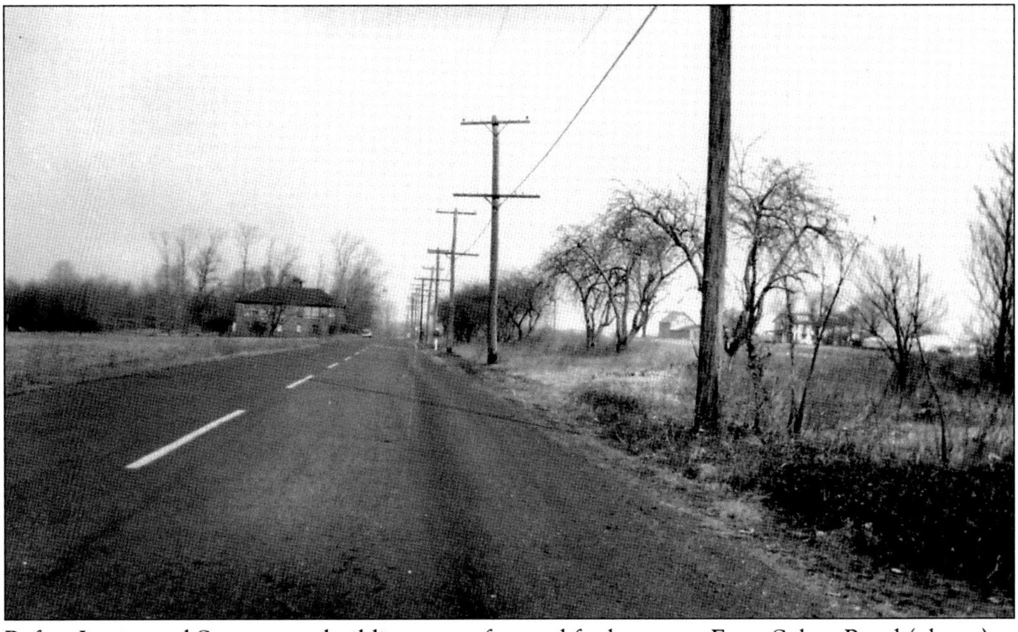

Before Levitt and Sons came, buildings were few and far between. Even Salem Road (above), a major thoroughfare because of the schoolhouse and municipal building, was largely devoid of traffic. (Courtesy Betty Sever.)

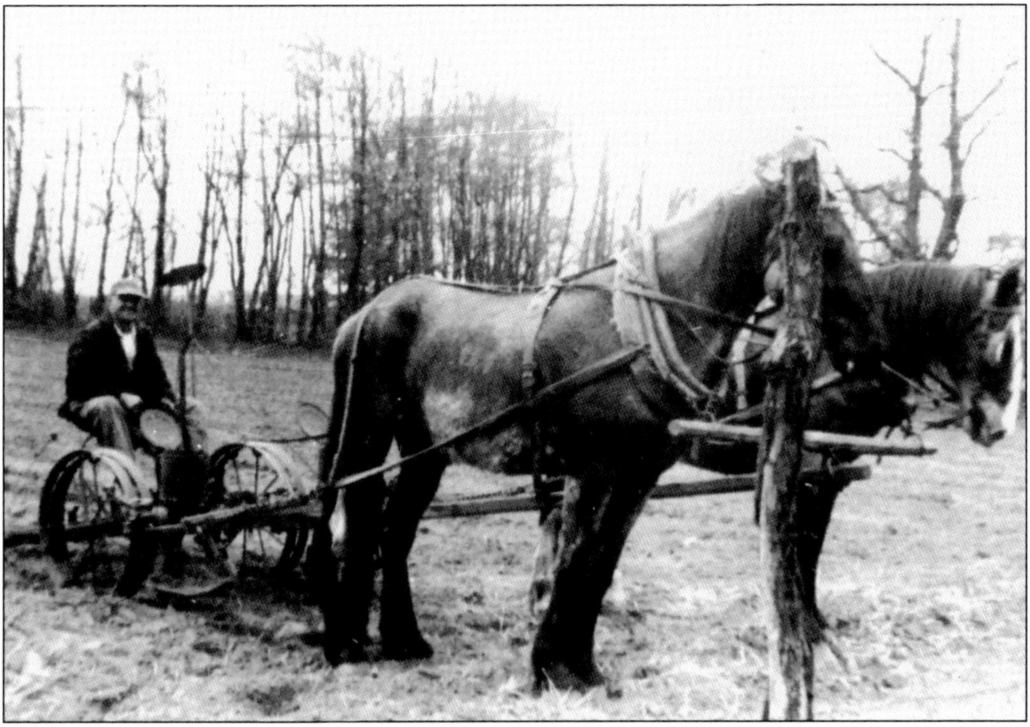

During the 1940s, Willingboro had three working dairy farms. Here a farmer works his team of horses. (Courtesy Carol J. Suplee/Betty Sever.)

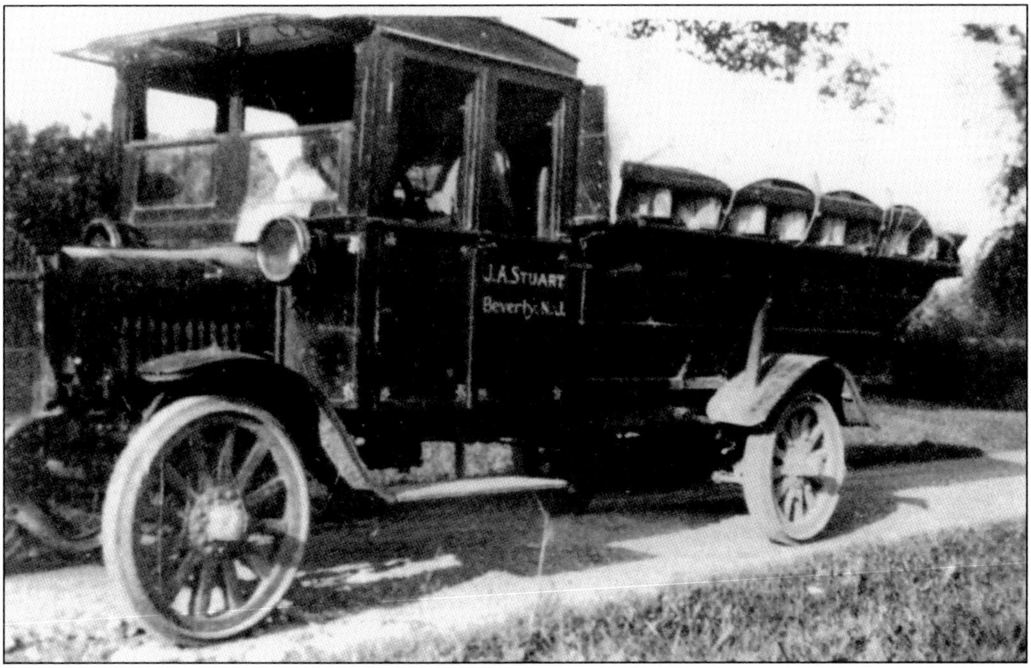

Farmer James A. Stuart's truck is loaded with baskets of apples in this *c.* 1916 photograph. Apples grown in Willingboro were a favorite snack in Philadelphia hotels. (Courtesy Carol J. Suplee/Stuart family.)

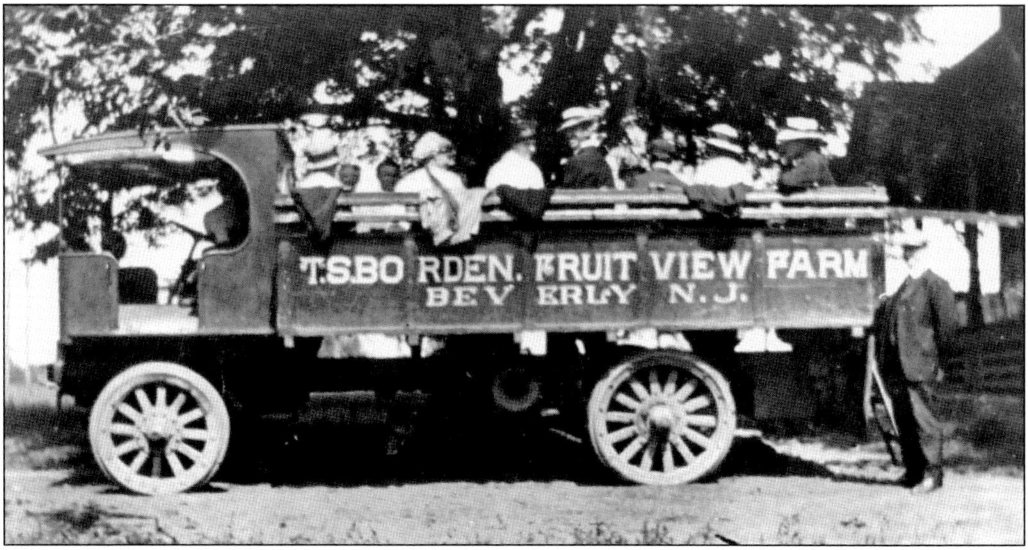

T.S. Borden operated a fruit farm at Charleston Road and Route 130 in Willingboro, although mail went through a post office in Beverly. In this *c.* 1930 photograph, a group of well-dressed Sunday school students prepares to leave for a picnic at Rancocas Park near Mount Holly. A featured attraction at the park was a merry-go-round. (Courtesy Carol J. Suplee/Stuart family.)

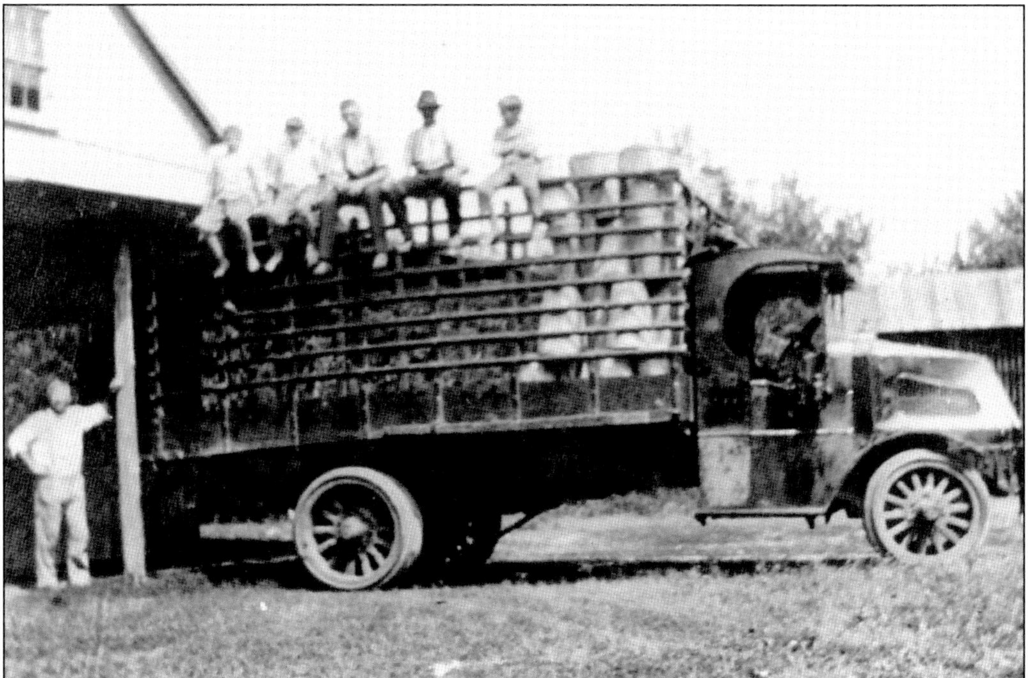

In the early 1900s, a group of farm hands sits atop a Bulldog Mack truck owned by James A. Stuart. The truck made many runs between rural Willingboro and Philadelphia. (Courtesy Carol J. Suplee/Stuart family.)

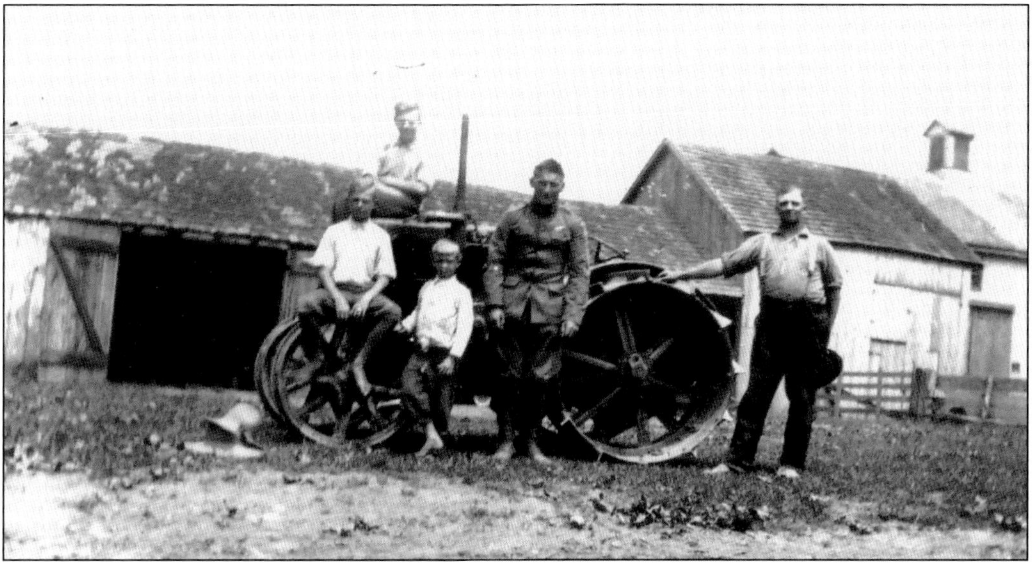

Warren, Stan, and Bill Perkins pose with their father, Warren Perkins, and an unidentified soldier on their farm on Park Road in 1926. The Perkins farm was down the road from the former William Franklin estate. (Courtesy Carol J. Suplee/Perkins family.)

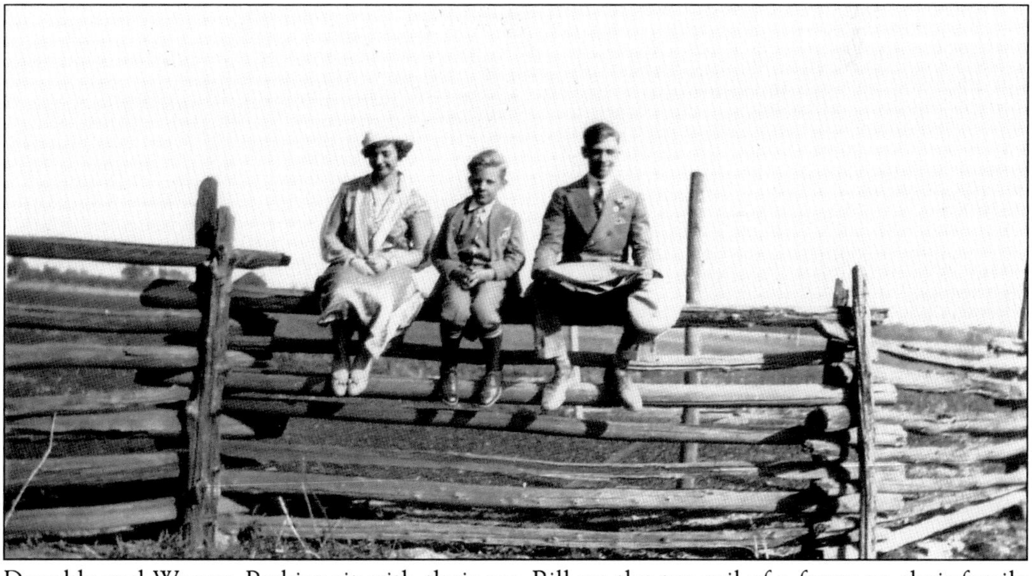

Donalda and Warren Perkins sit with their son Bill on the top rail of a fence on their family farm during the 1930s. Three decades later, John F. Kennedy High School was built on their land. (Courtesy Carol J. Suplee/Perkins family.)

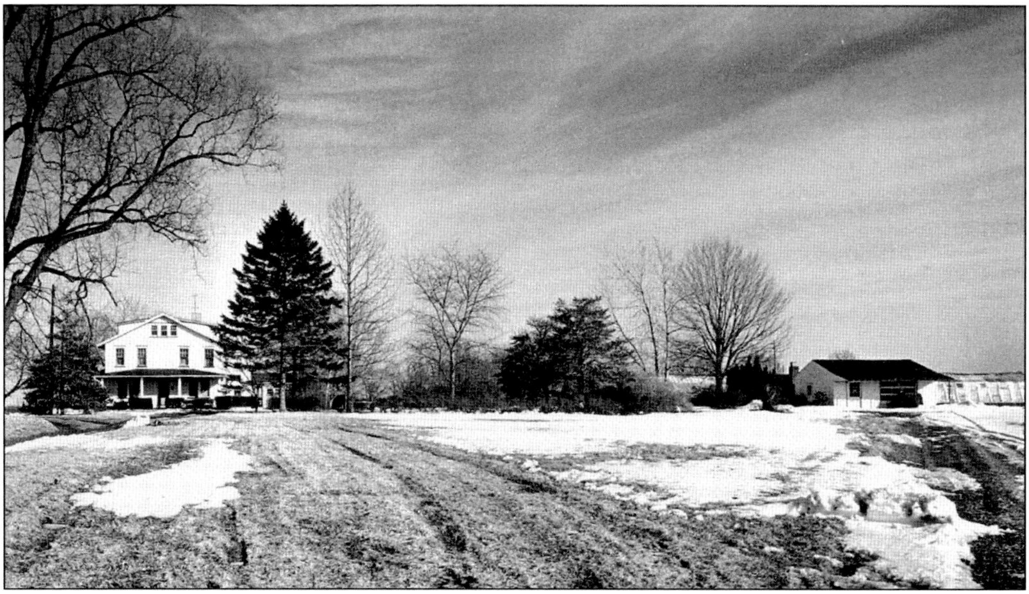

This is part of the farm off Salem Road that belonged to the Stuart family. It included the homestead and a greenhouse, shown here in a 1978 photograph. (Courtesy Burlington County Times.)

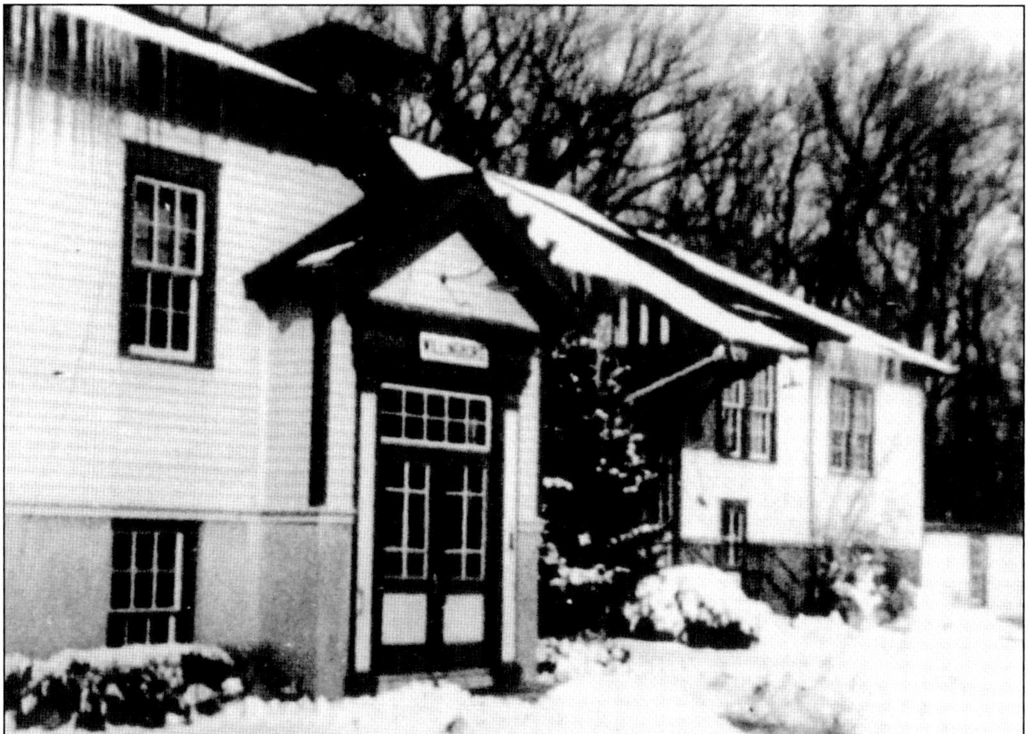

As Willingboro grew in the early 1900s, the old one-room schoolhouse became too small to accommodate all of the local children. In 1918, residents built the Consolidated School. The building served as both a school and home for municipal government. (Courtesy Dave Retzko.)

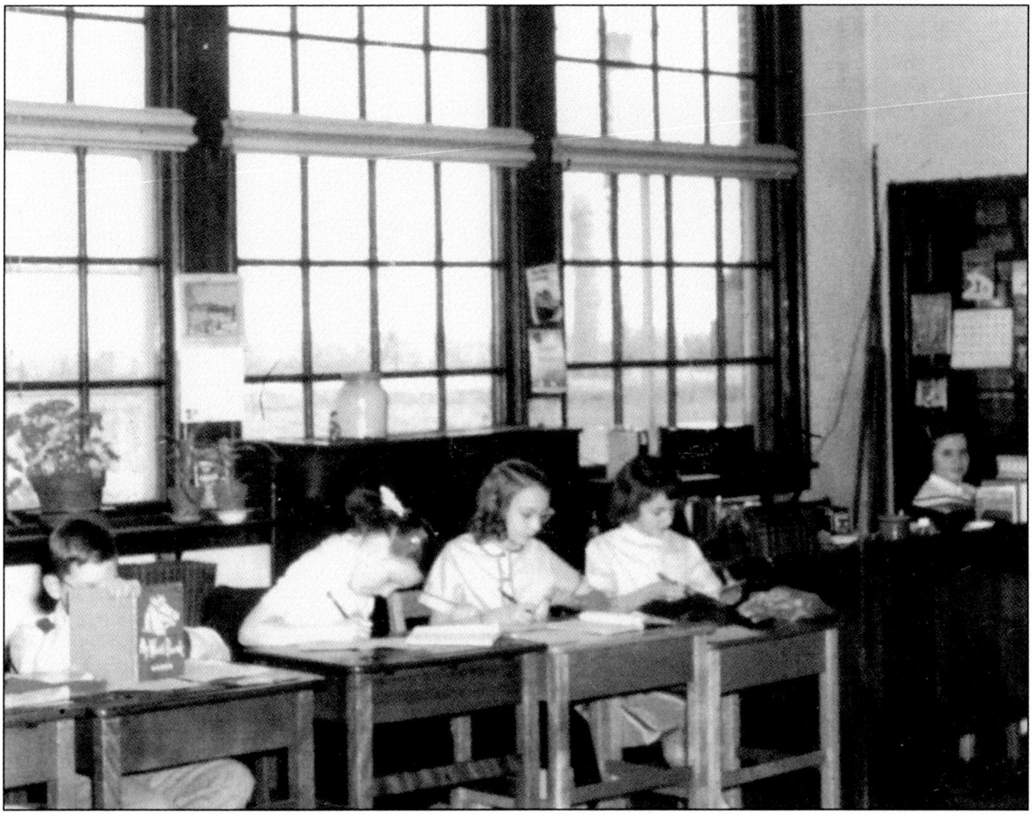

Students tend to their studies in a classroom in the Consolidated School on Salem Road. The structure also operated as the Willingboro Municipal Building until it burned down in the 1960s. (Courtesy Willingboro Public Library/Stuart family.)

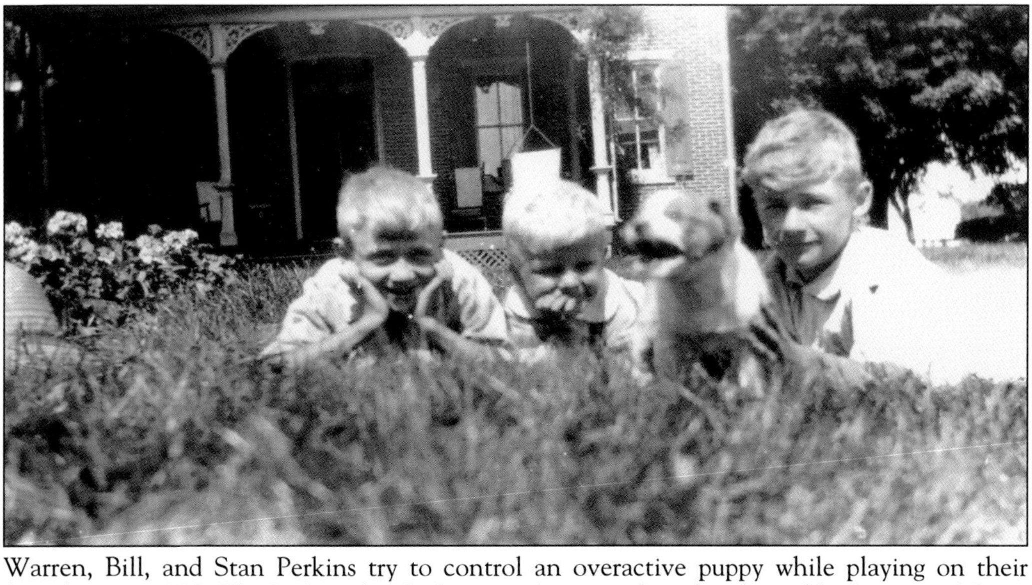

Warren, Bill, and Stan Perkins try to control an overactive puppy while playing on their front lawn *c.* 1920. The Perkins family farm was later purchased and razed by Levitt and Sons. (Courtesy Carol J. Suplee/Perkins family.)

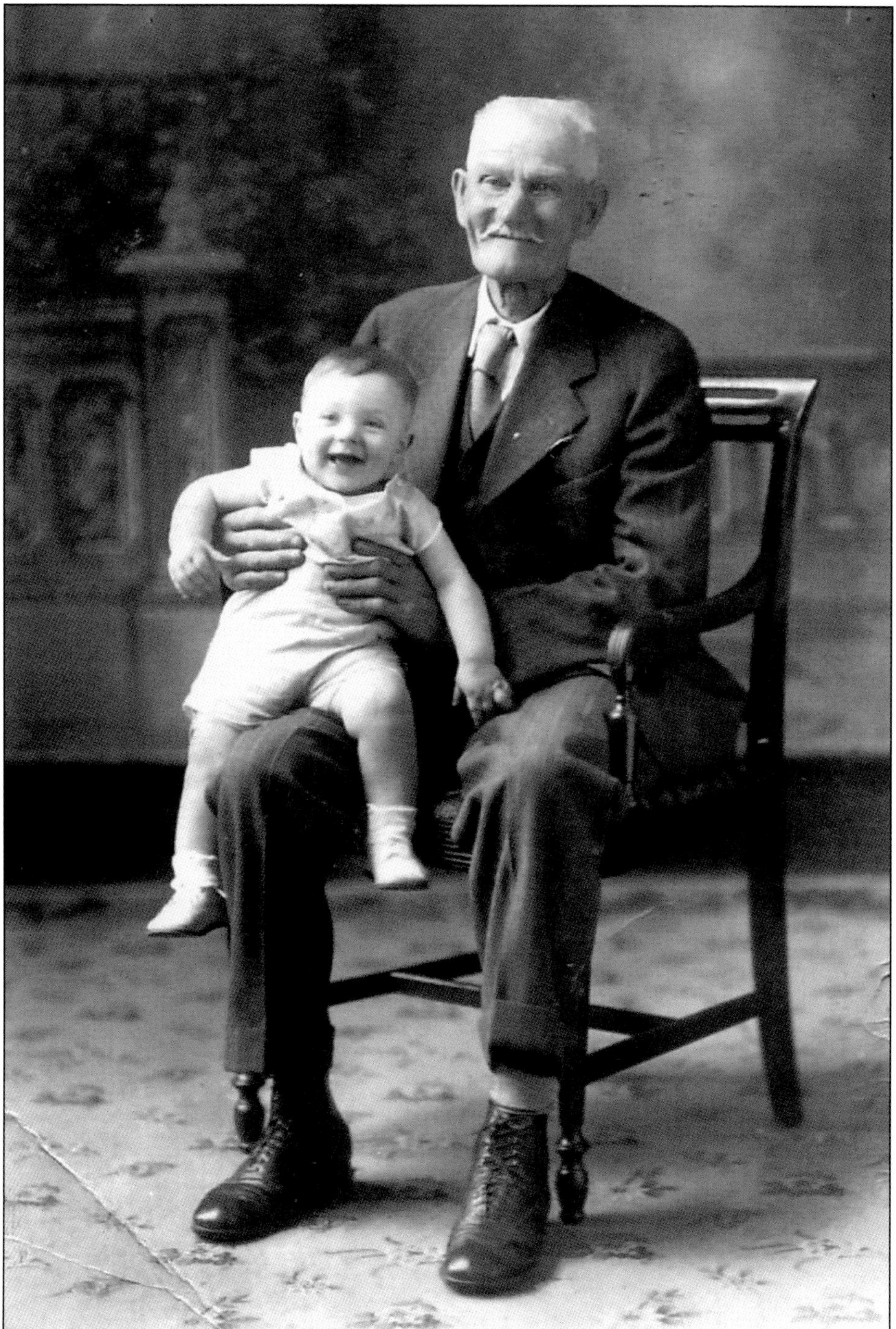

This 1936 photograph shows Edwin Van Sciver, a farmer who, in the late 1880s, was an East Coast–style Wyatt Earp. Constable Van Sciver rode around town on a white stallion—pistols at his side—and chased away any unruly visitors. The child on his lap is Richard Van Sciver, who eventually became chief of the Willingboro Police Department. (Courtesy Willingboro Historical Society.)

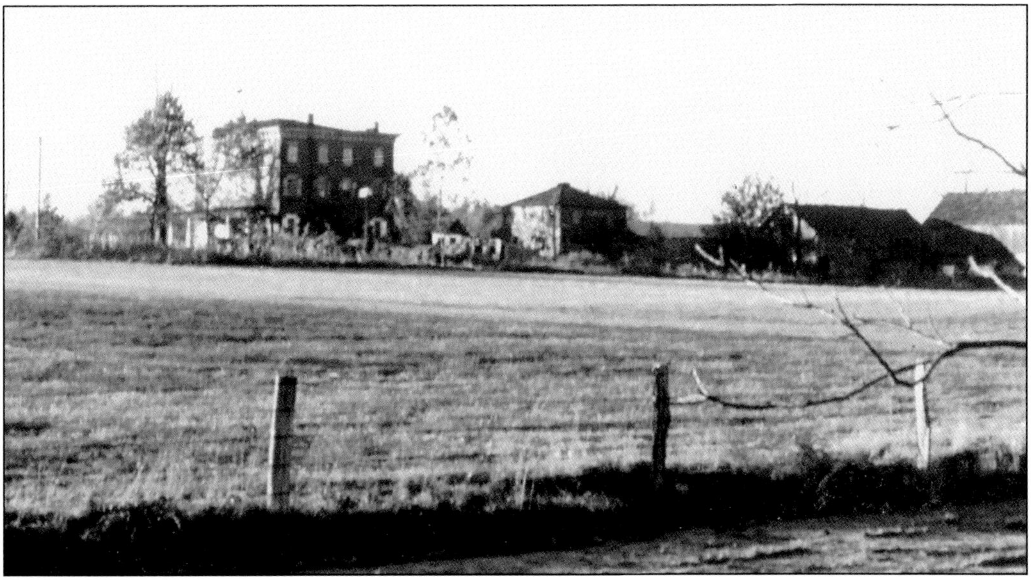

This house used to belong to Edward Grovatt and was an early stagecoach stop on what is now Levitt Parkway (at Hawthorne Park). The low building on the right was a bowling alley for the entertainment of travelers. (Courtesy Willingboro Public Library/Stuart family.)

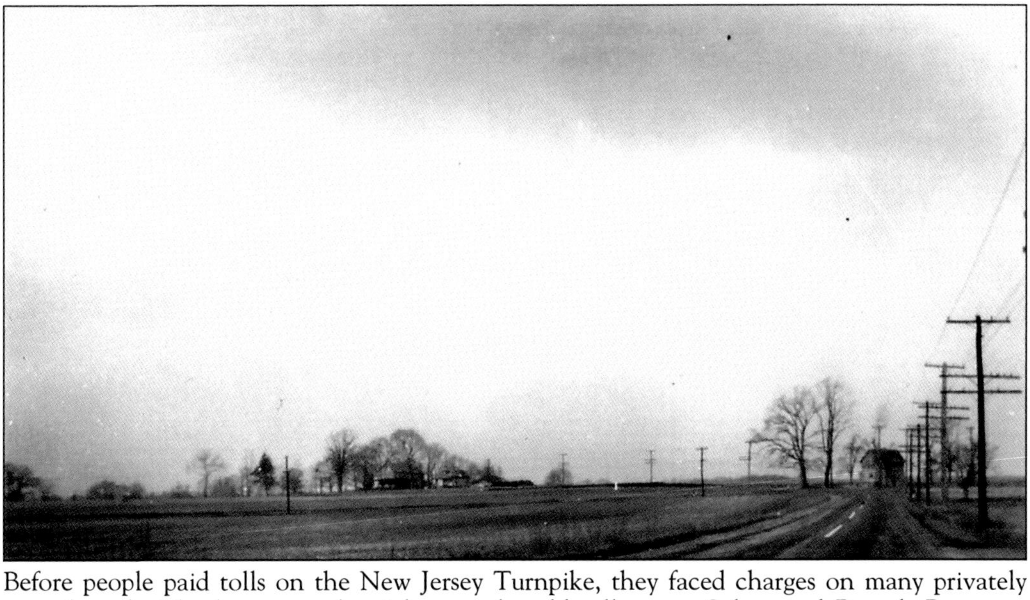

Before people paid tolls on the New Jersey Turnpike, they faced charges on many privately owned roads. The house on the right was the old tollgate at Salem and Beverly-Rancocas Roads. The home on the left belonged to the Brooks family. (Courtesy Betty Sever.)

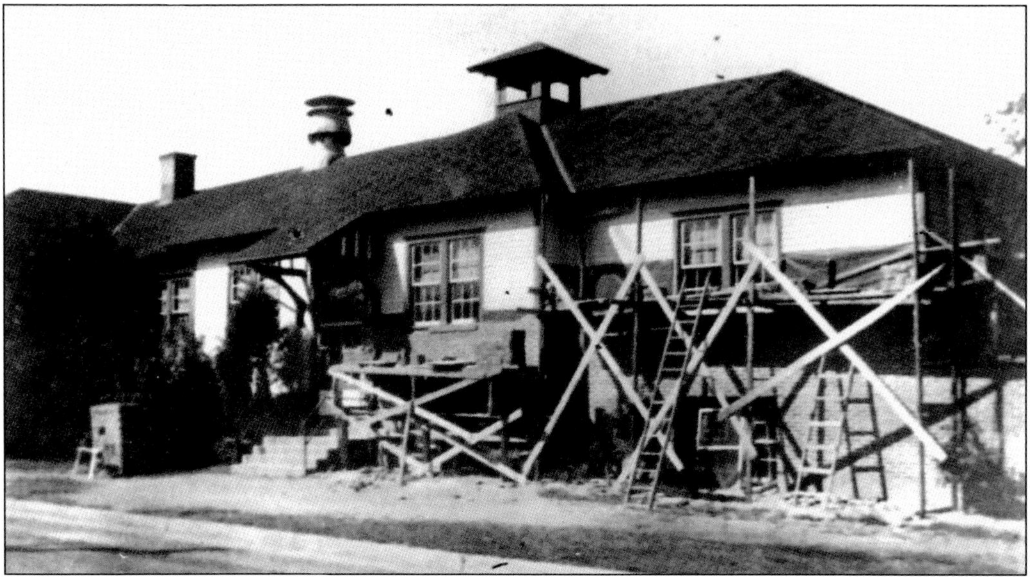

The Consolidated School on Salem Road was built in 1918, enlarged in 1930, and faced with brick (shown here in progress) in 1940 and 1941. The building, which also housed municipal offices, the library, and a community center, burned down in December 1964. (Courtesy Burlington County Times/Stuart family.)

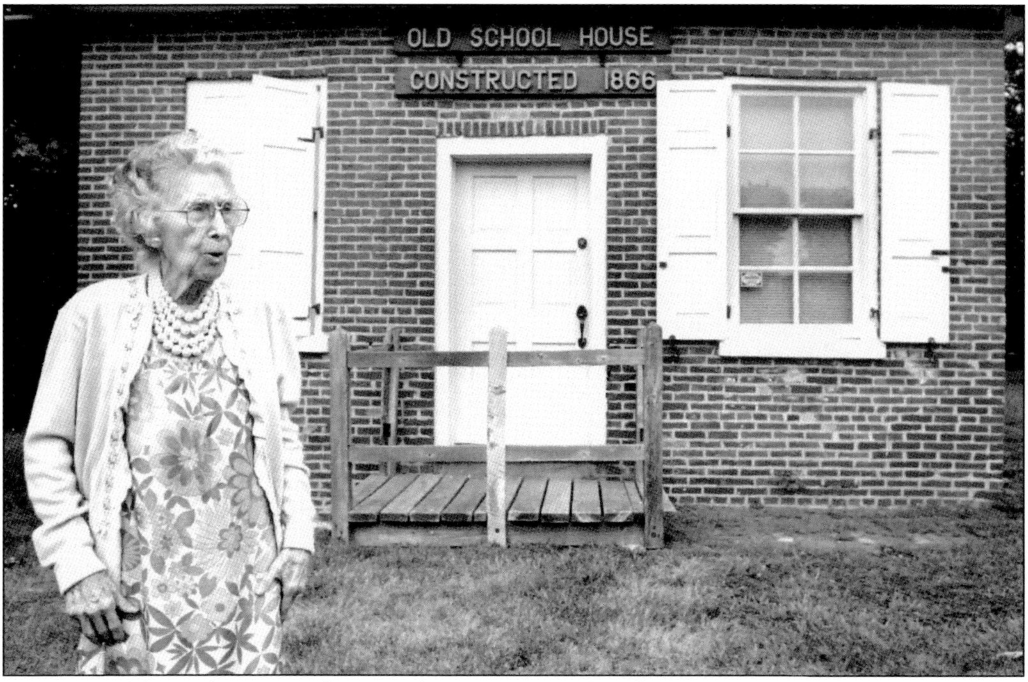

Marion Stehlinger began teaching in the one-room schoolhouse on Salem Road in 1921. She taught arithmetic, spelling, and phonics to 53 children in three grades. (Courtesy Burlington County Times.)

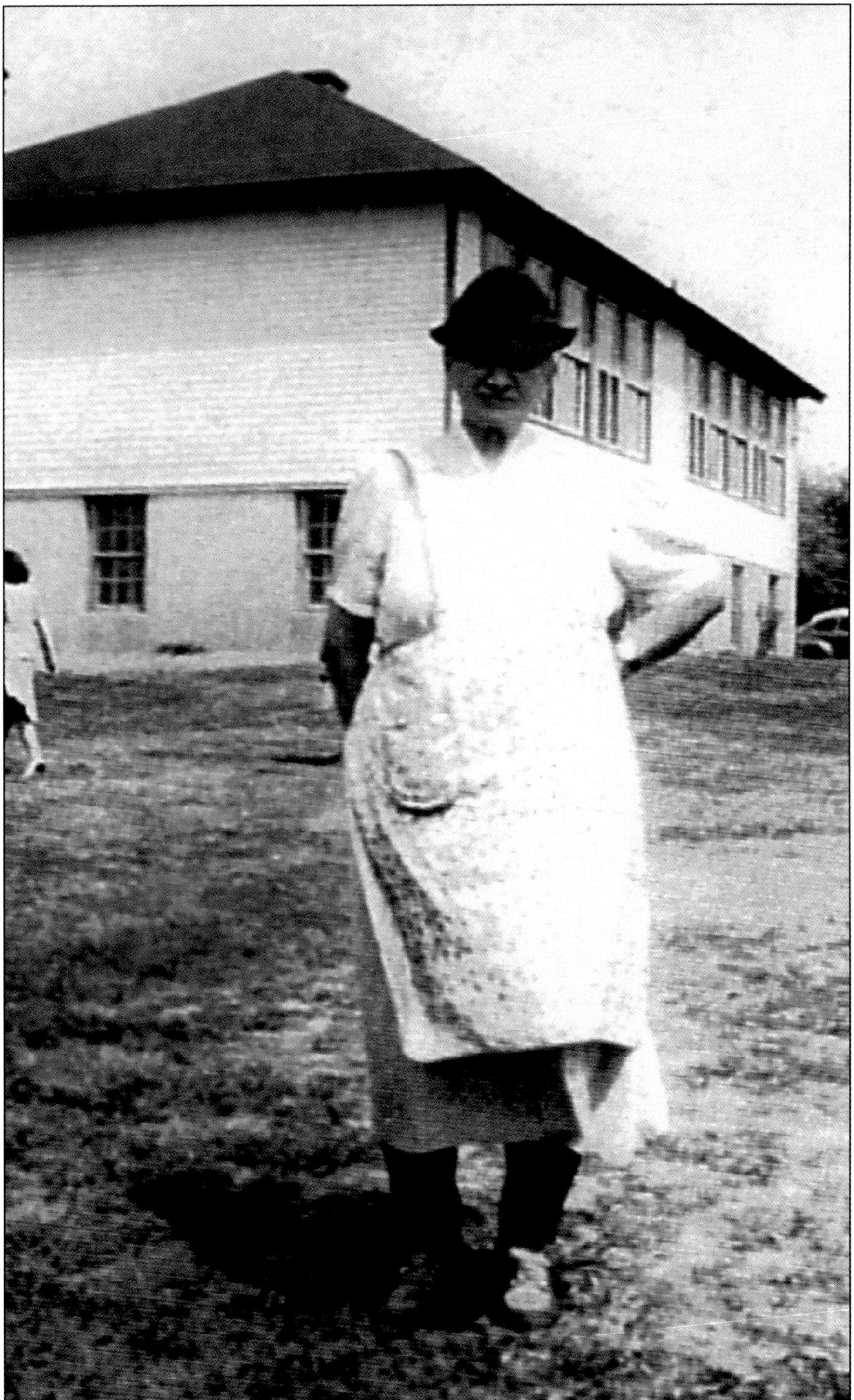

A woman identified as Mrs. Laun was the cook and janitor at the five-room schoolhouse on Salem Road. This picture of her was taken outside the school in 1941. (Courtesy Betty Sever.)

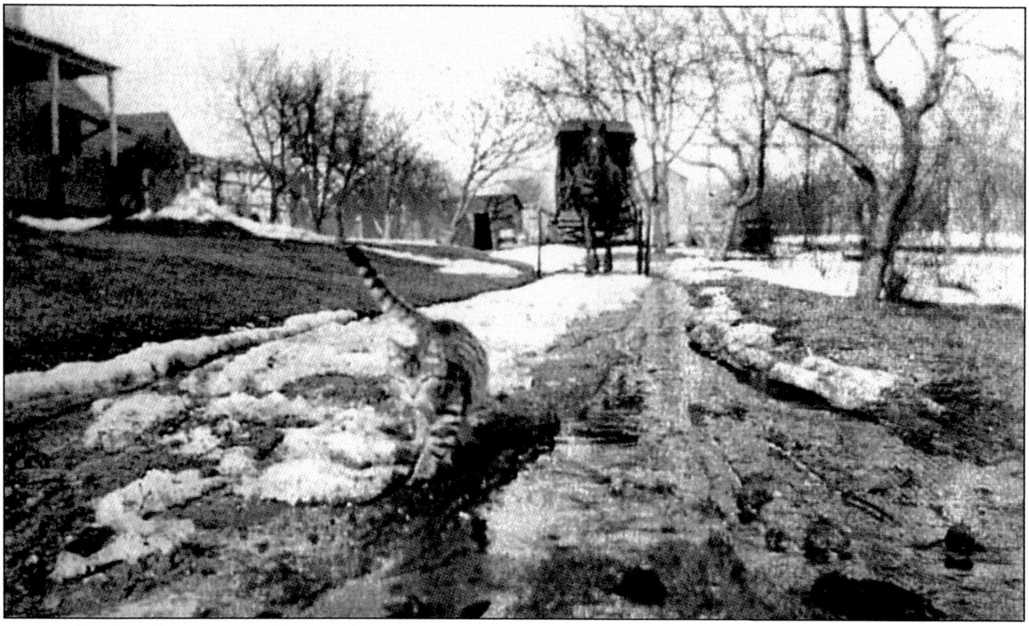

A cat leads a horse and buggy down the driveway of the Sever dairy farm during the 1940s. The horse and buggy delivered milk from the dairy, which was located off Charleston Road. (Courtesy Betty Sever.)

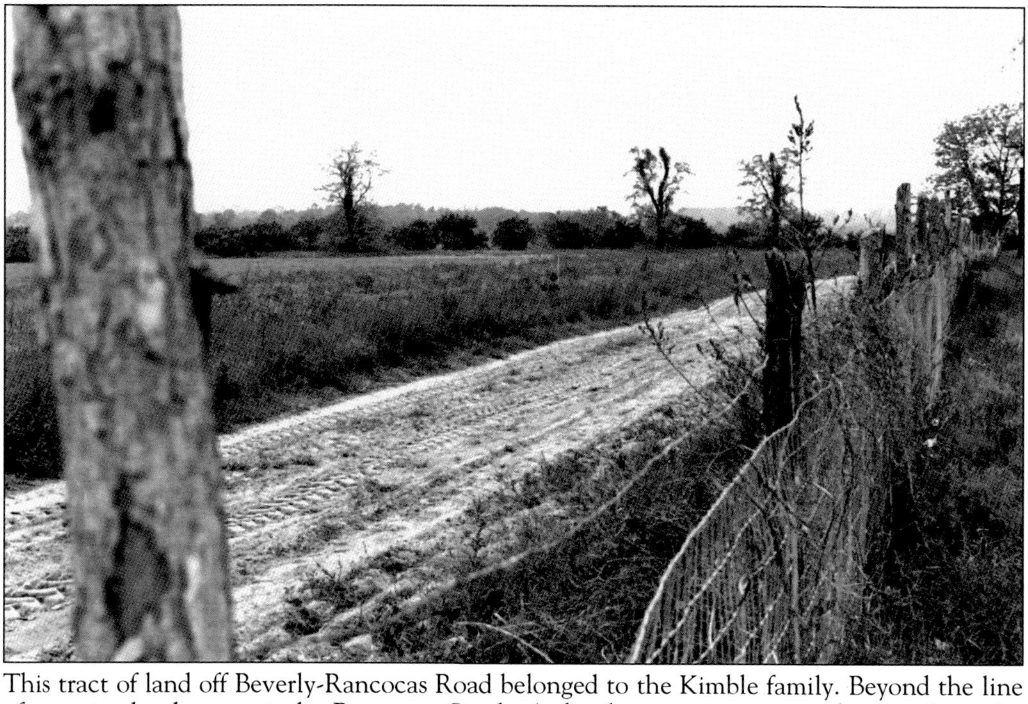

This tract of land off Beverly-Rancocas Road belonged to the Kimble family. Beyond the line of trees in the distance is the Rancocas Creek. A developer once attempted to purchase the land, but instead the township used state funds to buy the site and turn it into Mill Creek Park. (Courtesy Carol J. Suplee/Cramp family.)

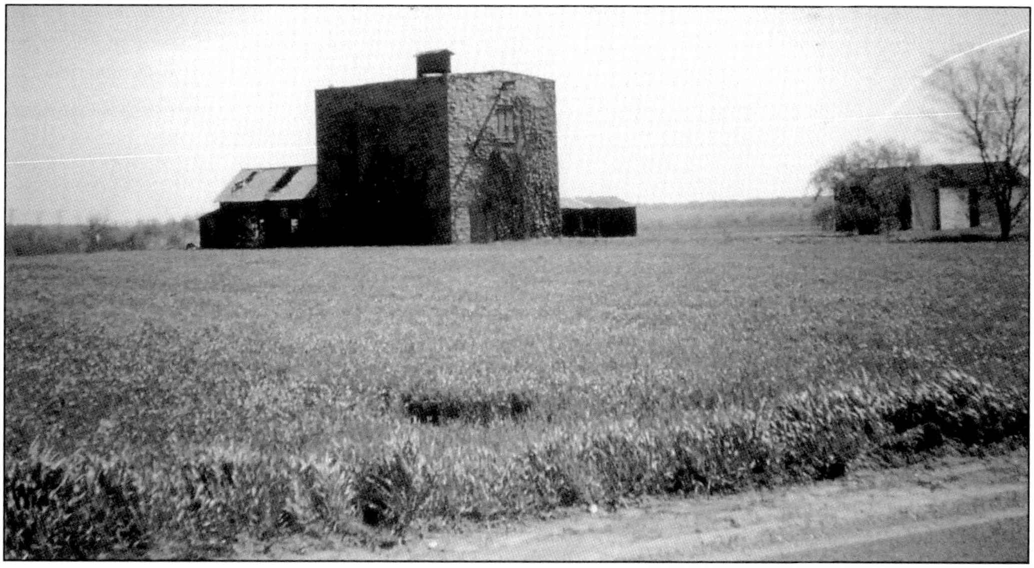

Today, we think nothing of grabbing a cold soda from the refrigerator or keeping leftovers for a few days. Yet, for a long time, such conveniences were difficult to accomplish. At the Buzby farm on Beverly-Rancocas Road (shown here), a tall stone building was used for cold storage. (Courtesy Carol J. Suplee.)

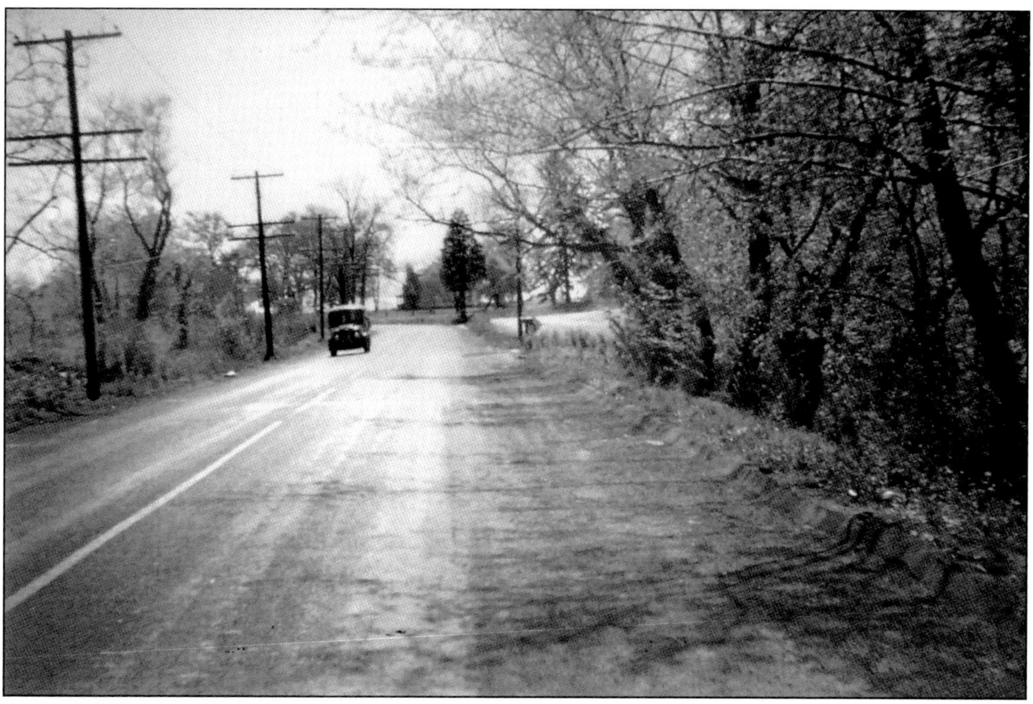

A truck belonging to Bishop's dairy farm travels on Beverly-Rancocas Road near the future site of Mill Creek Park. Levitt and Sons later expanded Beverly-Rancocas Road from two lanes to four. (Courtesy Carol J. Suplee/Cramp family.)

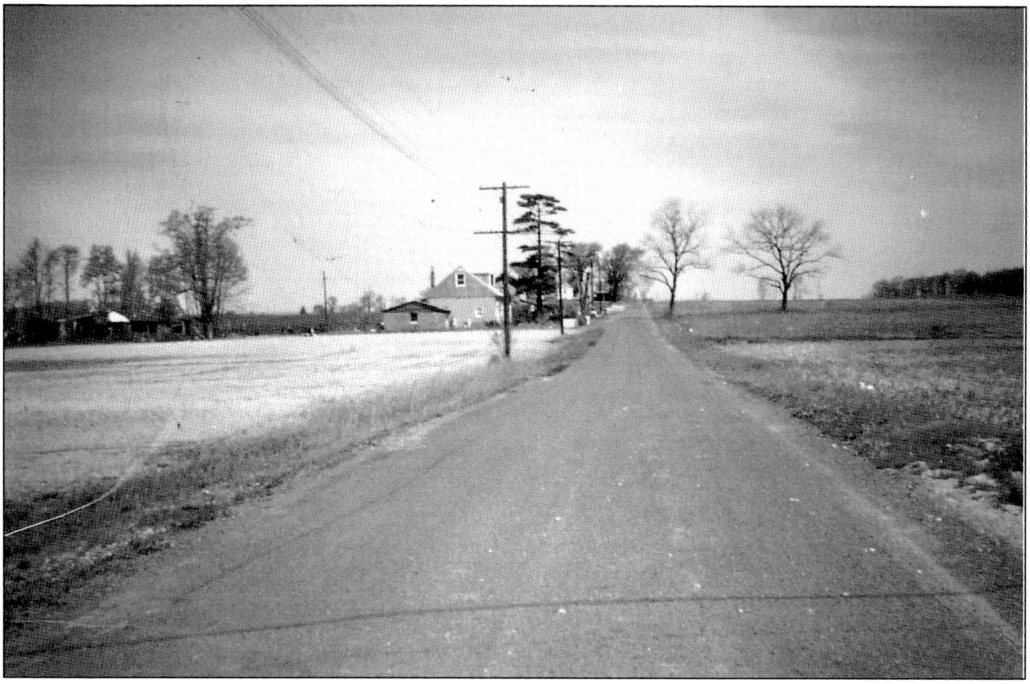

Shown in the mid-1950s is Park Road (Kennedy Way), as it approached the future site of Hawthorne Park. The house on the left eventually was razed to make way for the Tower Shopping Center. (Courtesy Carol J. Suplee/Cramp family.)

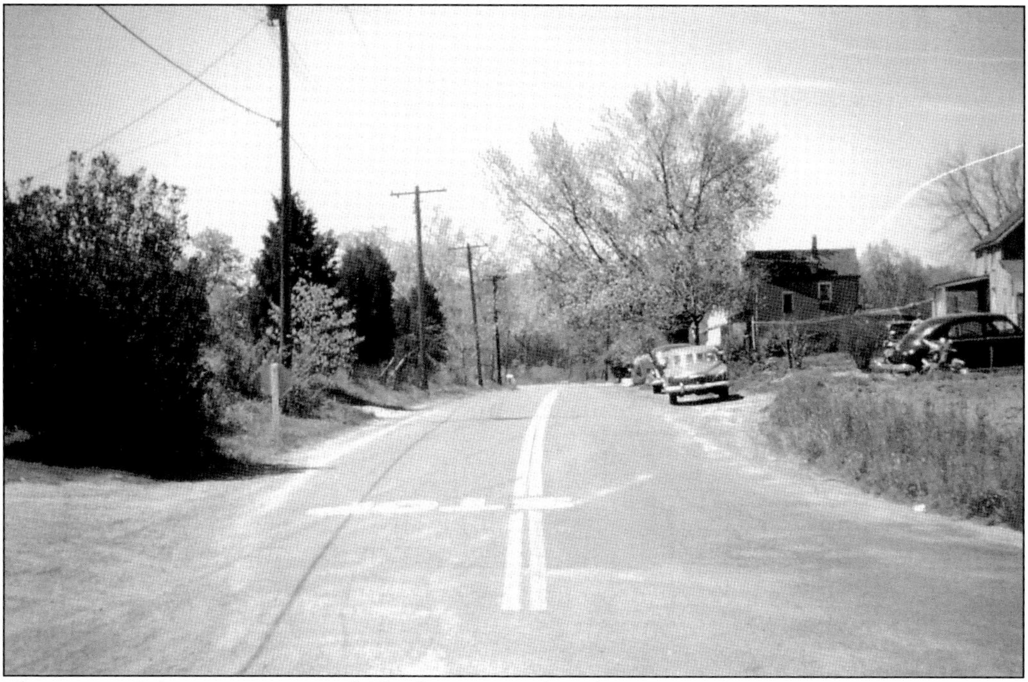

This view of the intersection of Charleston Road and Levitt Parkway was taken facing Mill Creek and Park Road. John F. Kennedy High School was later built just beyond where these cars were parked. (Courtesy Carol J. Suplee/Cramp family.)

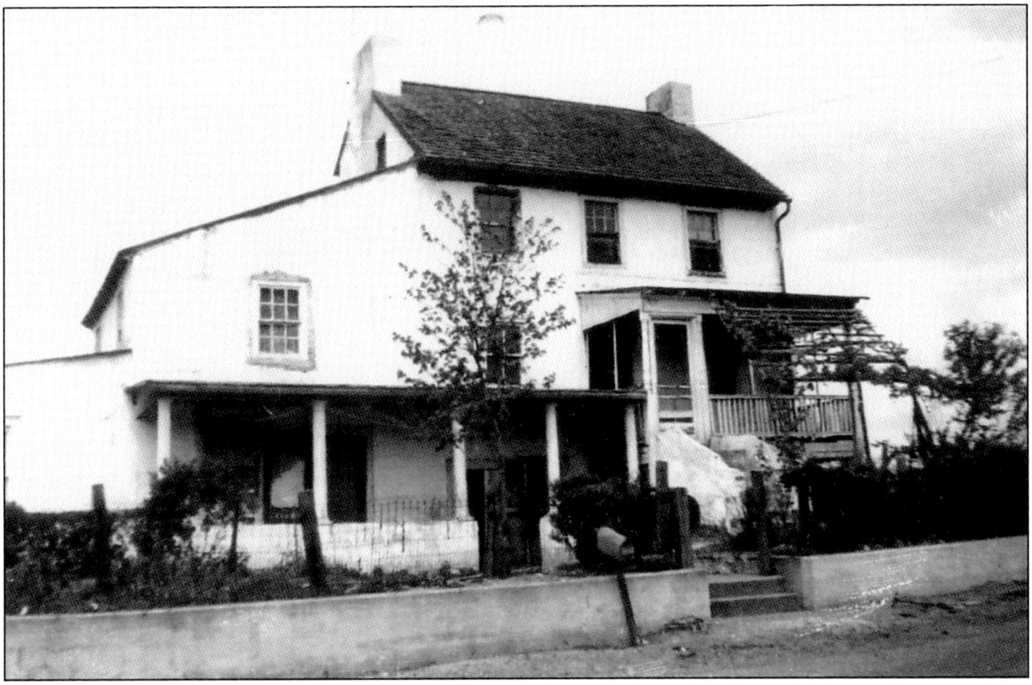

This multistory house belonging to the Lowther family sat on a hill at the intersection of Charleston and Salem Roads. The house was razed when Levitt and Sons began developing the town. (Courtesy Burlington County Times.)

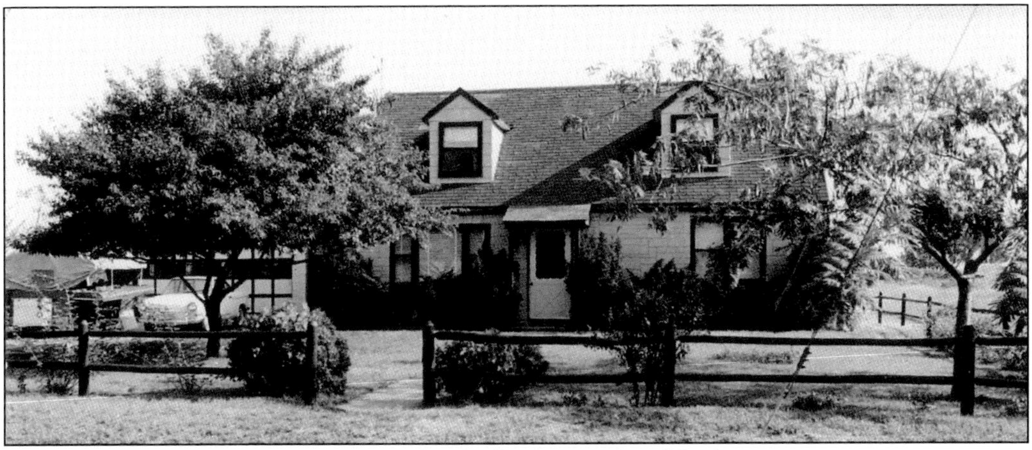

Each early Willingboro house was individually designed and had its own unique appearance. This house, shown in 1968, was located between Rose Street and Route 130. (Courtesy Burlington County Times.)

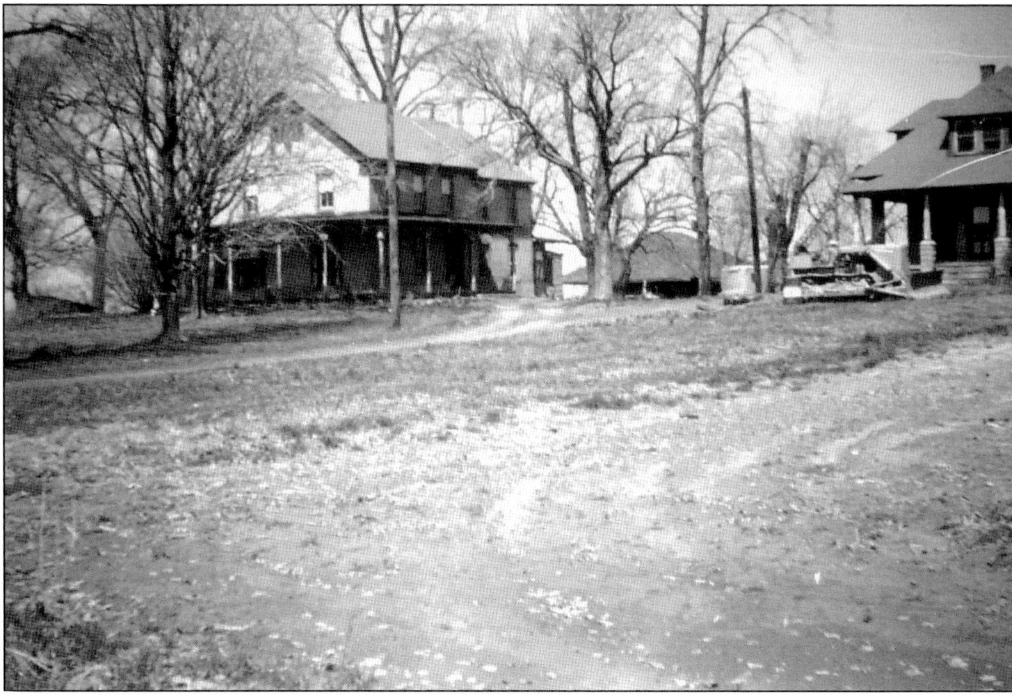

These two homes were located off Beverly-Rancocas Road near what would become Pageant Lane. Many large homes such as these were torn down to make way for the new Levittown community. (Courtesy Cramp family.)

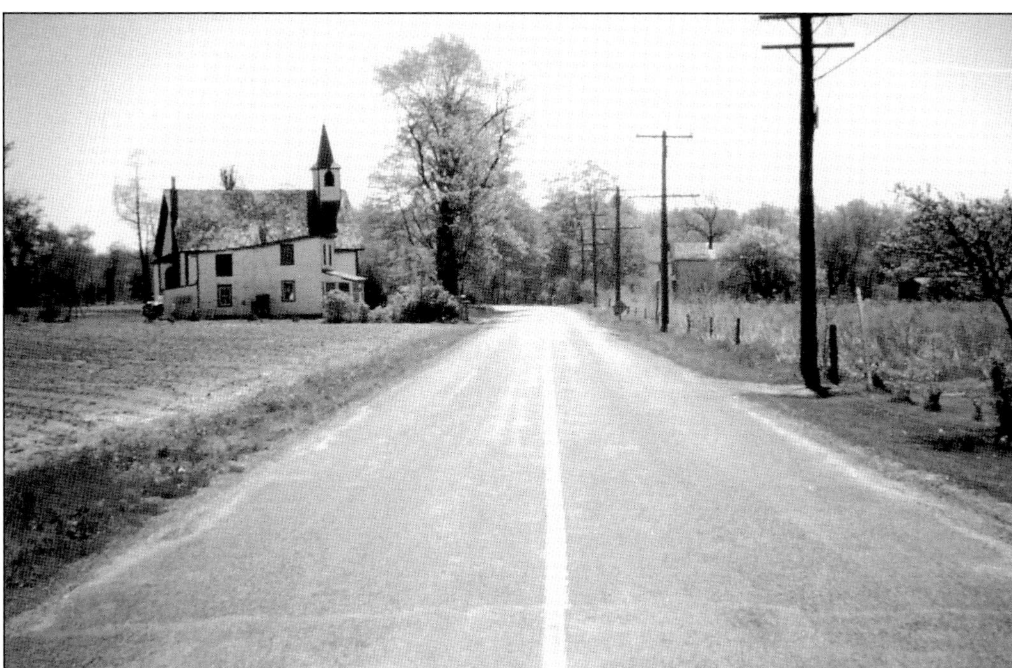

This photograph of Charleston Road was taken looking toward what would become Buckingham Way. The building on the left is a church. (Courtesy Cramp family.)

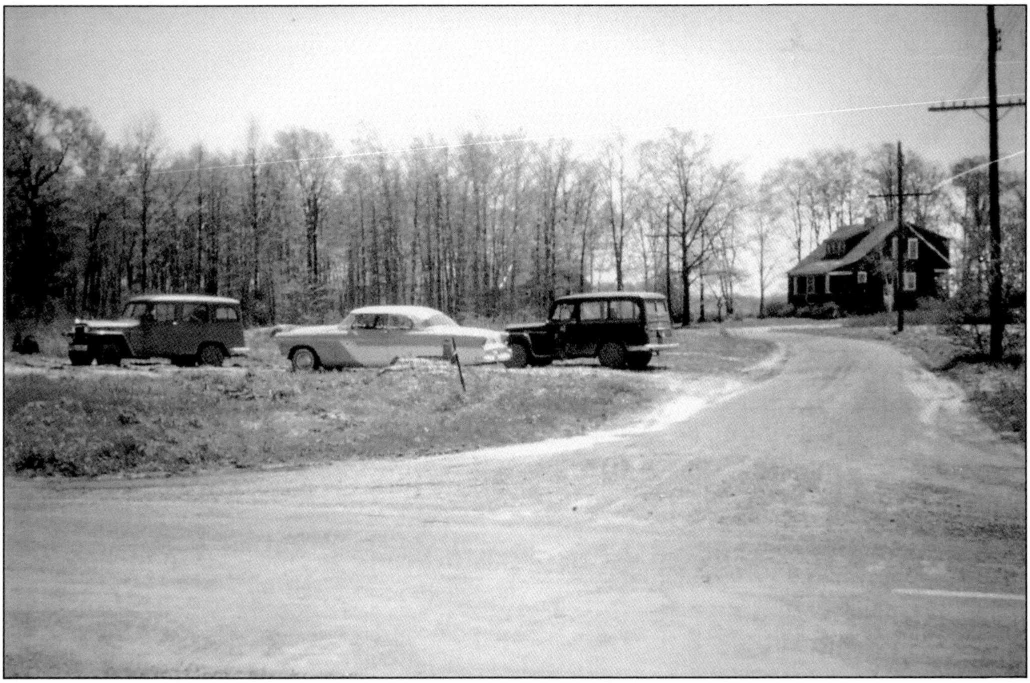

These 1950s-era vehicles were parked on what would become Baldwin Lane in Levitt's Buckingham Park neighborhood. Many of the tall trees in Willingboro would fall to the developer's bulldozers. (Courtesy Cramp family.)

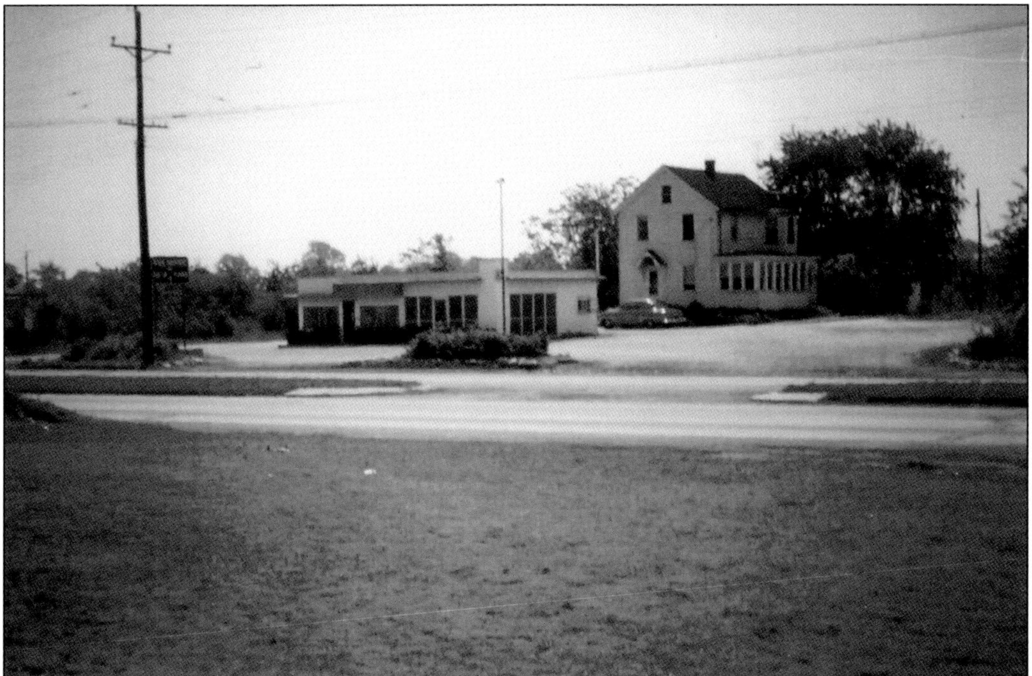

The Mark Restaurant was located on Route 130. Even in the days before Levitt, the highway was a heavily traveled thoroughfare. (Courtesy Carol J. Suplee/Cramp family.)

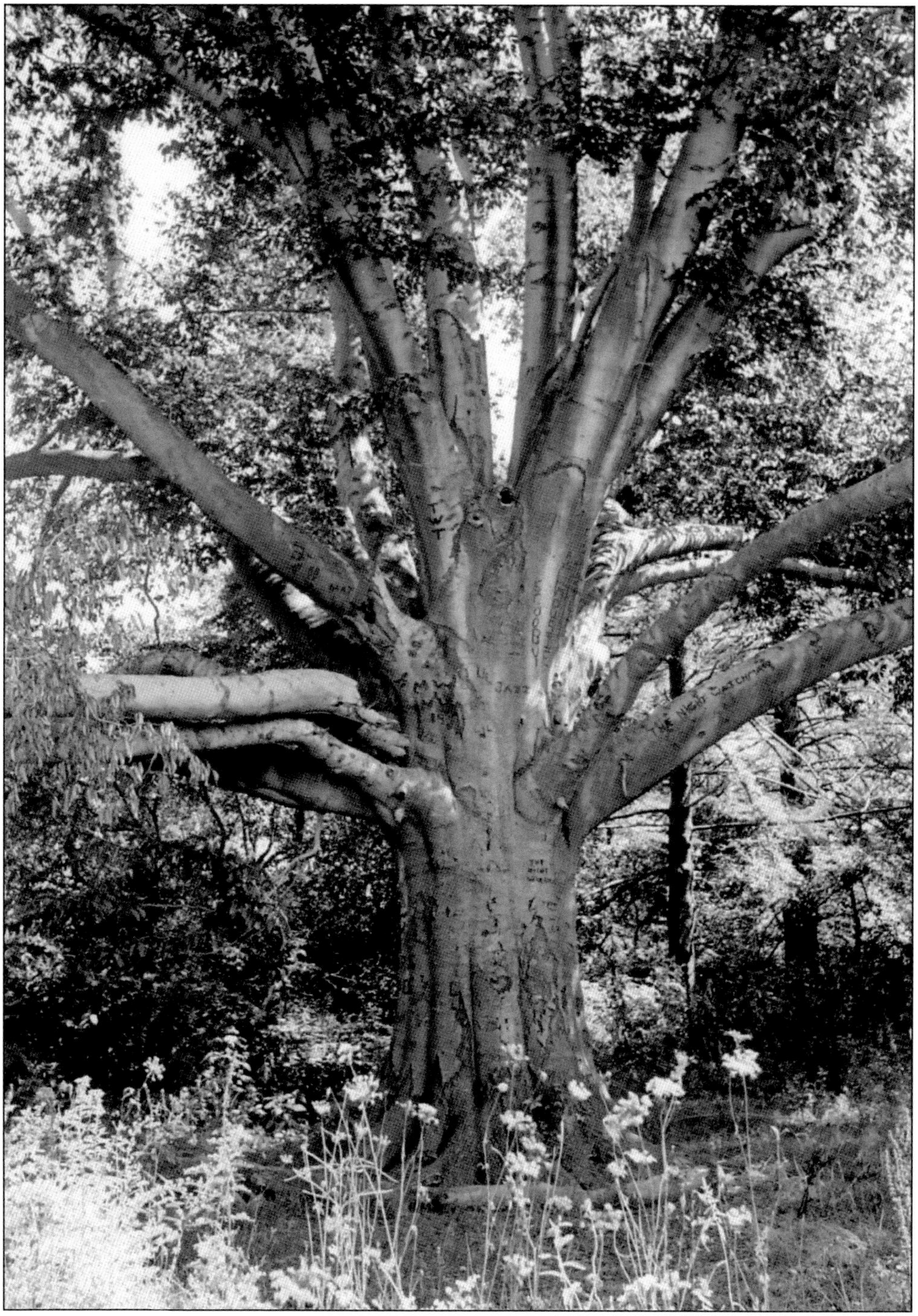

One of Willingboro's most famous residents lives in the Garfield Park neighborhood—but it is not a person. It is a more-than-300-year-old beech tree with a circumference of 14 feet and 4 inches. Township leaders contend that it is the second largest beech tree in the United States. A drawing of the tree is featured on the township's seal. (Courtesy Willingboro Township Manager's Office.)

Two

Rancocas Village
The Center of Commerce and Culture

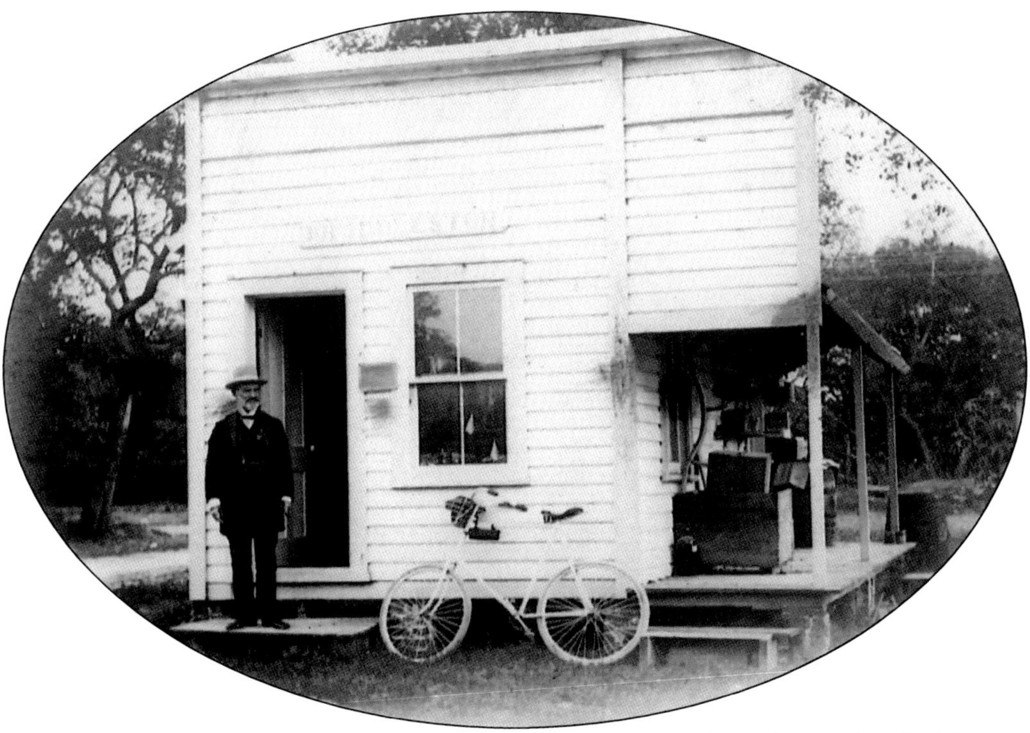

Ben Bishop and his wife were one of the village's entrepreneurial couples. In their building on West Main Street, they operated a candy store, an ice-cream parlor, and a harness shop. In this undated photograph, a man poses outside the shop. At that time, the name above the store's entrance was Huddleston. (Courtesy Rancocas Historical Society.)

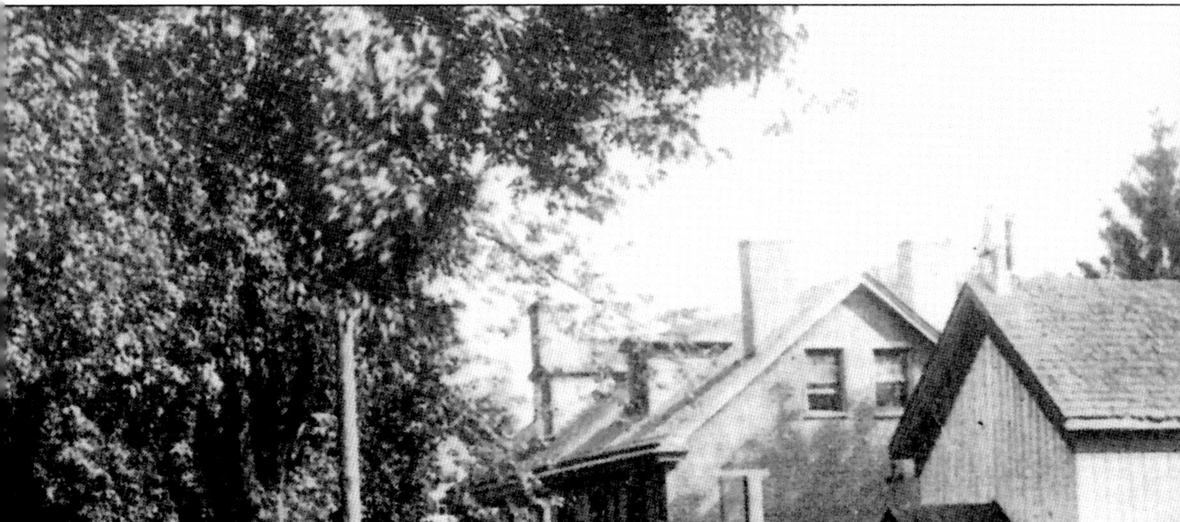

This is a photograph of Main Street in the early 1900s. At the time, the street was still made of dirt and filled with ruts. The building on the right, behind the child, served as the Episcopal church until it was torn down in the 1930s. (Courtesy Rancocas Historical Society.)

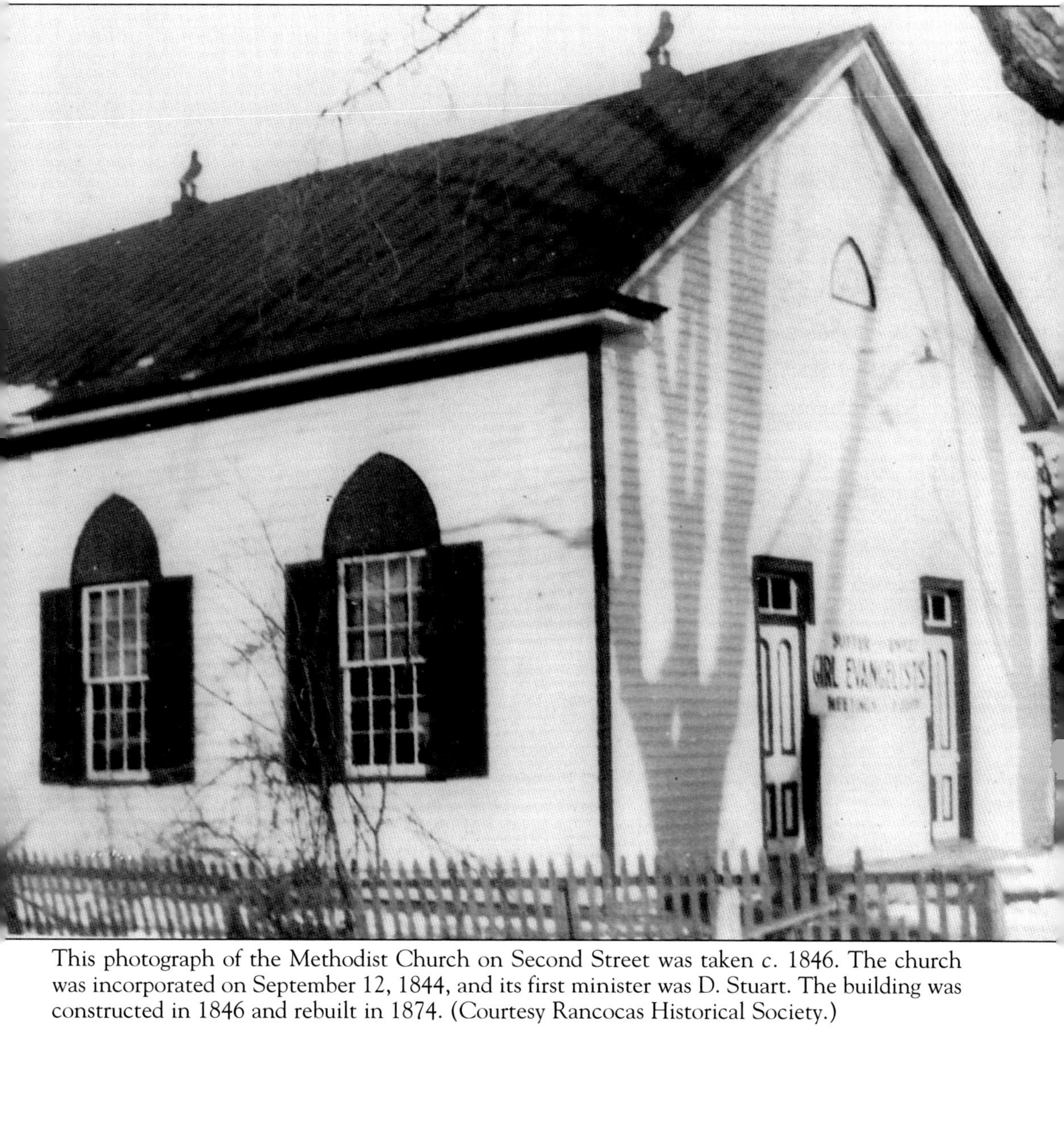

This photograph of the Methodist Church on Second Street was taken *c.* 1846. The church was incorporated on September 12, 1844, and its first minister was D. Stuart. The building was constructed in 1846 and rebuilt in 1874. (Courtesy Rancocas Historical Society.)

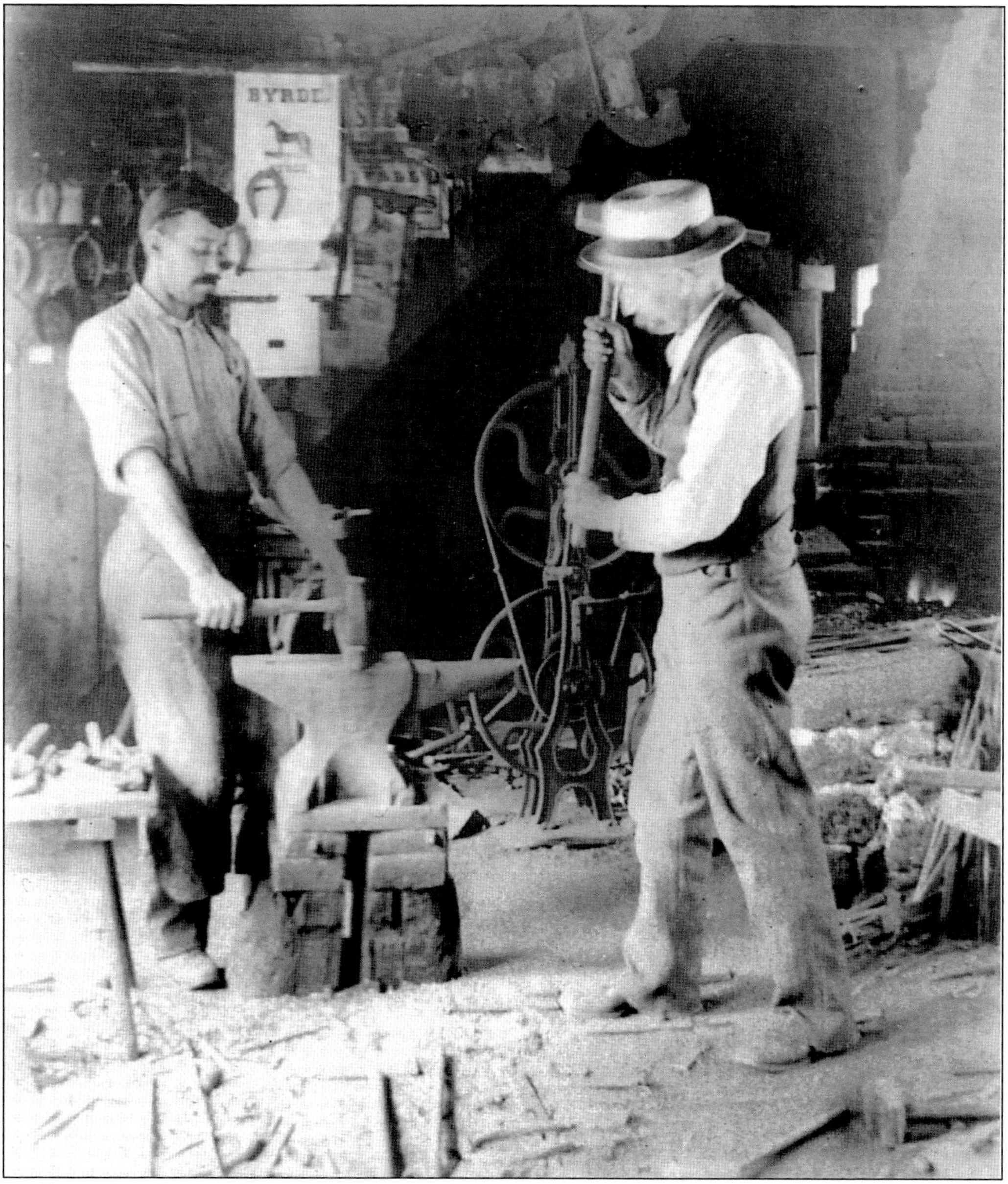

Wallis and William Fish work with a hammer and anvil in the blacksmith shop on Bridge Street in the late 1800s or early 1900s. William Fish and Theadore Whitcraft owned the blacksmith shop and the adjoining wheelwright shop until the 1930s. Both crafts were in heavy demand until cars took over the local roads. During the Civil War, the Union League of Rancocas met in a hall above the blacksmith shop. After the North won, the Order of United American Mechanics took over the hall. (Courtesy Rancocas Historical Society.)

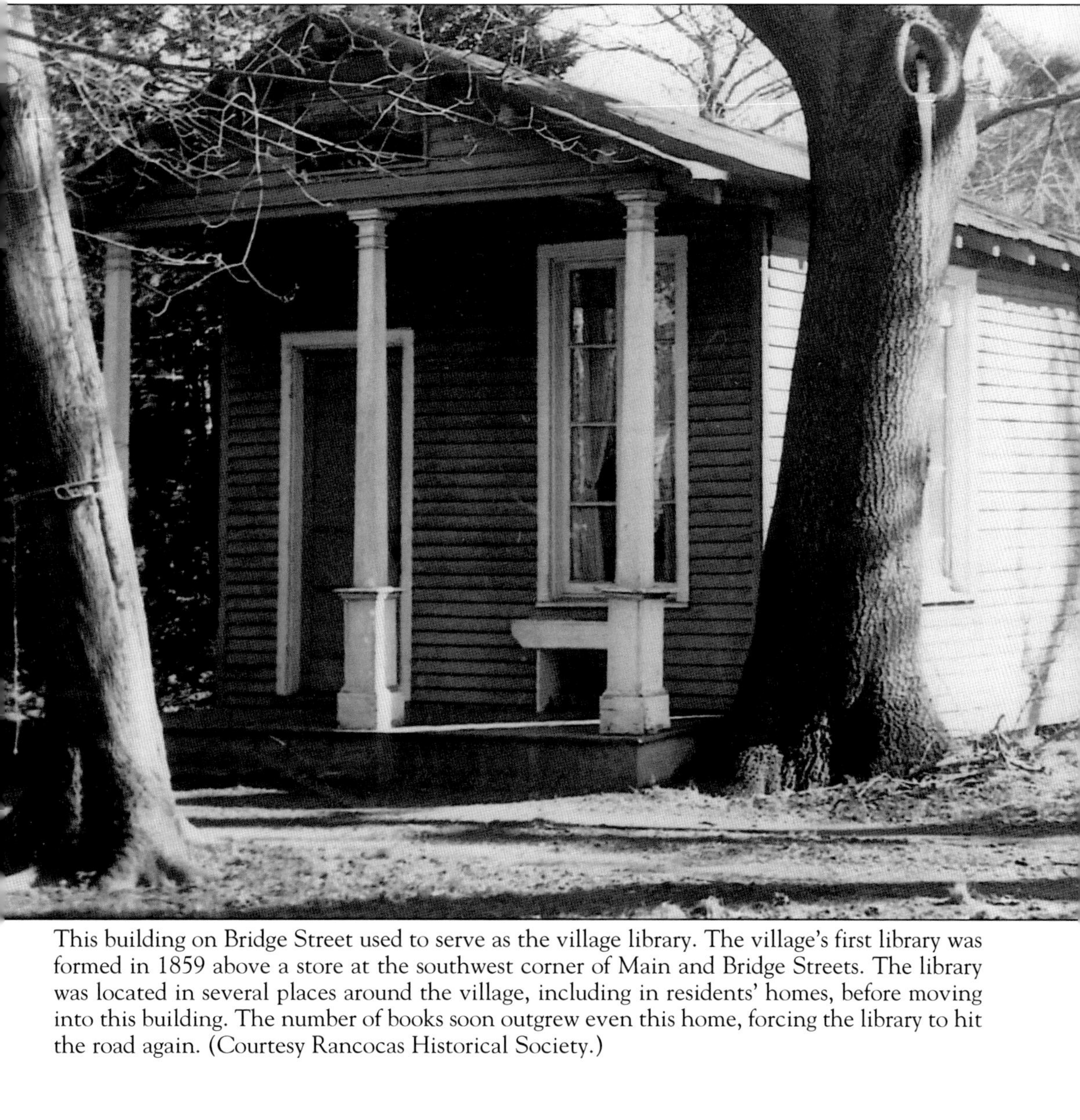

This building on Bridge Street used to serve as the village library. The village's first library was formed in 1859 above a store at the southwest corner of Main and Bridge Streets. The library was located in several places around the village, including in residents' homes, before moving into this building. The number of books soon outgrew even this home, forcing the library to hit the road again. (Courtesy Rancocas Historical Society.)

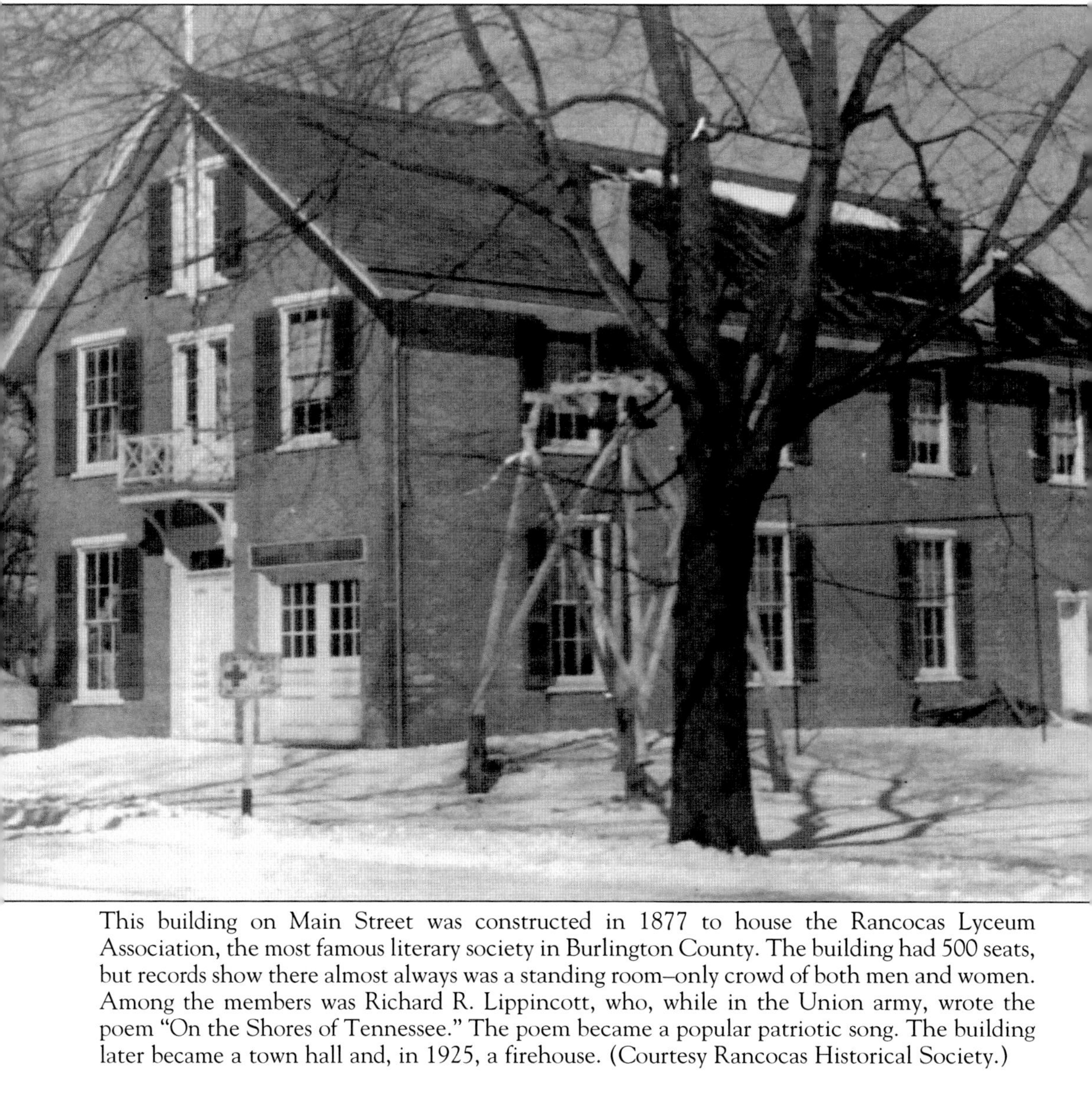

This building on Main Street was constructed in 1877 to house the Rancocas Lyceum Association, the most famous literary society in Burlington County. The building had 500 seats, but records show there almost always was a standing room–only crowd of both men and women. Among the members was Richard R. Lippincott, who, while in the Union army, wrote the poem "On the Shores of Tennessee." The poem became a popular patriotic song. The building later became a town hall and, in 1925, a firehouse. (Courtesy Rancocas Historical Society.)

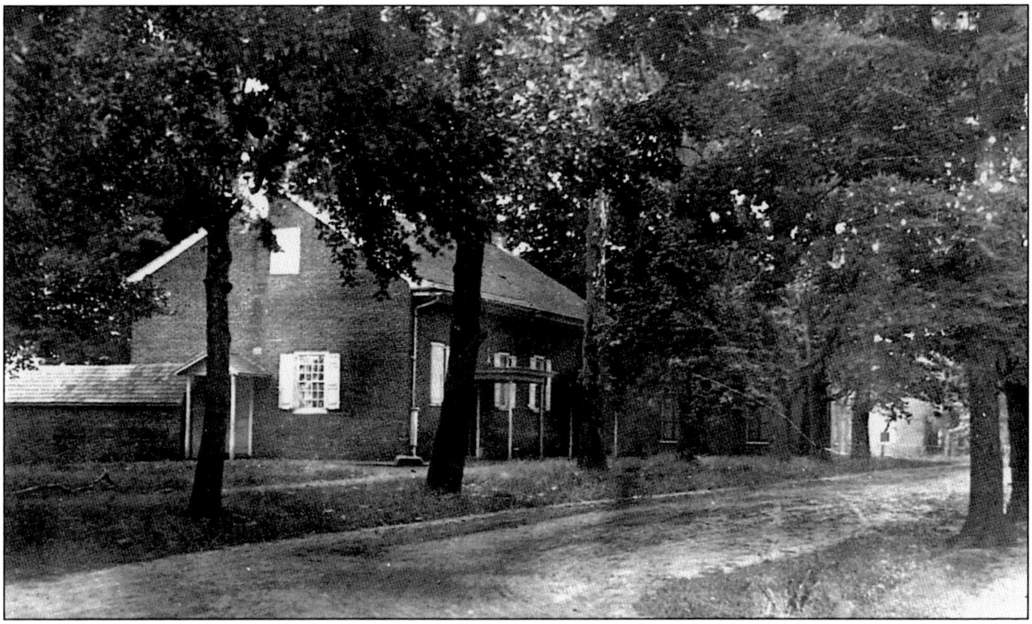

Shown is the Rancocas Friends Meeting House on East Main Street, as seen from Bridge Street. The first Rancocas meetinghouse was built in 1772 and an adjacent schoolhouse in 1773. The brick building was constructed in 1822 to replace the original wood frame structure. (Courtesy Rancocas Historical Society.)

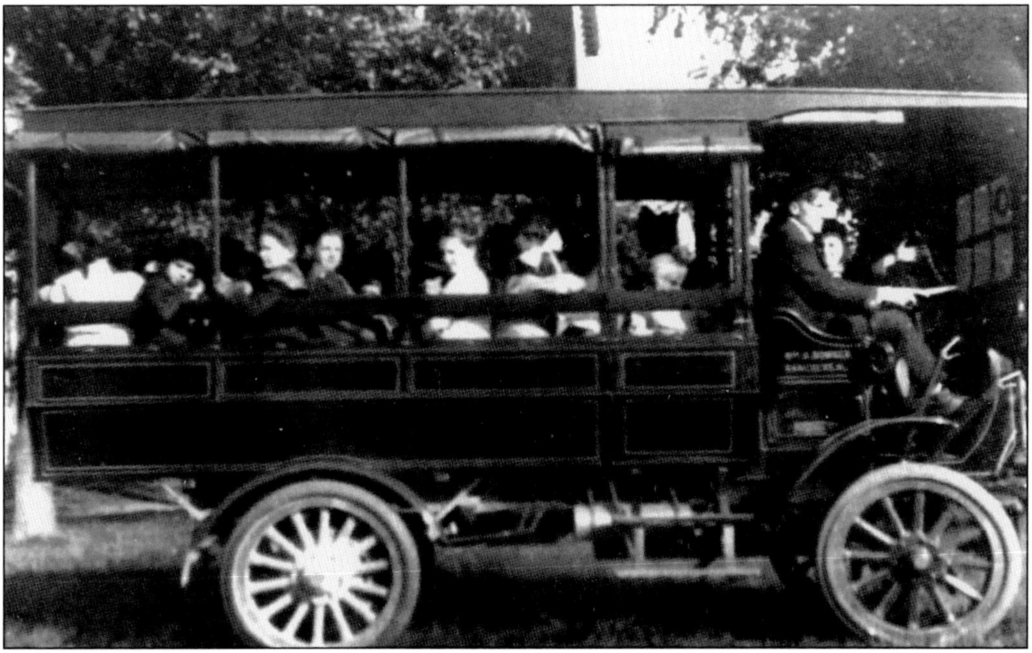

An early motorized school bus transports children to a school in Rancocas Village. The school was built in 1874 by the trustees of Willingboro School District No. 32 and later became Rancocas Grange No. 131. (Courtesy Rancocas Historical Society.)

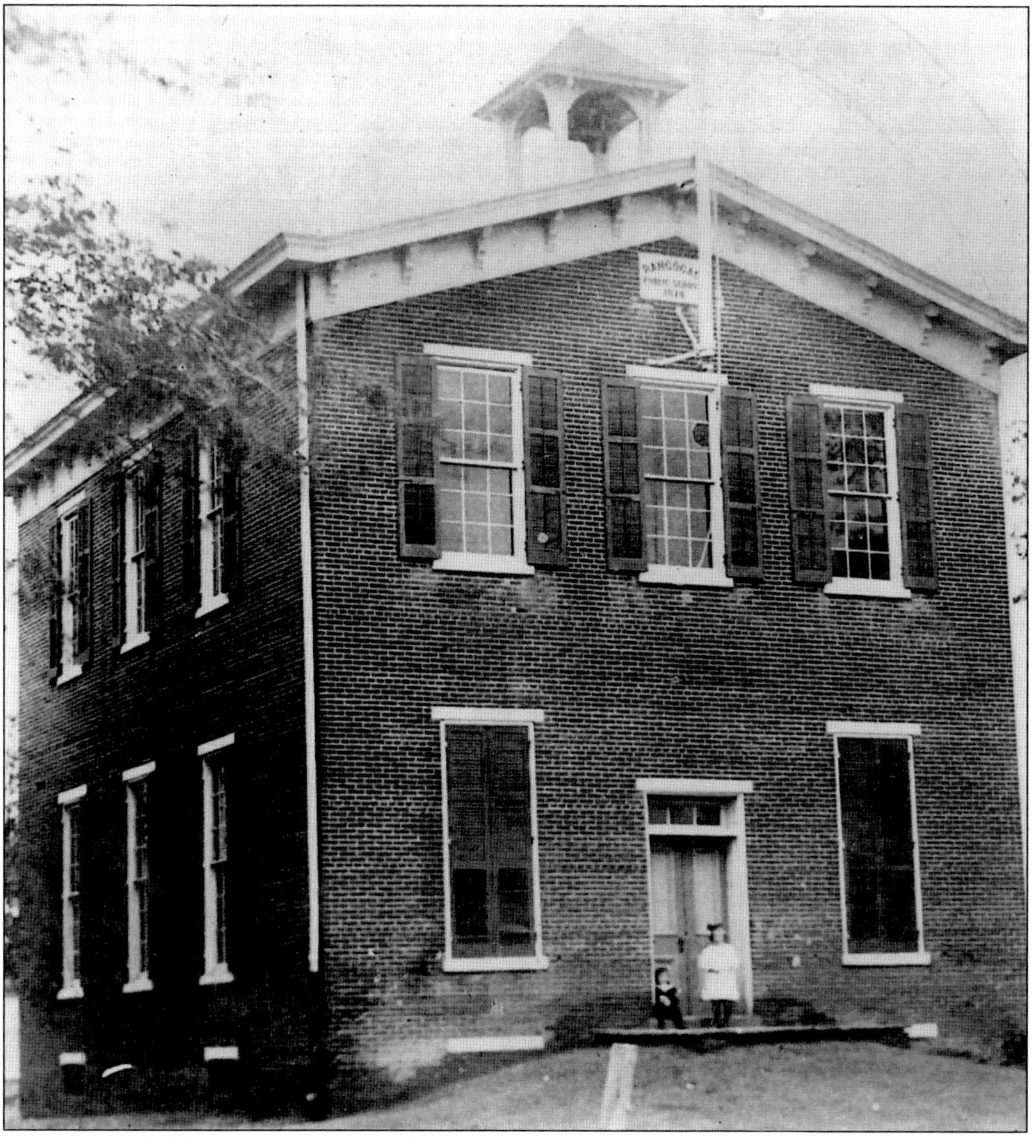

These two children were presumably two of the 86 children who attended Willingboro School District No. 32 when it opened in 1874, the year this photograph was taken. When the trustees constructed this large, two-story brick building, it was the first public school in the village. According to *The History of Burlington County*, by Maj. E.M. Woodward, teachers identified with the school were Jacob Knight, Susan Haines, Mordecai Matlack, Martha Haines, David Stokes, Merebiah Wright, Jarret Stokes, and William Stokes. The building was later purchased and operated as Rancocas Grange No. 131 from 1918 to 1968. (Courtesy Rancocas Historical Society.)

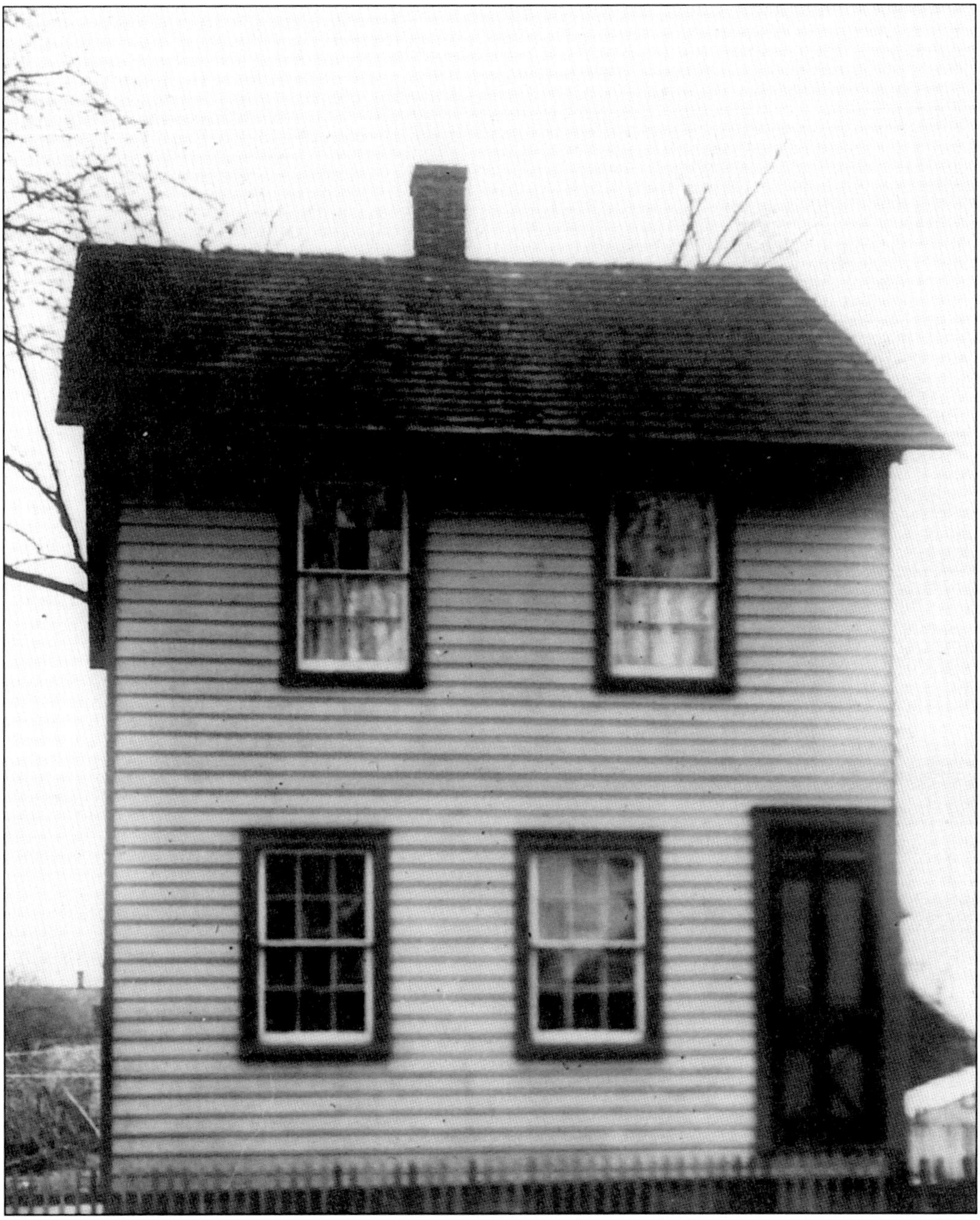

This house at 122 West Second Street was likely built along with the Steam Flour Grist Mill in 1854 and 1855 by William Brock. (Courtesy Rancocas Historical Society.)

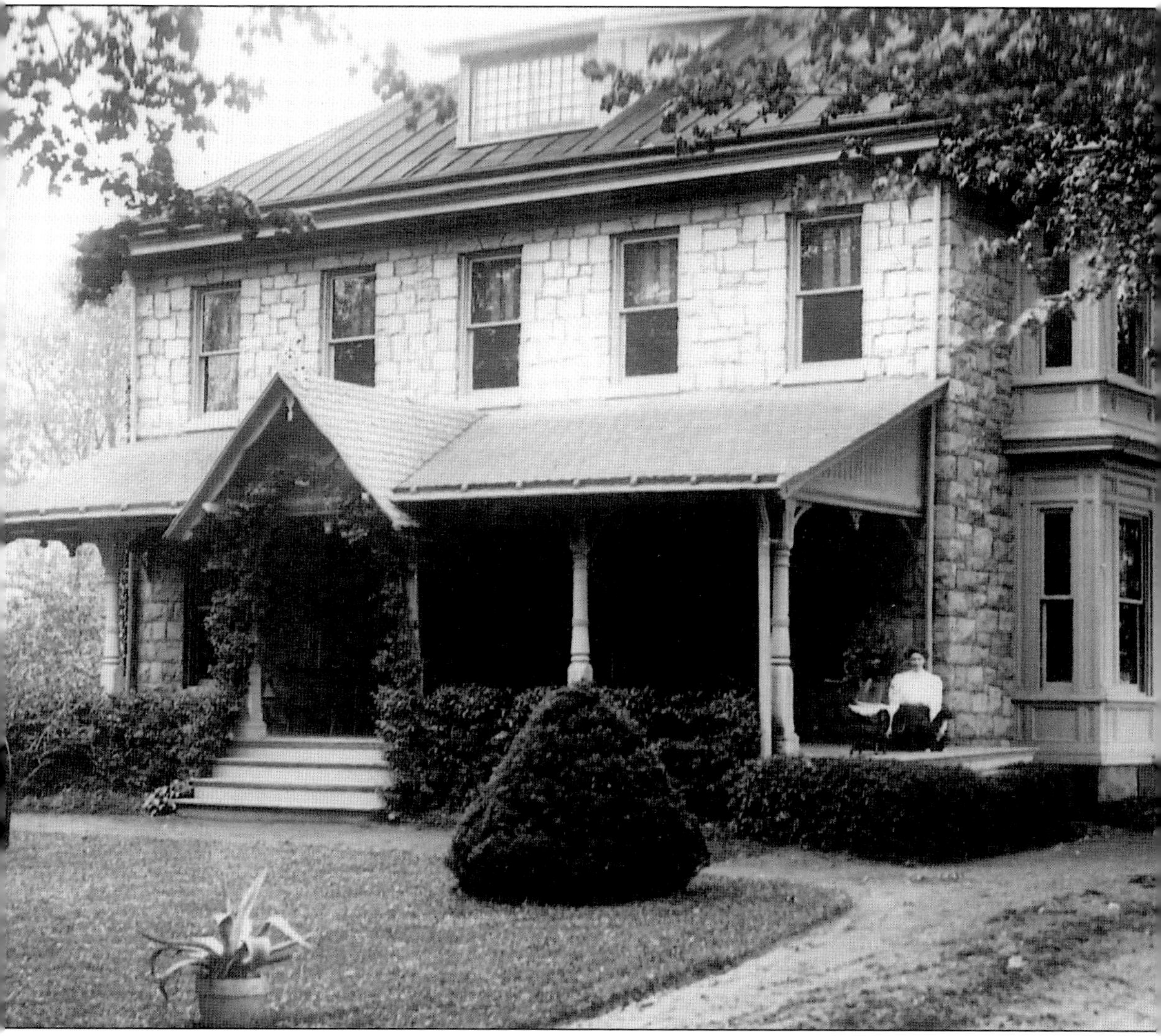

Stones imported from Pennsylvania by barge were used to build this house in Rancocas Village, once part of a very large estate owned by Elwood Hart. According to the records of the Rancocas Historical Society, Ella M. Lippincott sold the house to Joseph and John Wills in 1883 or 1884. (Courtesy Rancocas Historical Society.)

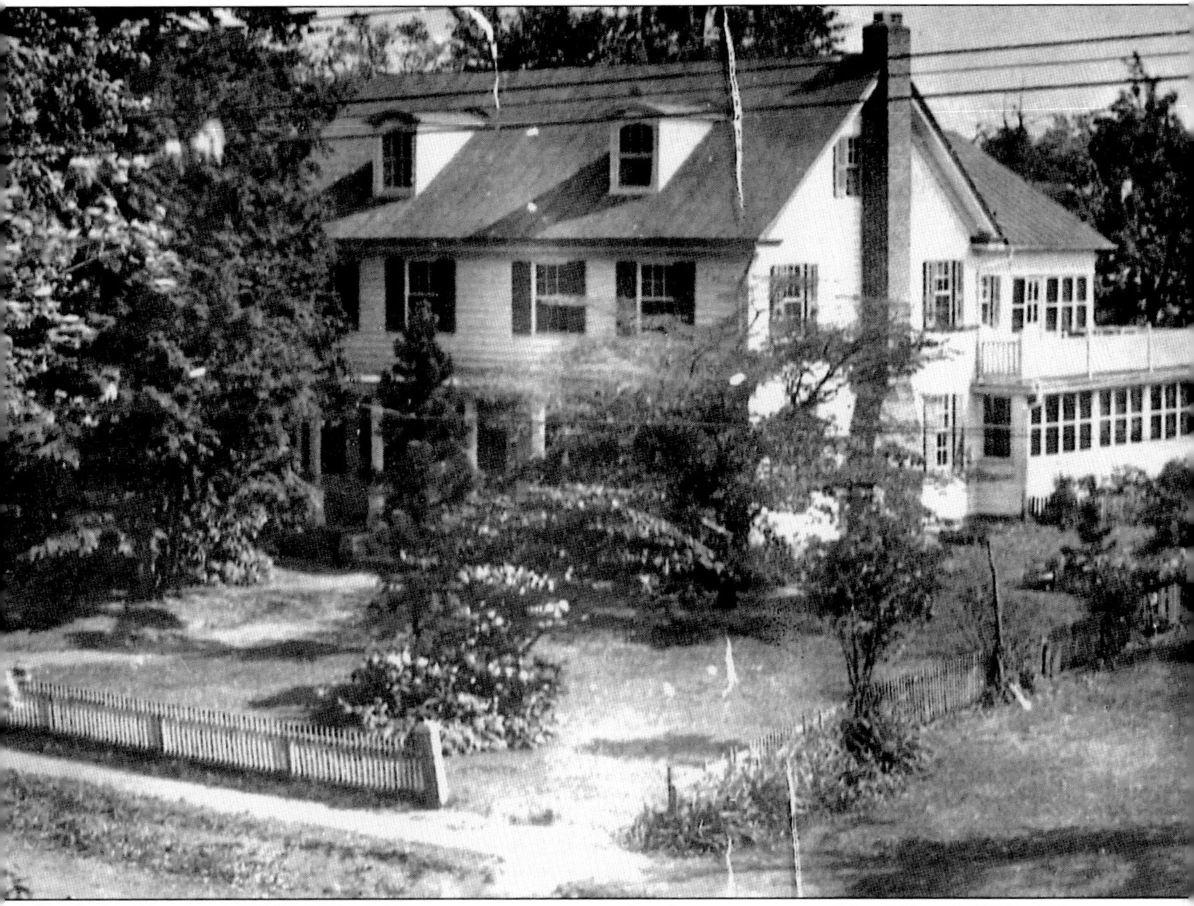

This house at 110 West Main Street was once part of a plantation owned by Samuel Wills. The property ran from the Rancocas Creek on the west side of Bridge Street to Main Street. Samuel Wills sold the land to Samuel Ellis. Joseph Lundy bought the land from Ellis in 1805, who in turn sold it to Ezra Haines in 1837. Village records indicate a house has been standing there since 1810. Several additions were constructed, the last being in 1936. All of the property's owners have been part of the Stokes family, either directly or through marriage. (Courtesy Rancocas Historical Society.)

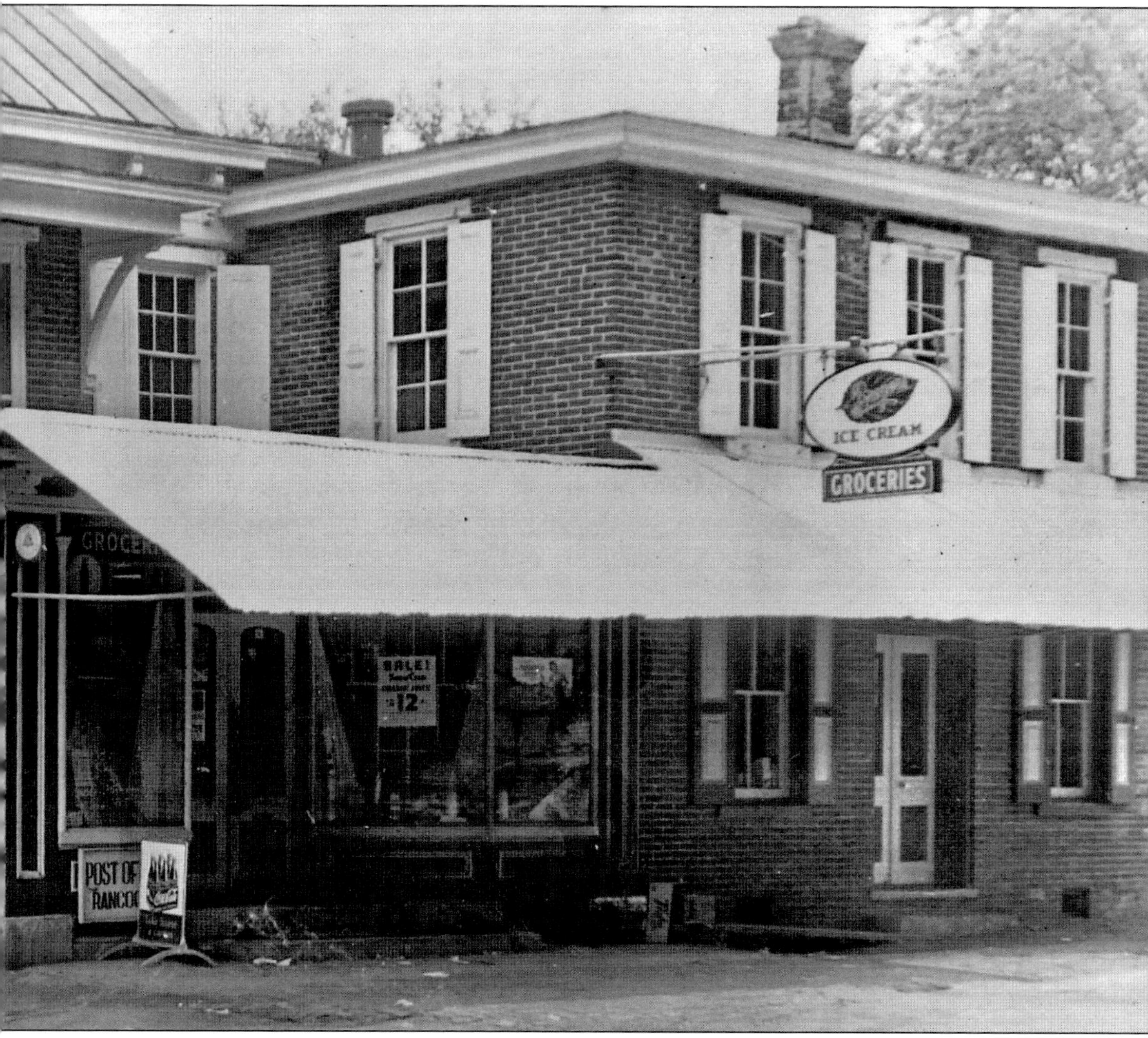

Before the age of supermarkets and shopping malls, people relied on general stores. In the early to mid-1900s, Stevens General Store stood at the corner of Bridge and Main Streets in Rancocas Village. Various signs on the store advertised Breyer's Ice Cream, groceries, Coca-cola, a public telephone, and orange juice on sale for 12¢. The store also contained a post office and Billy Bowker's Barber Shop. (Courtesy Rancocas Historical Society.)

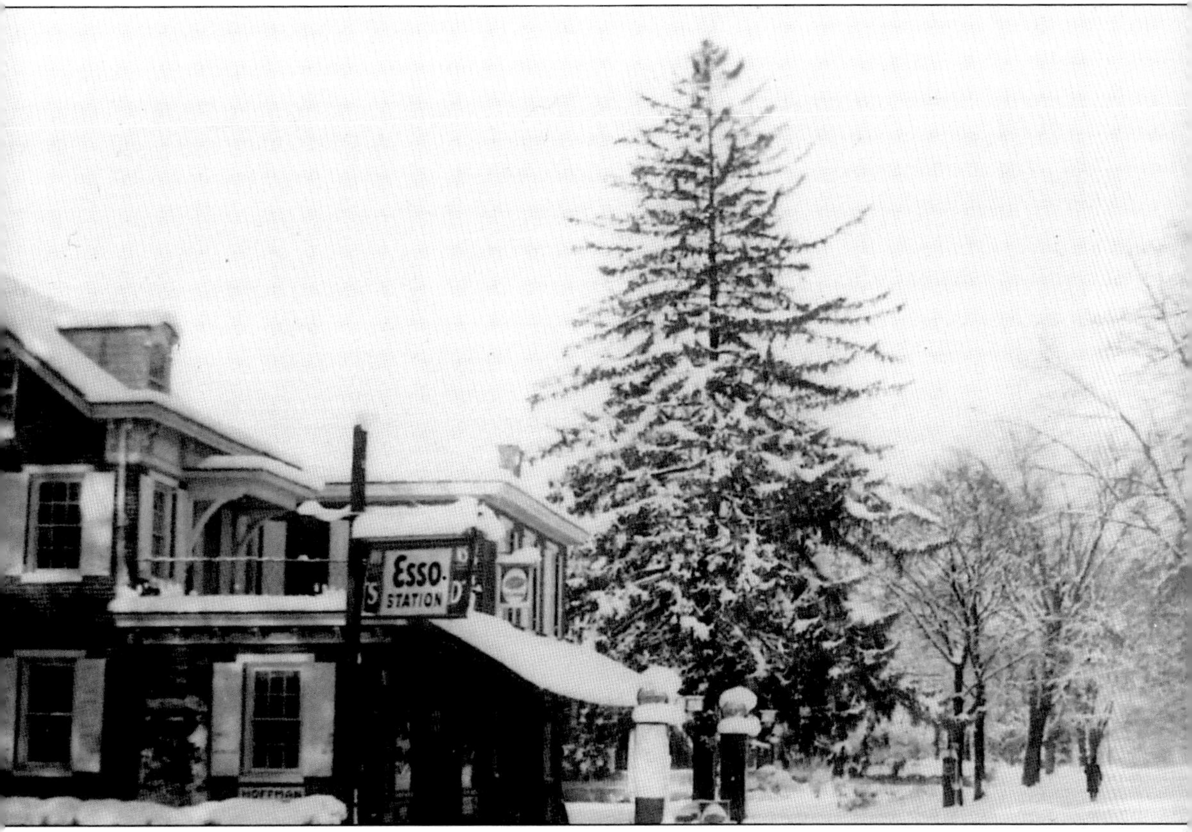

From 1928 to 1940, Stevens General Store served as an Esso gas station. Perhaps the winter snow shown here prevented people from filling up their automobiles. (Courtesy Rancocas Historical Society.)

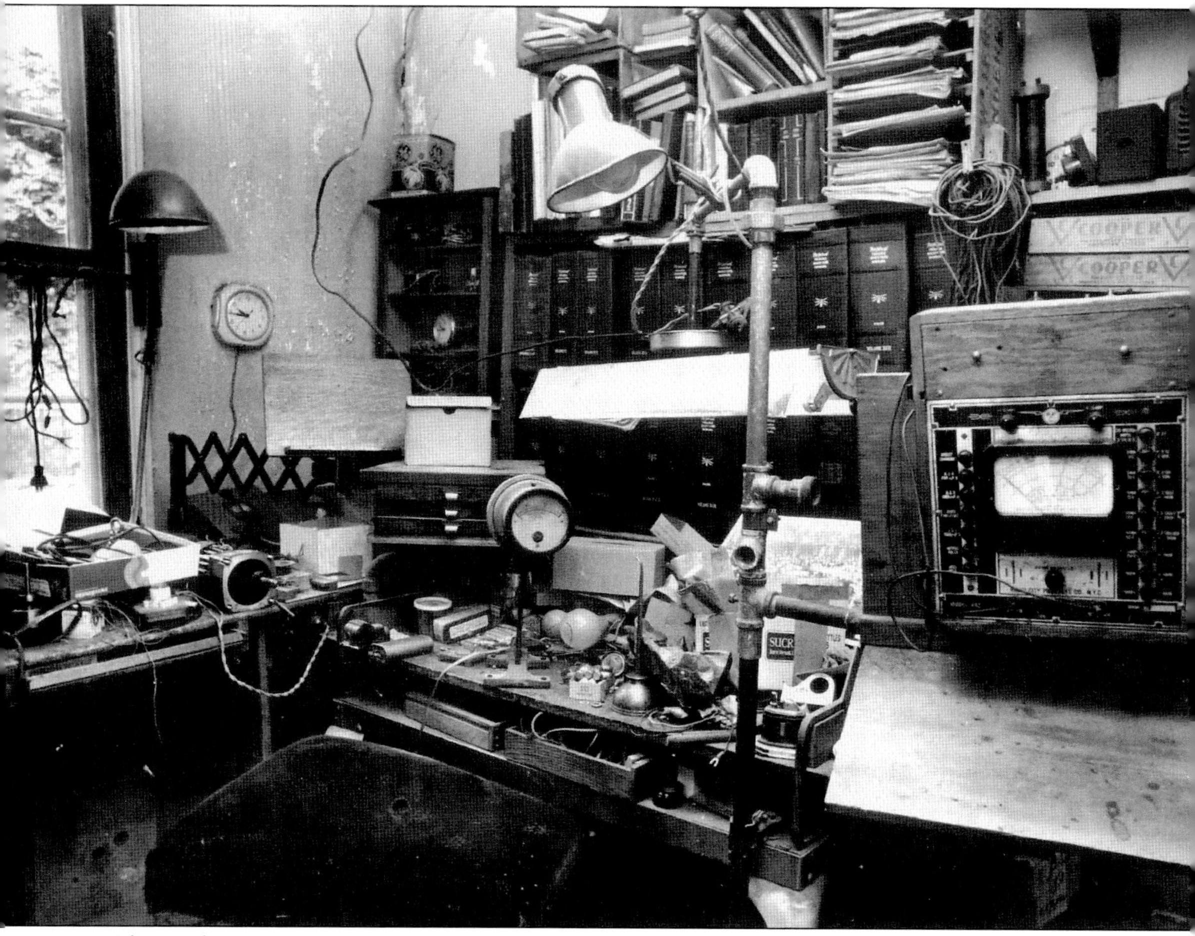

Above the general store, Mr. Stevens had a workshop in which he repaired radios. This photograph depicts the radio room's appearance during the 1940s. (Courtesy Rancocas Historical Society.)

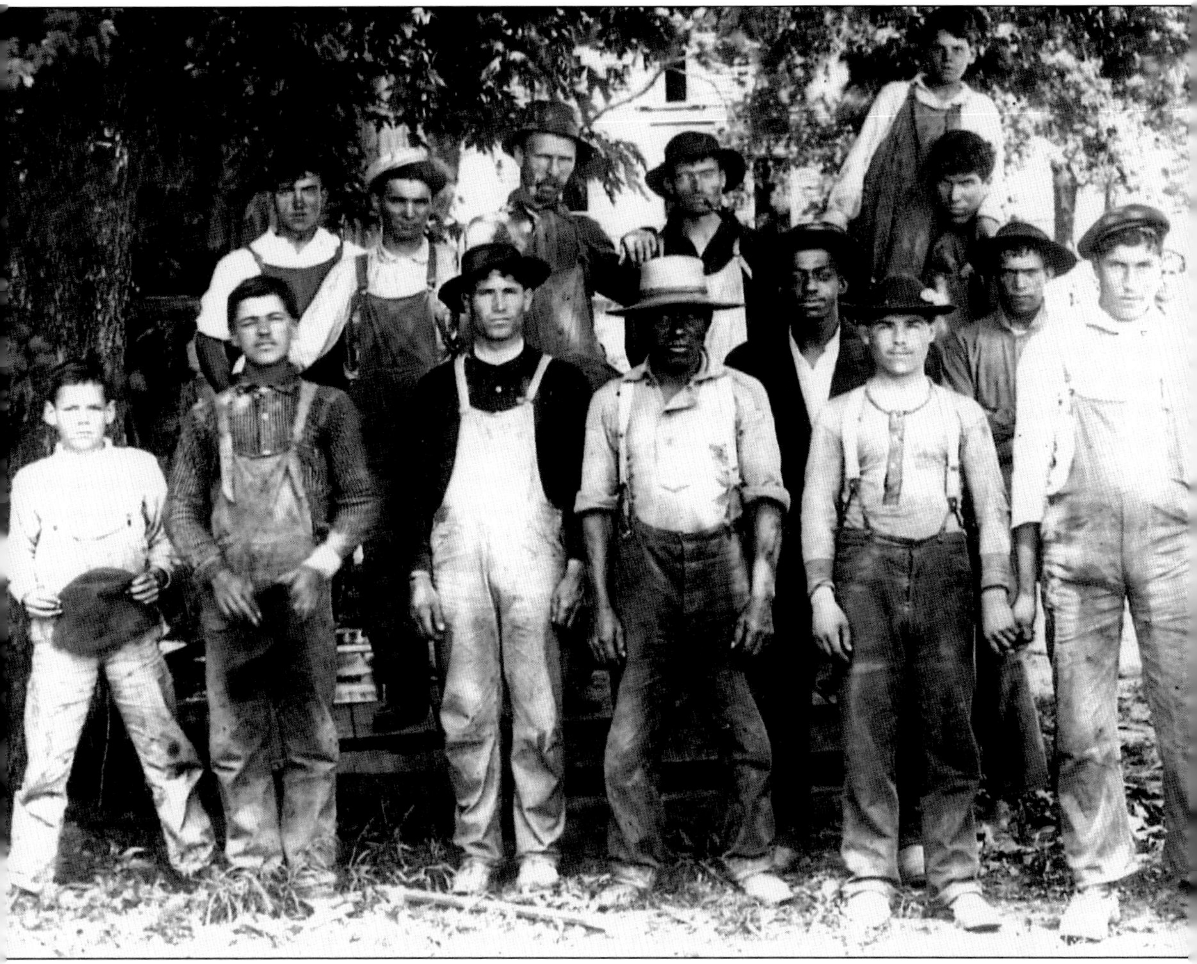

Residents of Rancocas Village worked on the railroad in the 19th and early 20th centuries. A train owned by James Stokes was used to transport gravel from a pit in what is now the Timbercrest development to barges on the Rancocas Creek. The tracks ran along the east side of Bridge Street and Centerton Road. A train trestle ran east of the Centerton Bridge to Texas Avenue in the Centerton section of Mount Laurel. Trucks brought gravel from the pit to the train. A tugboat named *Annie*—possibly after Stokes's mother, Annie McIlvain Stokes—piloted the gravel-laden barges down the creek. (Courtesy Rancocas Historical Society.)

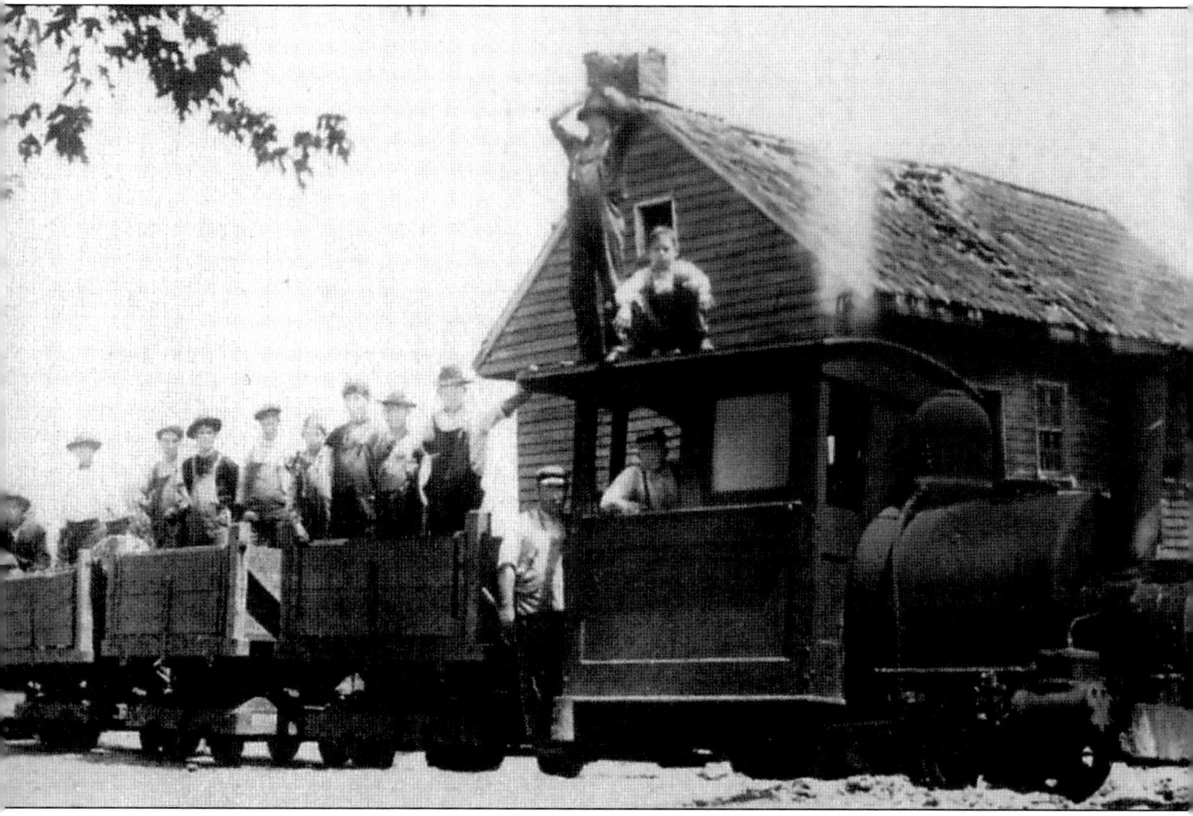

More than a dozen railroad workers take a break on the train owned by Jim Stokes. Among the Rancocas Village family names associated with the train were North, Poole, Gaconey, Johnson, Haines, Buck, Kimble, and Rodgers. (Courtesy Rancocas Historical Society.)

Three

The Levittown Transformation

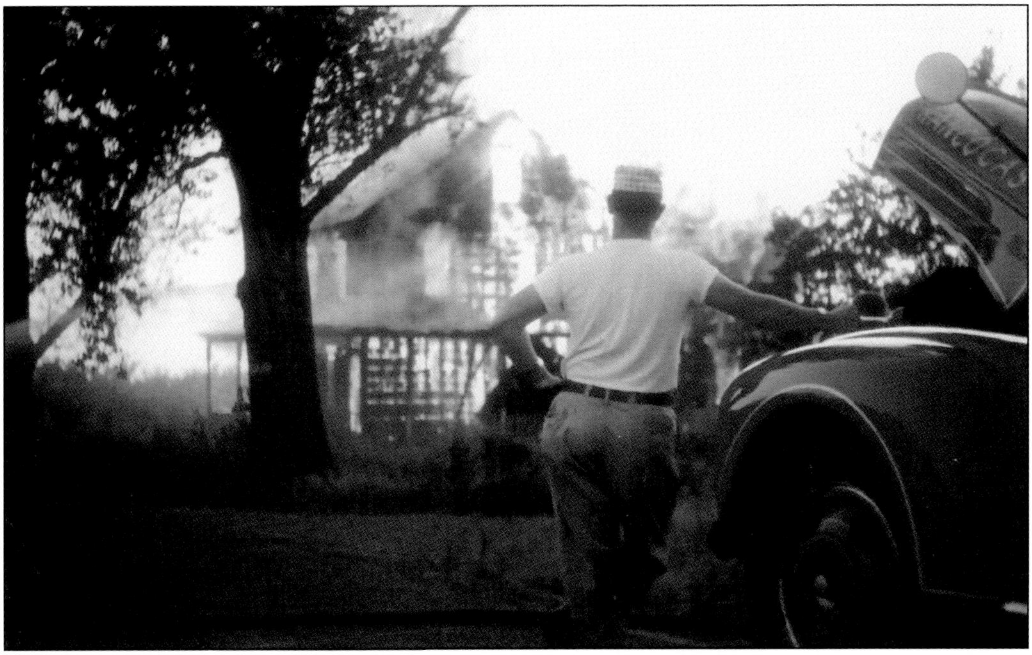

Levitt and Sons purchased most of the farms that comprised Willingboro in order to build the new development. As a result, many of the structures that had existed here for hundreds of years were burned to the ground. In this photograph, a man leans against a Rancocas fire engine as a house goes up in flames. (Courtesy Betty Sever.)

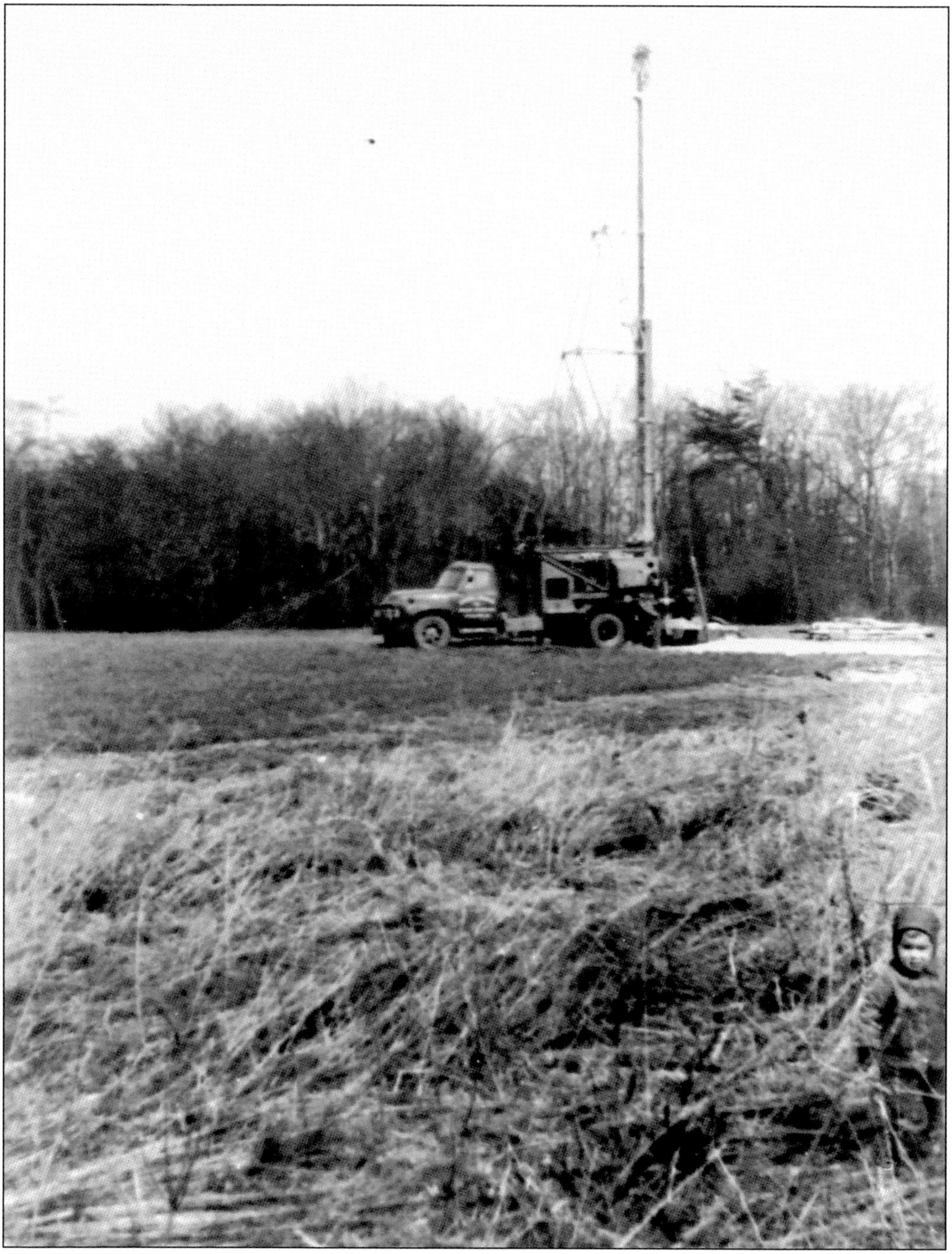

Workers for Levitt and Sons drill a well in the middle of a farm behind Sylvan Lane in March 1955. The girl in the corner has been identified as Jeanne Platt. (Courtesy Burlington County Times/Cramp family.)

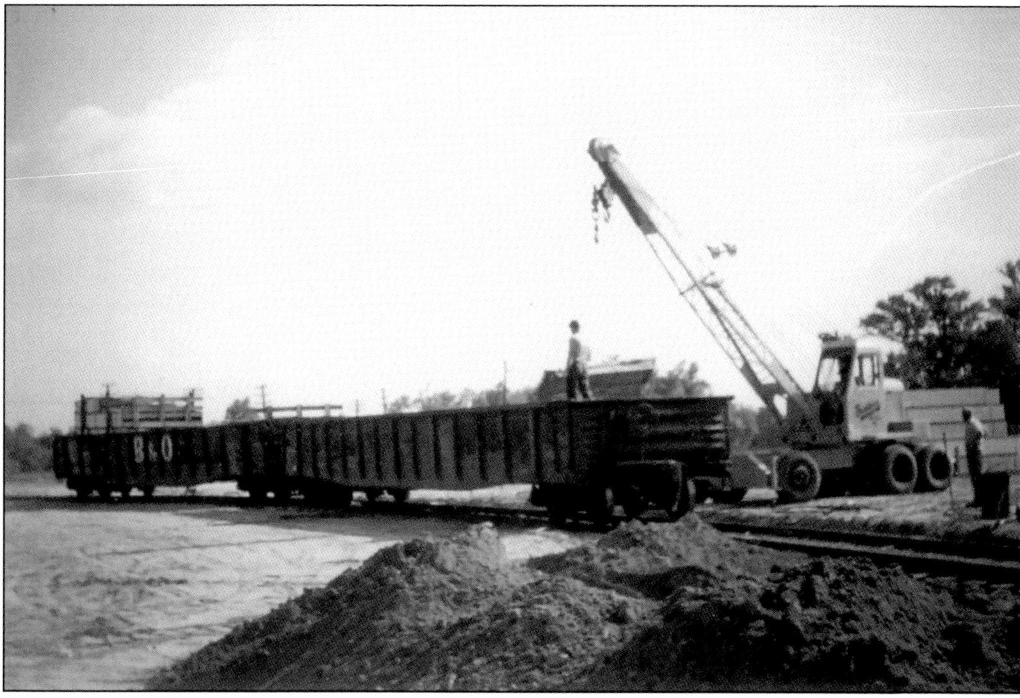

Levitt and Sons' houses were built quickly because they were made of prefabricated materials. Many of the materials were shipped by boat to Delanco and then loaded onto railroad cars for final transport to Willingboro. (Courtesy Carol J. Suplee/Cramp family.)

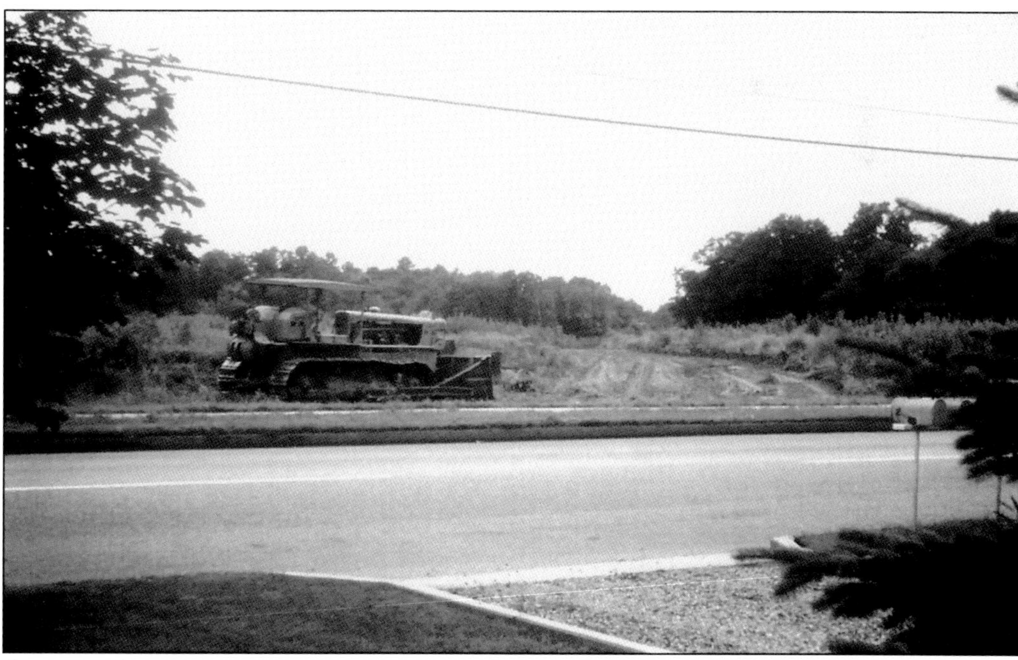

A piece of construction equipment paves the way for what would later become Somerset, Pennypacker, and Fairmount Parks. Within a few years, the land would be filled with houses. (Courtesy Betty Sever.)

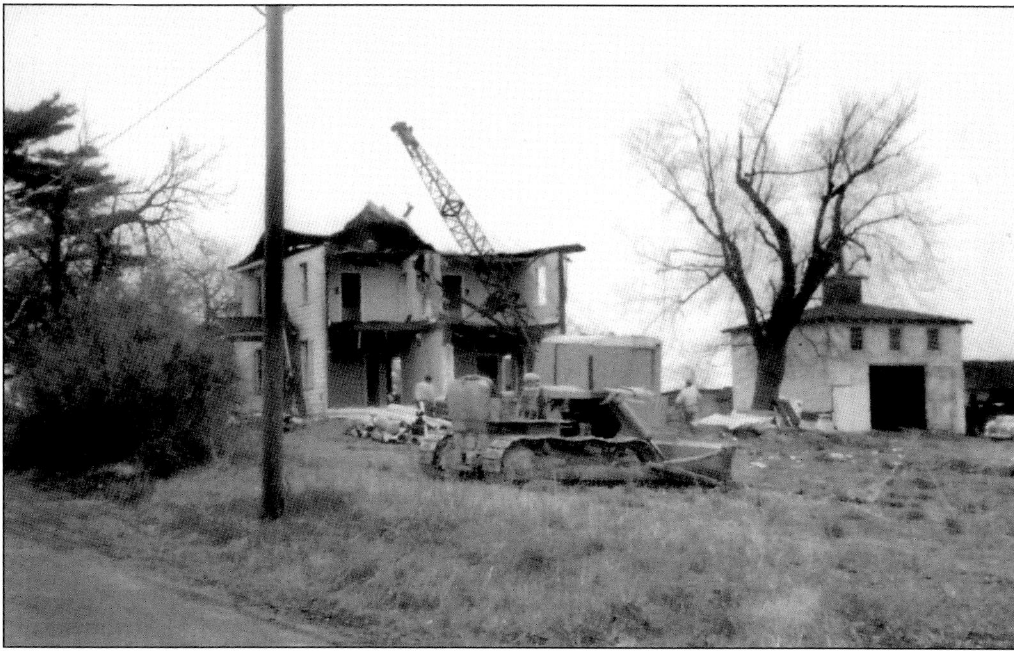

Another old Willingboro farmhouse falls victim to Levitt and Sons' wrecking ball. (Courtesy Betty Sever.)

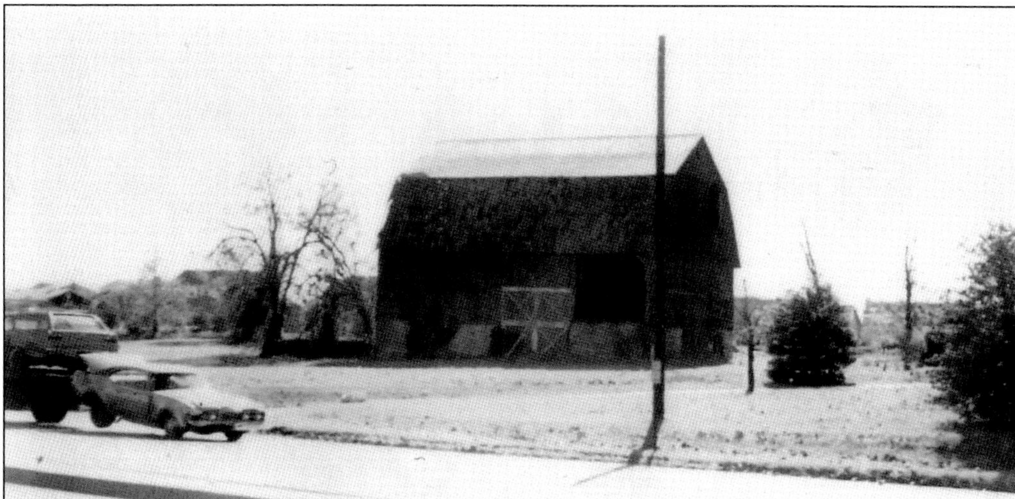

For a while, the farms and Levitt's new homes managed to coexist. In this photograph from the 1960s, a tow truck drives past a barn. (Courtesy Betty Sever.)

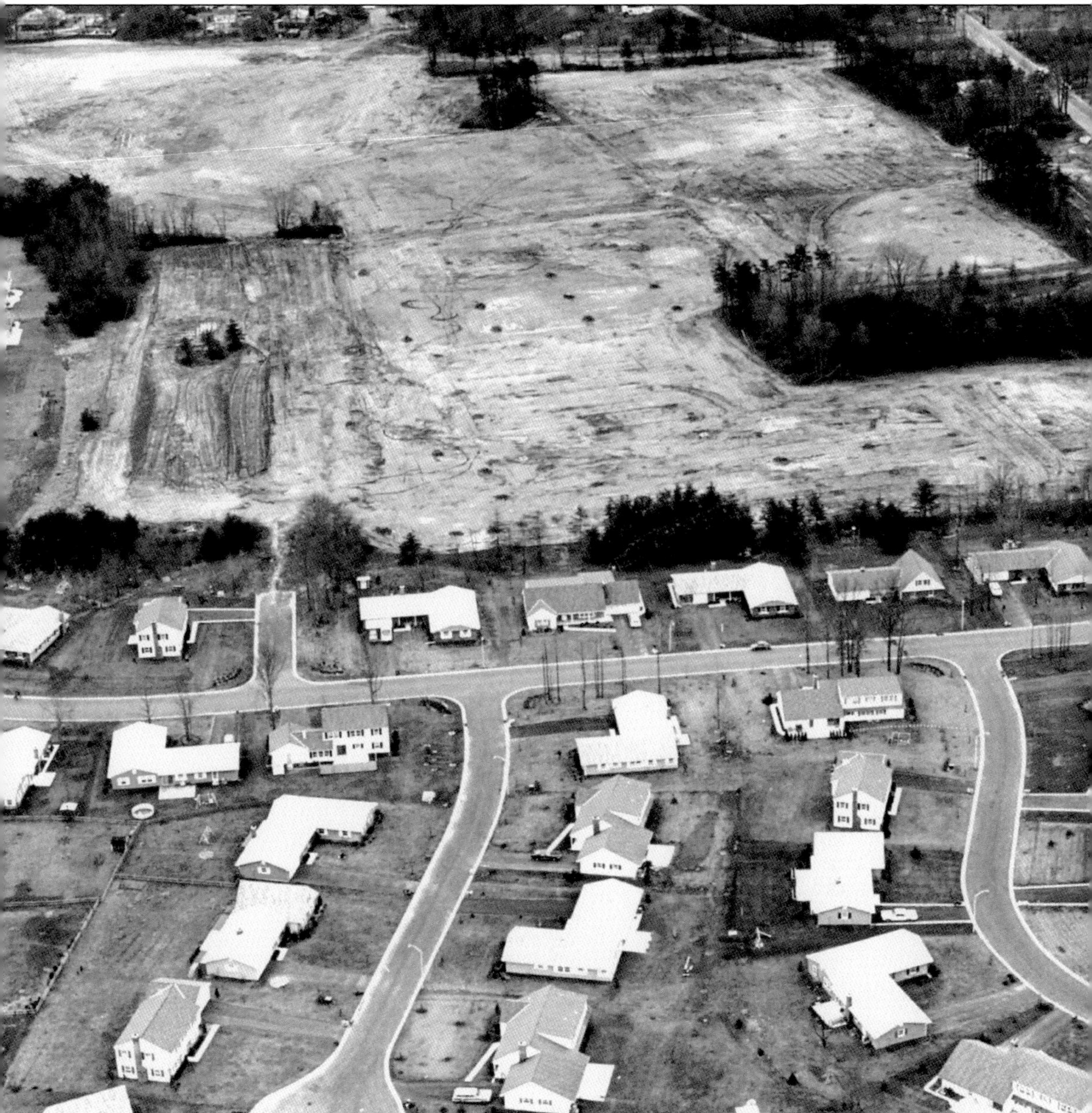

As Levitt's homes sprang up, open land became more and more rare. In this photograph, a farm that once belonged to the Perkins family was cleared to make way for a new high school. The road in the upper right was Park Road, which later became known as John F. Kennedy Way. (Courtesy Burlington County Times.)

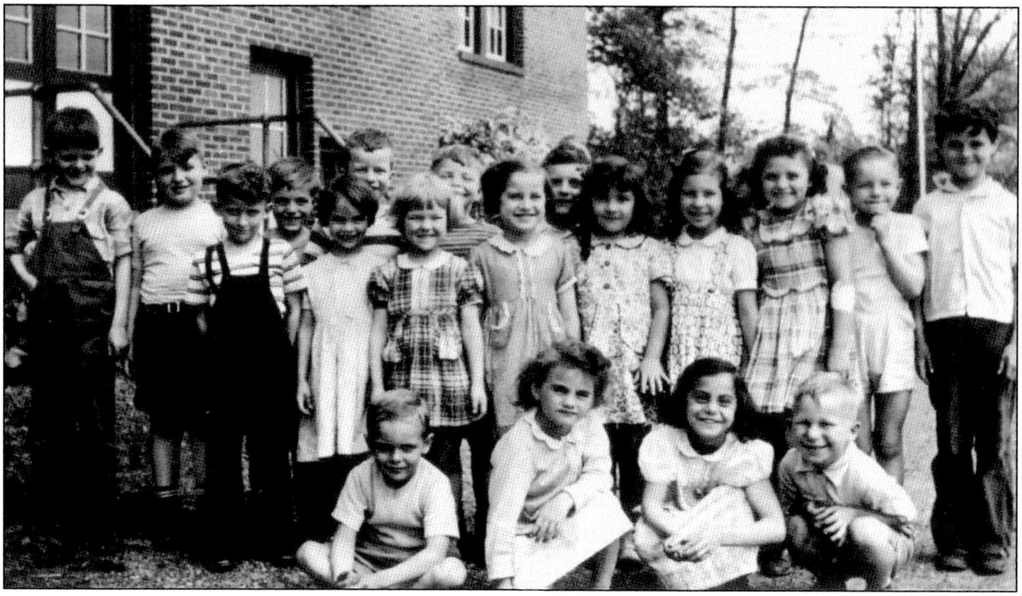

A group of children poses for a class photograph during the 1950s. The children attended the two-story Consolidated School on Salem Road, which was built in 1917 and 1918. The building was expanded three times between 1922 and 1939 to accommodate more classrooms, a stage, and a kitchen. (Courtesy Carol J. Suplee.)

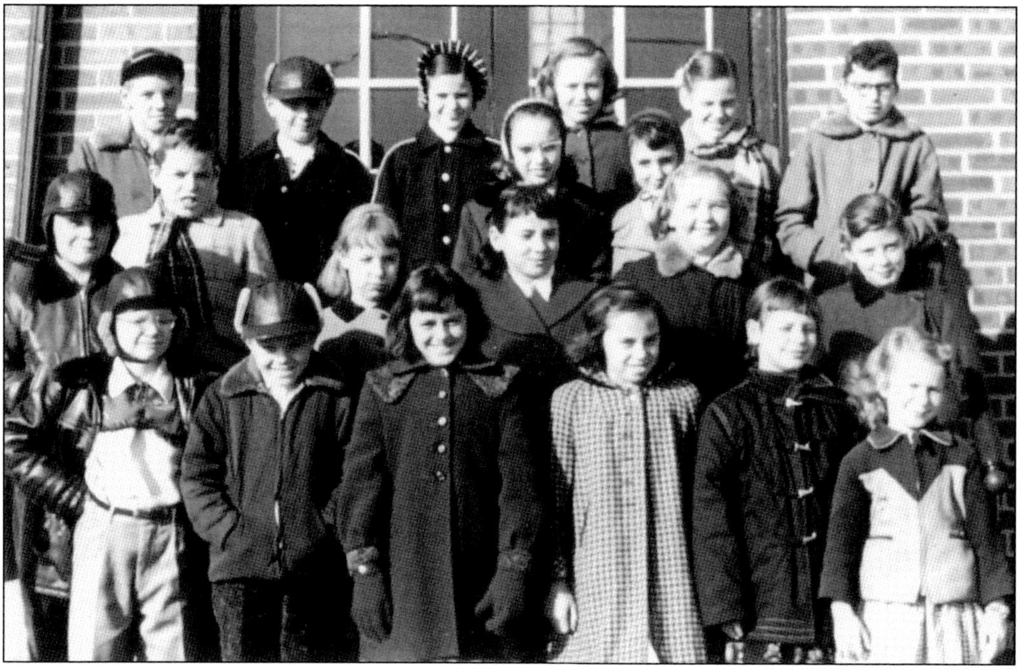

William Levitt and Sons began acquiring land in the township in 1954. Even as the community started to change, life went on for the children who attended the Consolidated School on Salem Road. This class photograph was taken *c.* 1956. (Courtesy Willingboro Public Library/ Stuart family.)

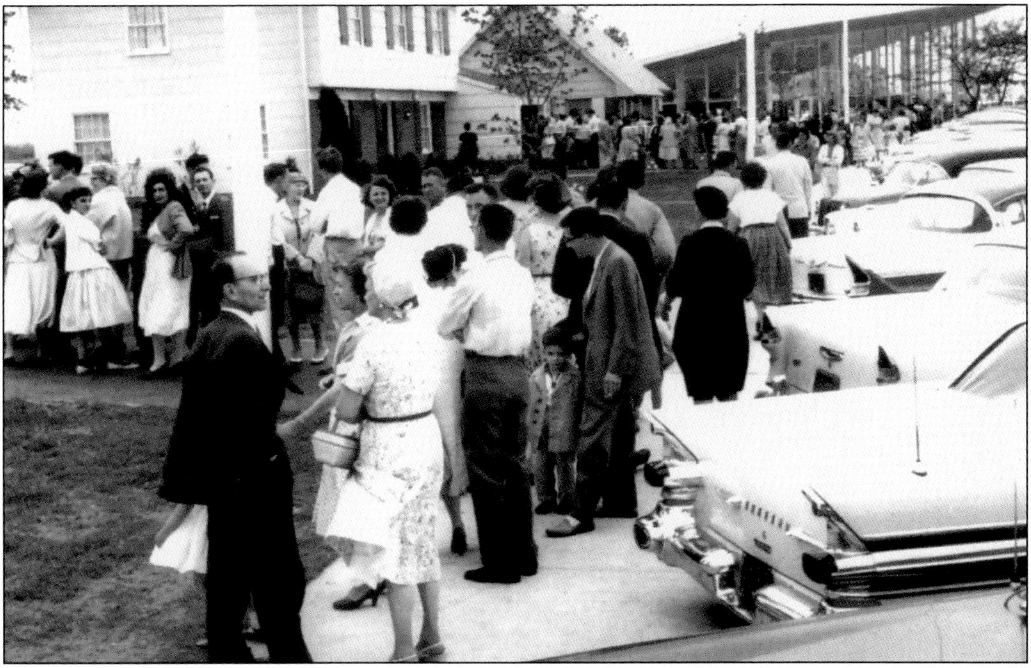

Thousands of people turned out to tour Levitt and Sons' model homes when they opened in 1958. The homes were affordable, costing between $11,900 and $14,500, and came with basic appliances attractive to young families with children. Prior to coming to Willingboro, Levitt had built 26,000 homes in nearby Bucks County, Pennsylvania. (Courtesy Willingboro Public Library.)

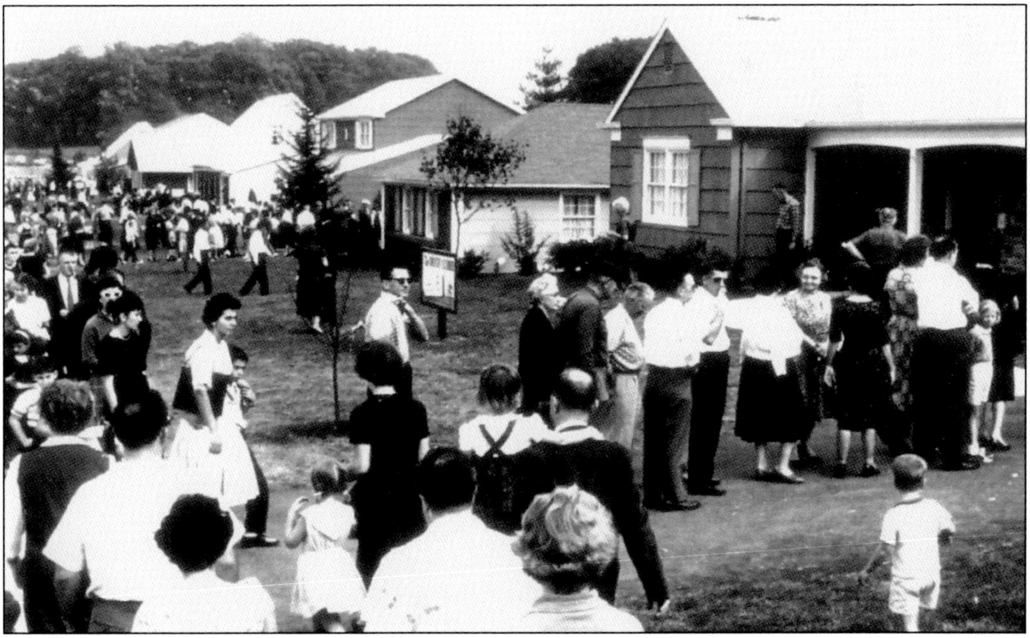

Crowds flocked to the new community every time Levitt and Sons debuted new model homes. In this photograph from 1965, potential residents look at models on Rockland Drive that would be built in Garfield Park. (Courtesy Willingboro Public Library.)

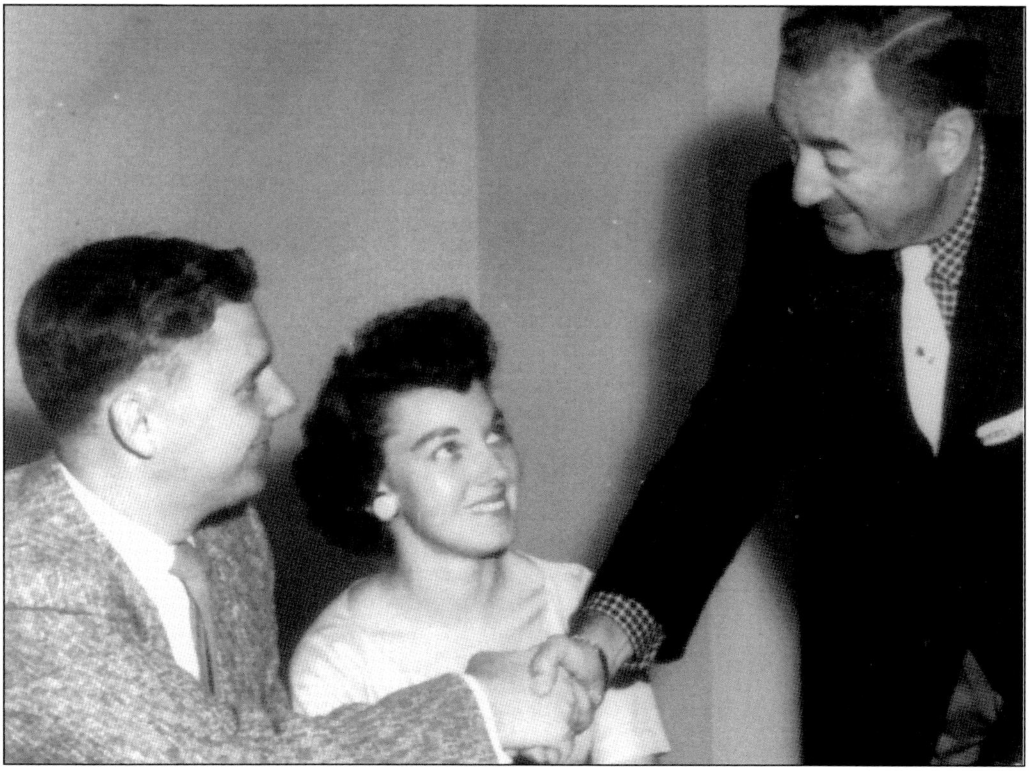

Leo Mount, 26, and his wife, Joan, were the first family to make final settlement on a home in Willingboro in 1958. The couple occupied a house at 51 Sussex Drive in the township's Somerset Park section. William Levitt (right) supervised the closing. (Courtesy Willingboro Public Library.)

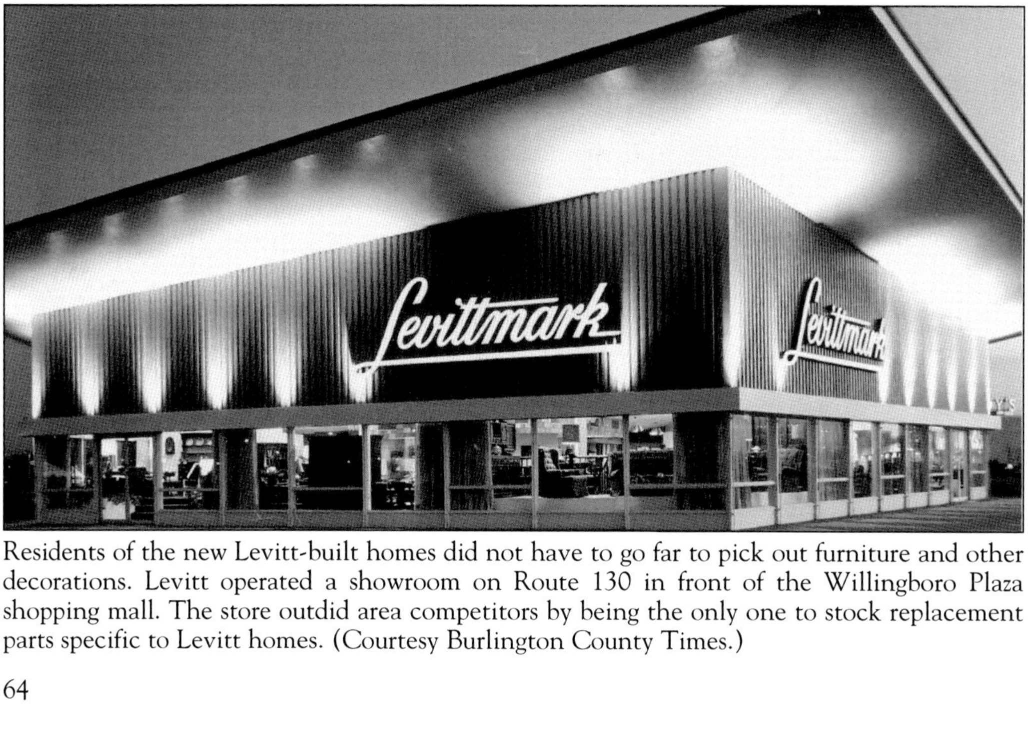

Residents of the new Levitt-built homes did not have to go far to pick out furniture and other decorations. Levitt operated a showroom on Route 130 in front of the Willingboro Plaza shopping mall. The store outdid area competitors by being the only one to stock replacement parts specific to Levitt homes. (Courtesy Burlington County Times.)

Just how much did it cost to purchase a house in Levittown? Signs like these posted in the model homes provide the answer: a Cape Cod cost $12,990, a Rancher $13,500, a Colonial $14,500 to $14,990, and the Country Clubber an expensive $22,990. (Courtesy Dave Retzko.)

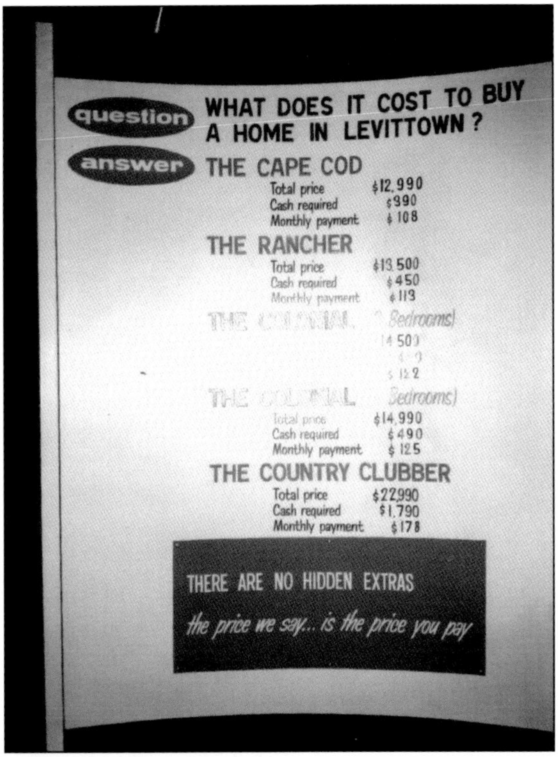

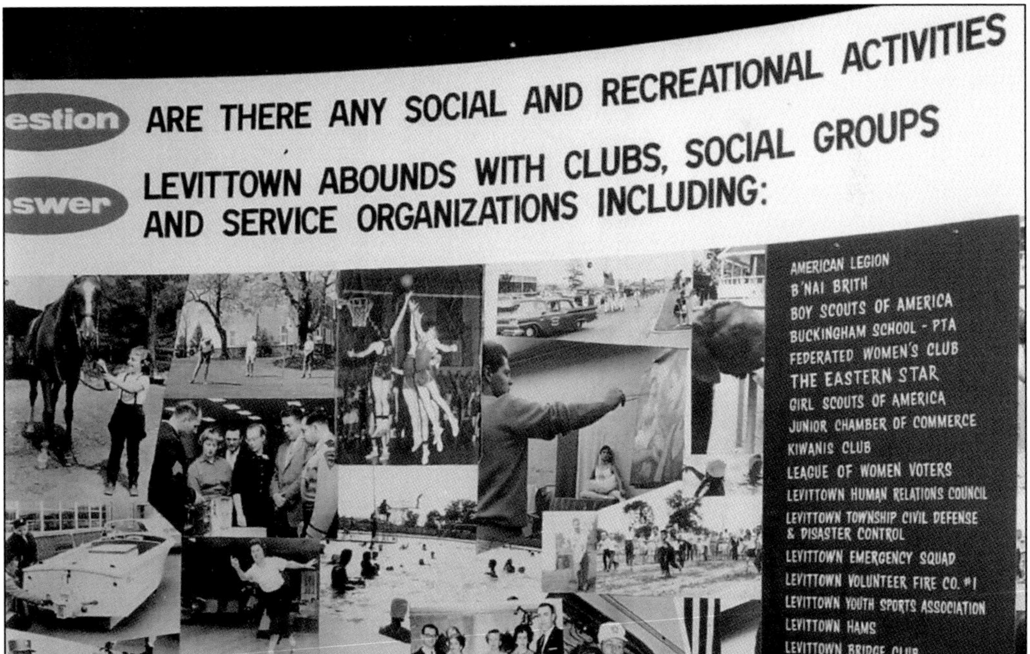

What could residents become involved with if they moved to Levittown? This sign, in a model home *c.* 1960, gives a short list: the American Legion, B'nai Brith, Girl Scouts, Boy Scouts, the Democrat and Republican Clubs, and the Rod and Gun Club. (Courtesy Dave Retzko.)

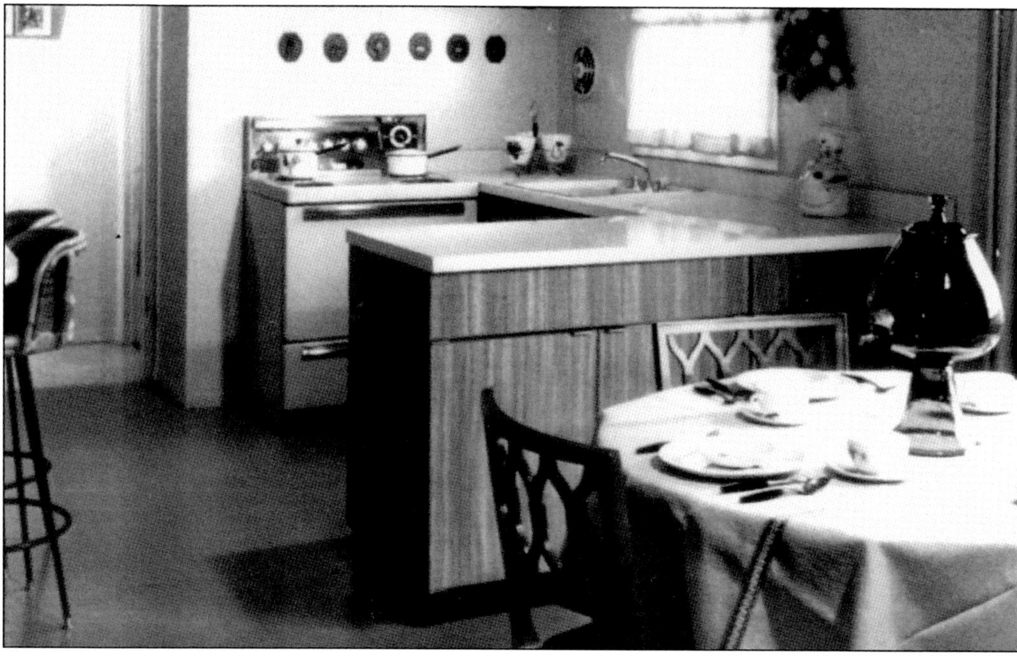

Those people who waited in long lines in 1958 to tour Levitt's homes would have seen an interior like this one. This is a kitchen and dining room from a Cape Cod model, which at the time cost $12,990. The kitchen contained basic appliances, but as in all the new houses, could be upgraded. (Courtesy Willingboro Public Library.)

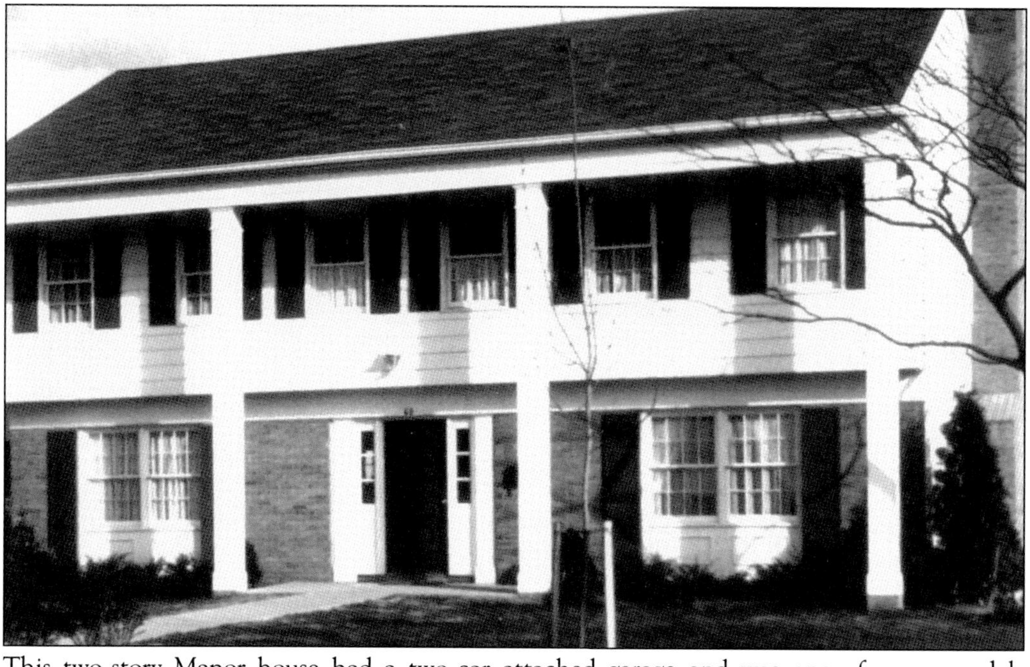

This two-story Manor house had a two-car attached garage and was one of many models Levitt and Sons offered in Willingboro. Levitt's homes were affordable and attracted many middle-class residents. Levitt reportedly set his profit margin on each home at 5 percent. (Courtesy Willingboro Public Library.)

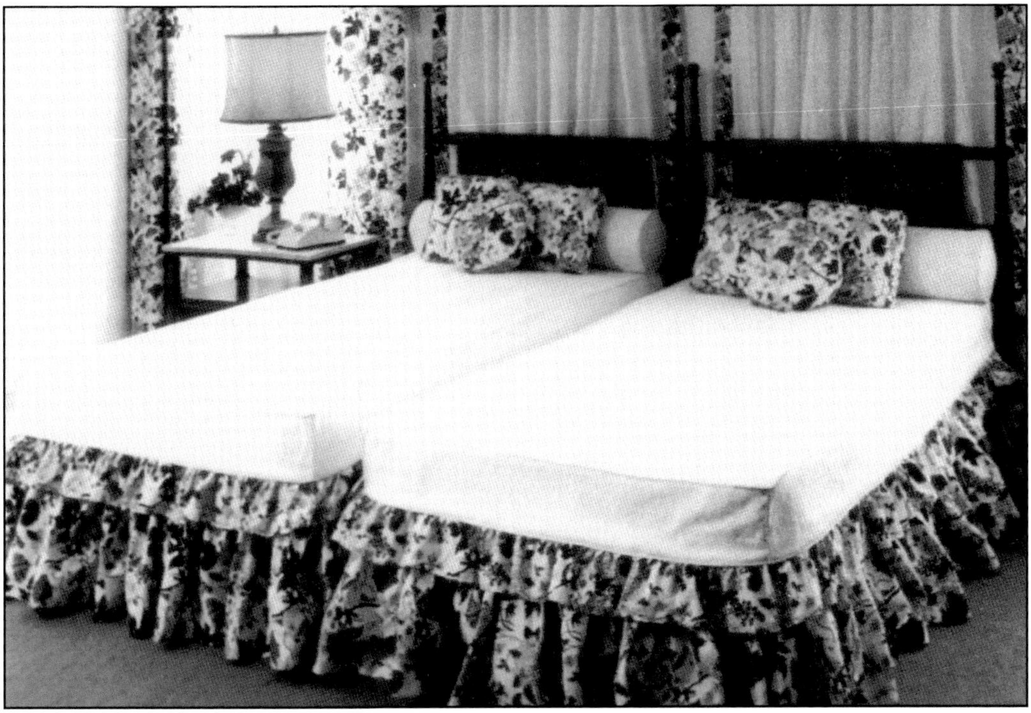

This was the master bedroom in the Manor house model. As befitting the conservative times, the room had two twin beds. (Courtesy Willingboro Public Library.)

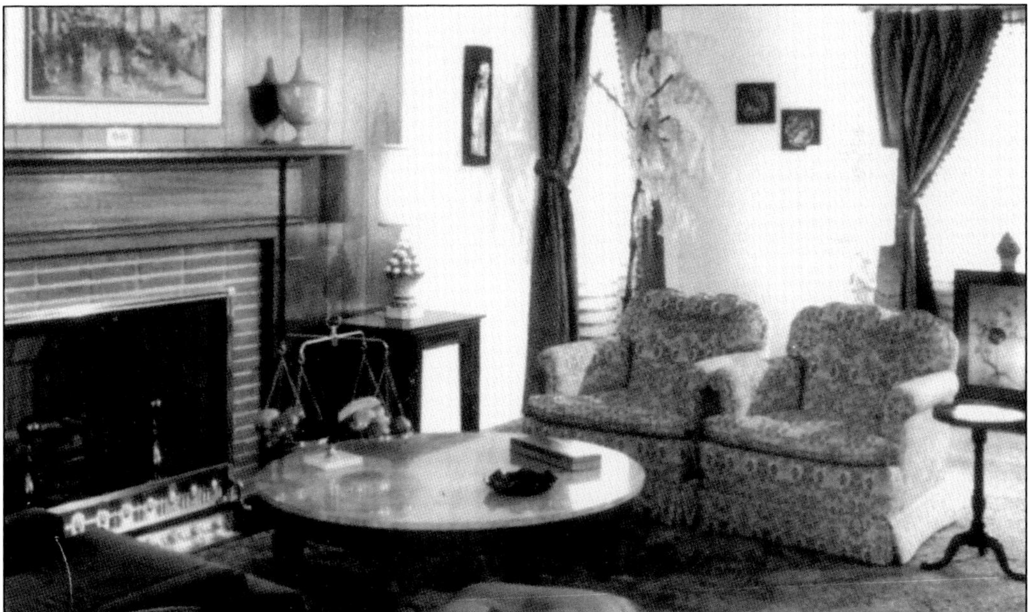

The Manor house model featured plenty of windows for natural light to come in. To deal with cold winters, the living room had a fireplace. Just as the bedroom had twin beds, the living room had identical chairs for the husband and wife to sit in and enjoy the fire. (Courtesy Willingboro Public Library.)

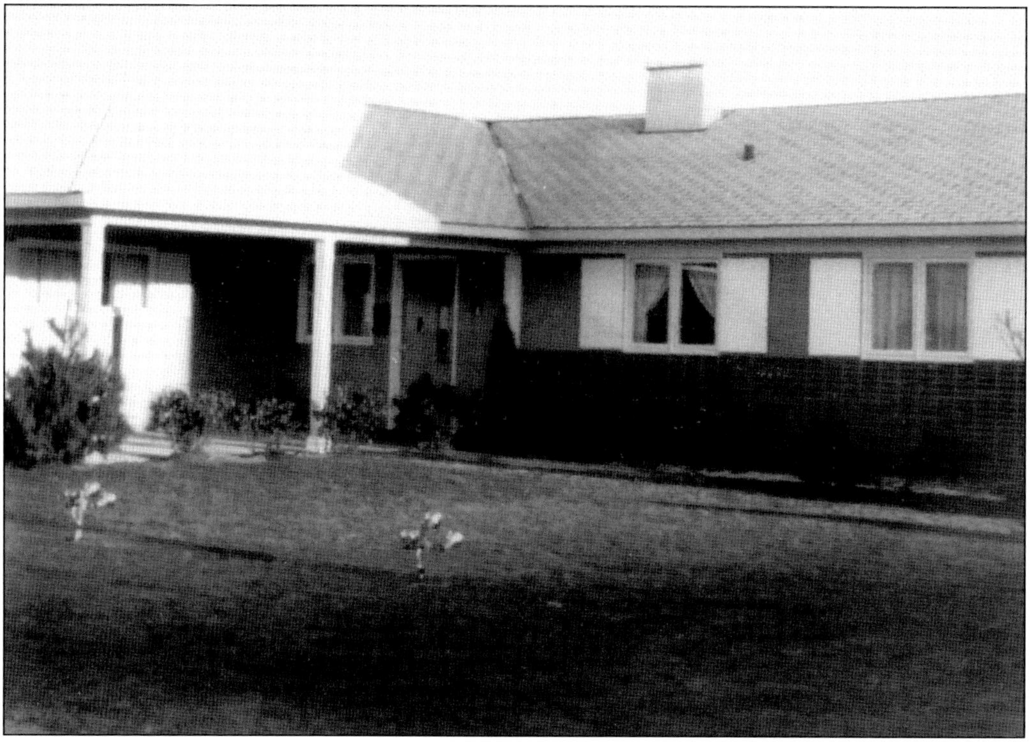

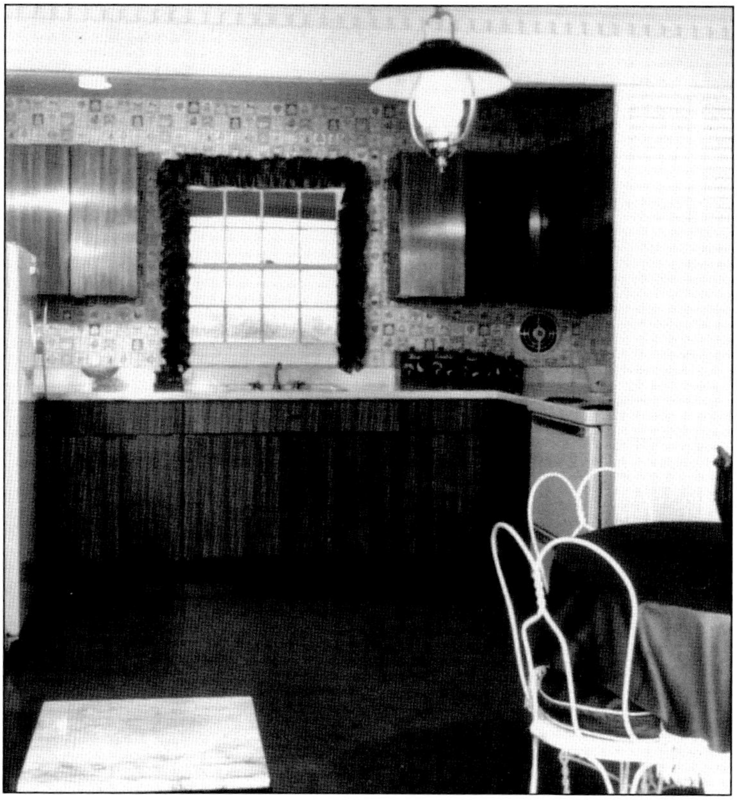

The one-story Rancher (above), one of the first models offered by Levitt and Sons, had 1,200 square feet of finished floor space and an oversized garage. It bore an exterior of brick and paneling, with a roof of asbestos shingles. The house cost $12,740, with a down payment of $400 and a monthly mortgage of $91. Aluminum screens and landscaping were included in the price. The interior included a kitchen and dining area (left). (Courtesy Willingboro Public Library.)

The Rancher had three bedrooms, two bathrooms, and a 21-foot-long living room (right). Heat in the home was provided by a gas-fired hot water radiant system. (Courtesy Willingboro Public Library.)

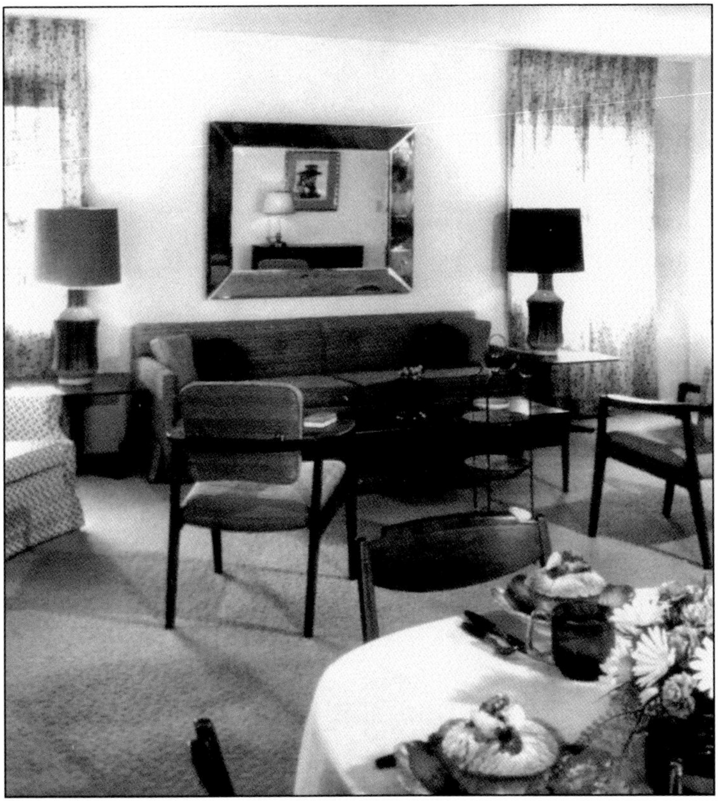

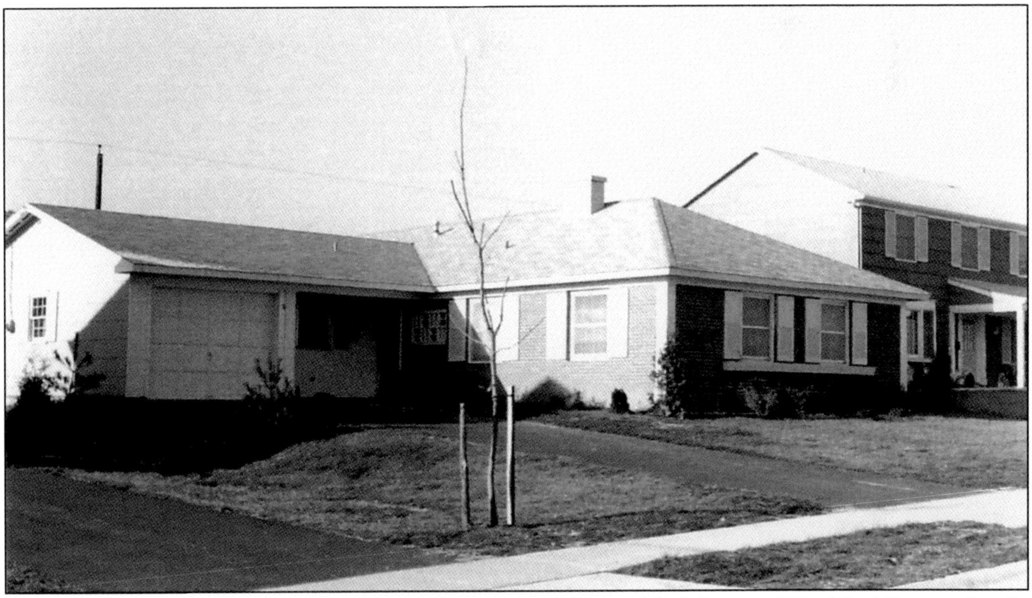

This L-shaped home on Montrose Lane belongs to Marion Huddleston. The Huddleston family moved to Willingboro's Millbrook Park neighborhood in 1960. Millbrook was among the first neighborhoods built by Levitt and Sons. (Courtesy Marion Huddleston.)

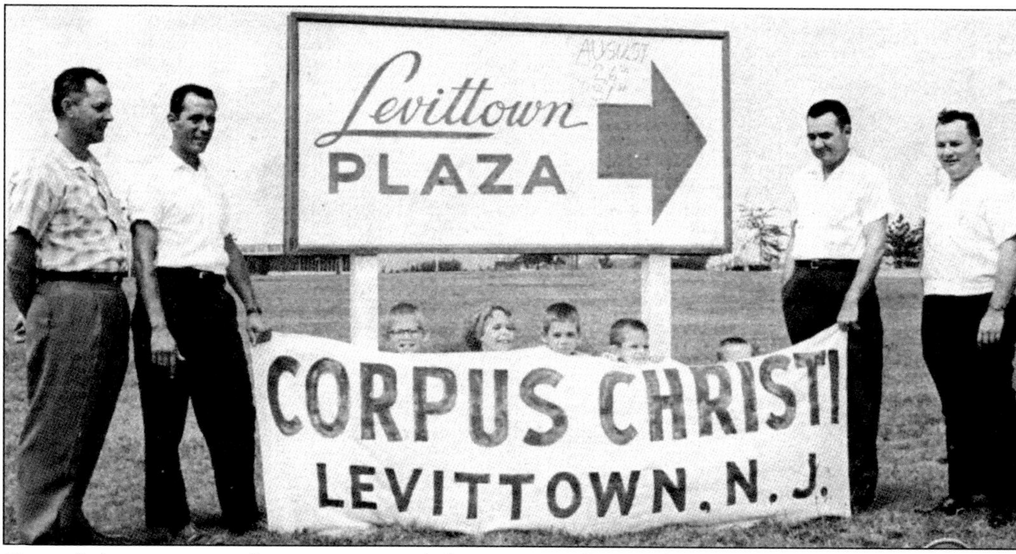

One of the common characteristics of the new residents of Levittown was that many were Roman Catholic. However, the town did not have a Catholic church or school, forcing residents to travel out of town. After petitioning the Diocese of Trenton, the Corpus Christi Church was established in April 1959. In this photograph, congregation members stand in front of a sign for the developing Levittown Plaza shopping center on Route 130. (Courtesy Corpus Christi Church.)

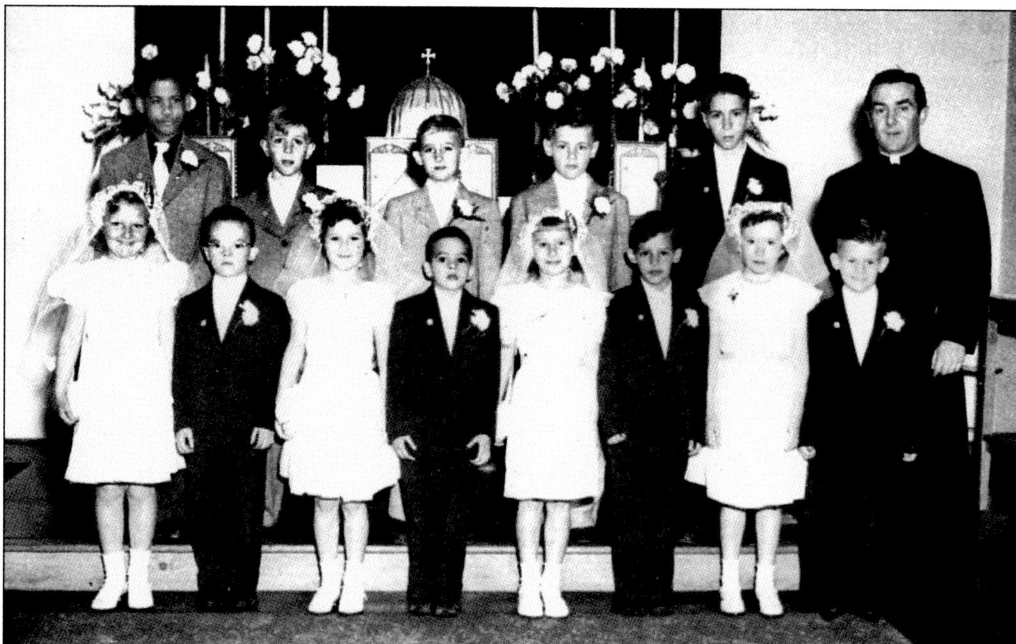

Corpus Christi members first held Mass in the nearby Somerset Park School. In November 1959, members broke ground for a church and school at Charleston and Sunset Roads. The first Mass was held in the new building's cafeteria in September 1960. In this 1959 photograph, children celebrating their First Communion pose with Rev. Francis Coan. (Courtesy Corpus Christi Church.)

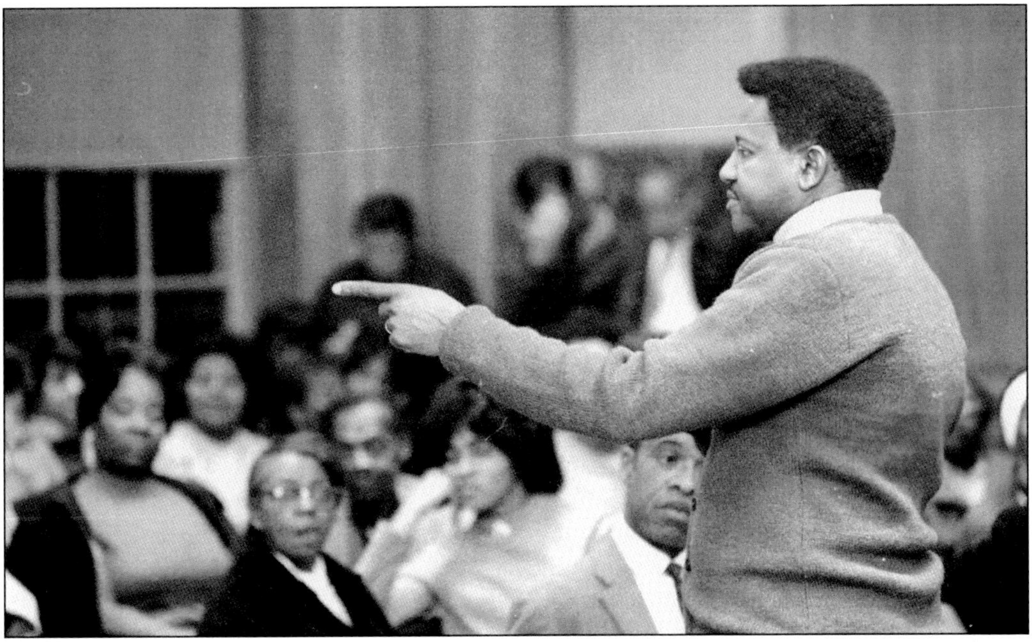

In 1958, Rev. Willie James was a soldier at nearby Fort Dix, looking for a place to settle down. When he went to buy one of Levitt and Sons' new homes, he was flatly turned down. William Levitt's housing developments were segregated, and the deeds stated that the homes would not be sold to blacks. With the encouragement of the U.S. attorney, Reverend James sued. The U.S. Supreme Court ruled in his favor, forcing Levitt to open Willingboro and his other communities to minorities. Reverend James, who headed the local National Association for the Advancement of Colored People chapter, is seen here speaking to a crowd in 1969. (Courtesy Burlington County Times.)

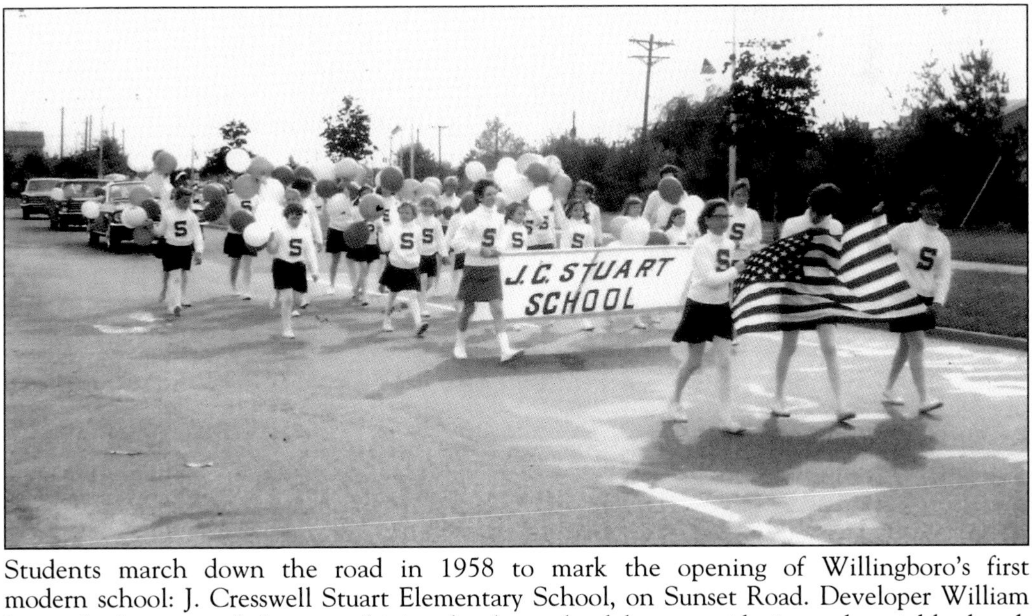

Students march down the road in 1958 to mark the opening of Willingboro's first modern school: J. Cresswell Stuart Elementary School, on Sunset Road. Developer William Levitt built many of the township's schools on land he set aside in each neighborhood. (Courtesy Betty Sever.)

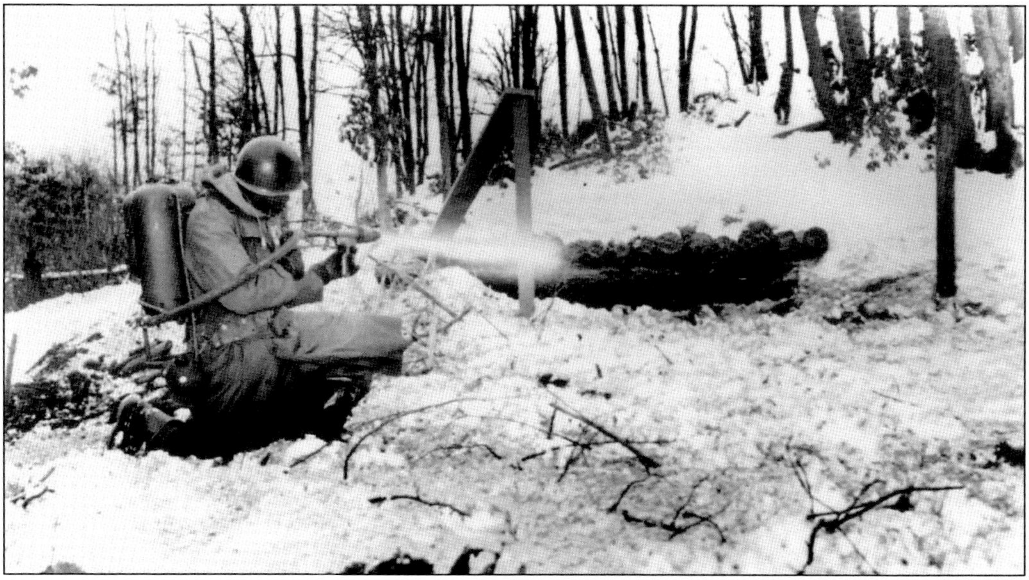

Many of the new Levittown's first residents were military personnel stationed at nearby Fort Dix and McGuire Air Force Base. In this photograph from January 1954, a soldier with the 364th Infantry Regiment, 9th Division, conducts flamethrower practice in the Fort Dix woods. (Courtesy Burlington County Times/Fort Dix Museum.)

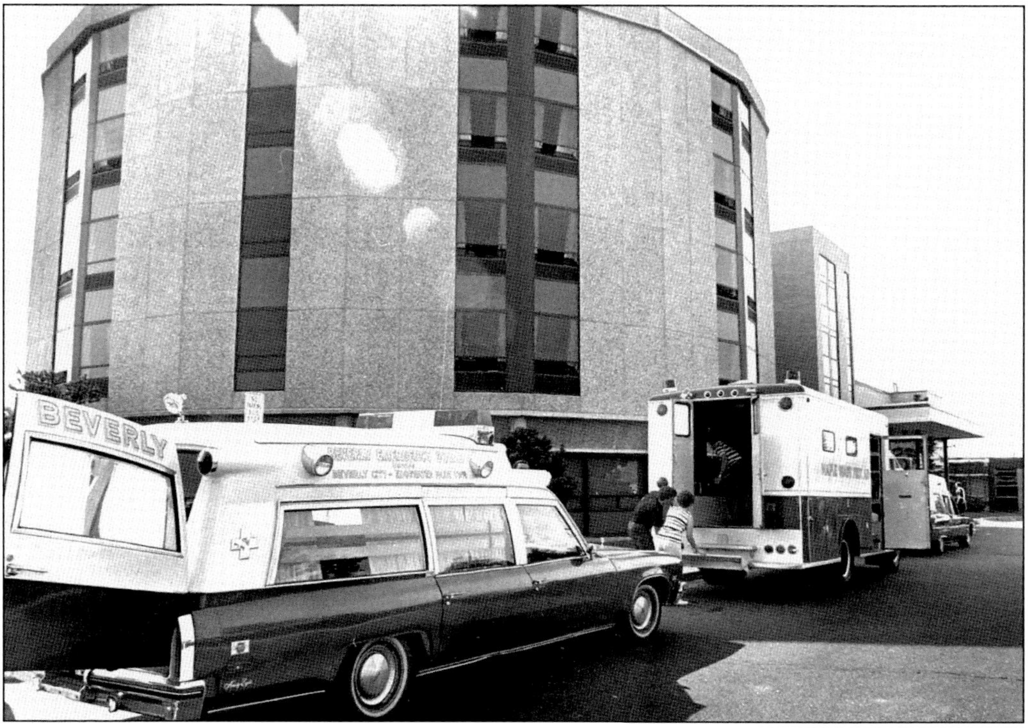

In 1961, 14 local doctors—many of the Jewish faith—founded Rancocas Hospital, on Sunset Road, after being unable to practice at other area medical facilities. In this photograph, ambulances from the Beverly-Edgewater Park and Maple Shade emergency squads wait outside the hospital. (Courtesy Burlington County Times.)

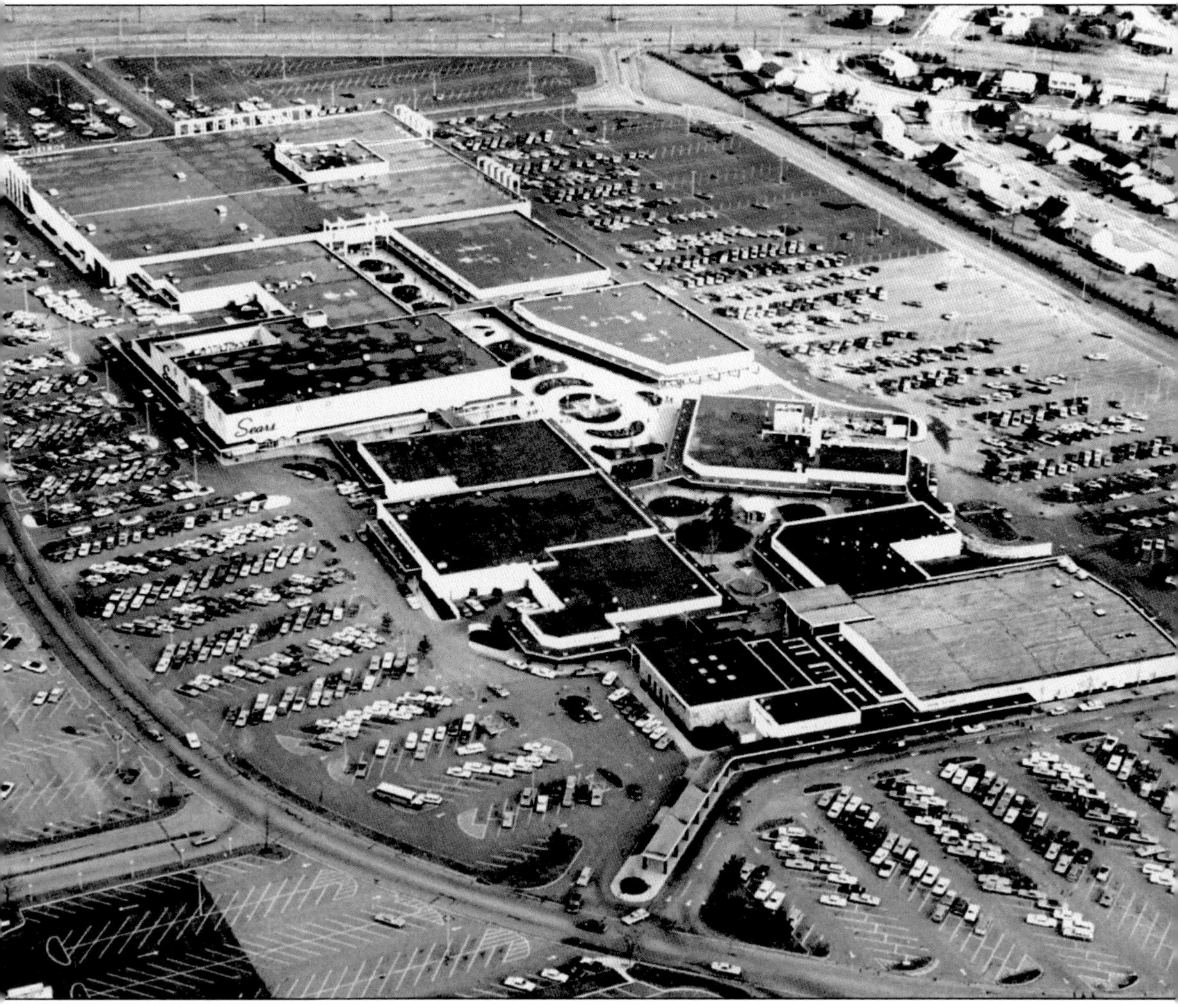

This aerial shot shows the Willingboro Plaza, which opened in 1959. It featured a Sears, Pomeroy's, Food Fair, and Woolworth's and was by far the township's largest commercial property. (Courtesy Dave Retzko/Levitt Corporation.)

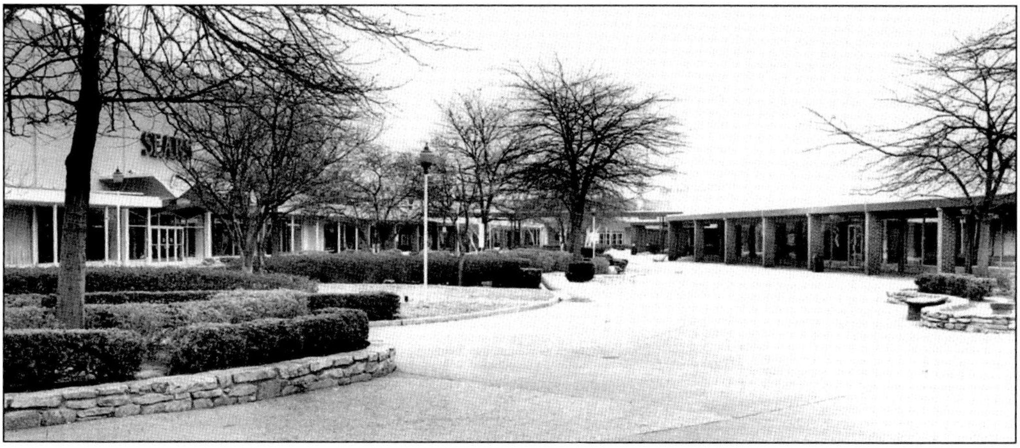

On busy days, the outdoor areas between the Willingboro Plaza's anchor stores such as Sears and the smaller retailers were jammed with shoppers. (Courtesy Burlington County Times.)

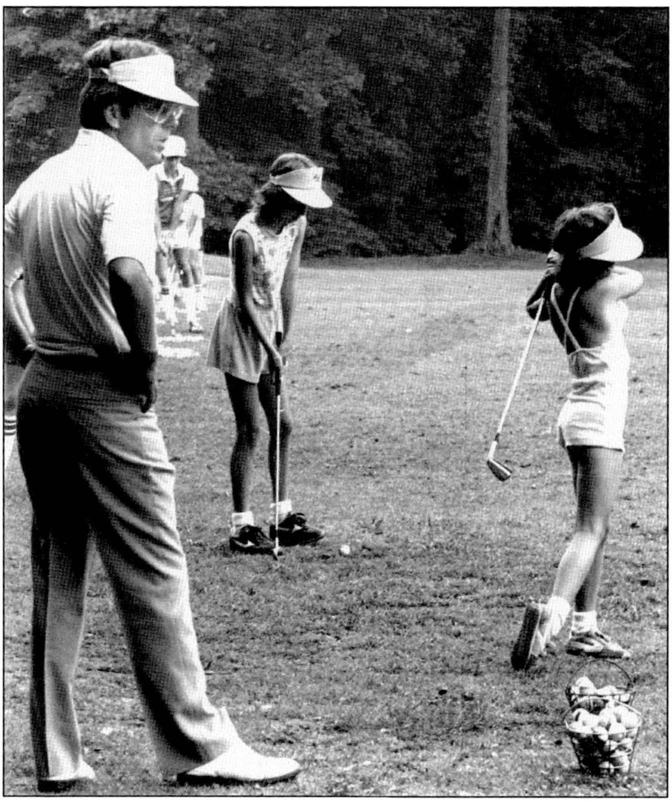

Levitt and Sons built the Willingboro Country Club in 1965 on 130 acres of land in Country Club Ridge Park. Robert Trent Jones designed the 18-hole course, which won wide acclaim for its challenging layout. The site also featured four tennis courts and an Olympic-sized swimming pool. The course's name was later changed to the Rancocas Country Club. (Courtesy Burlington County Times.)

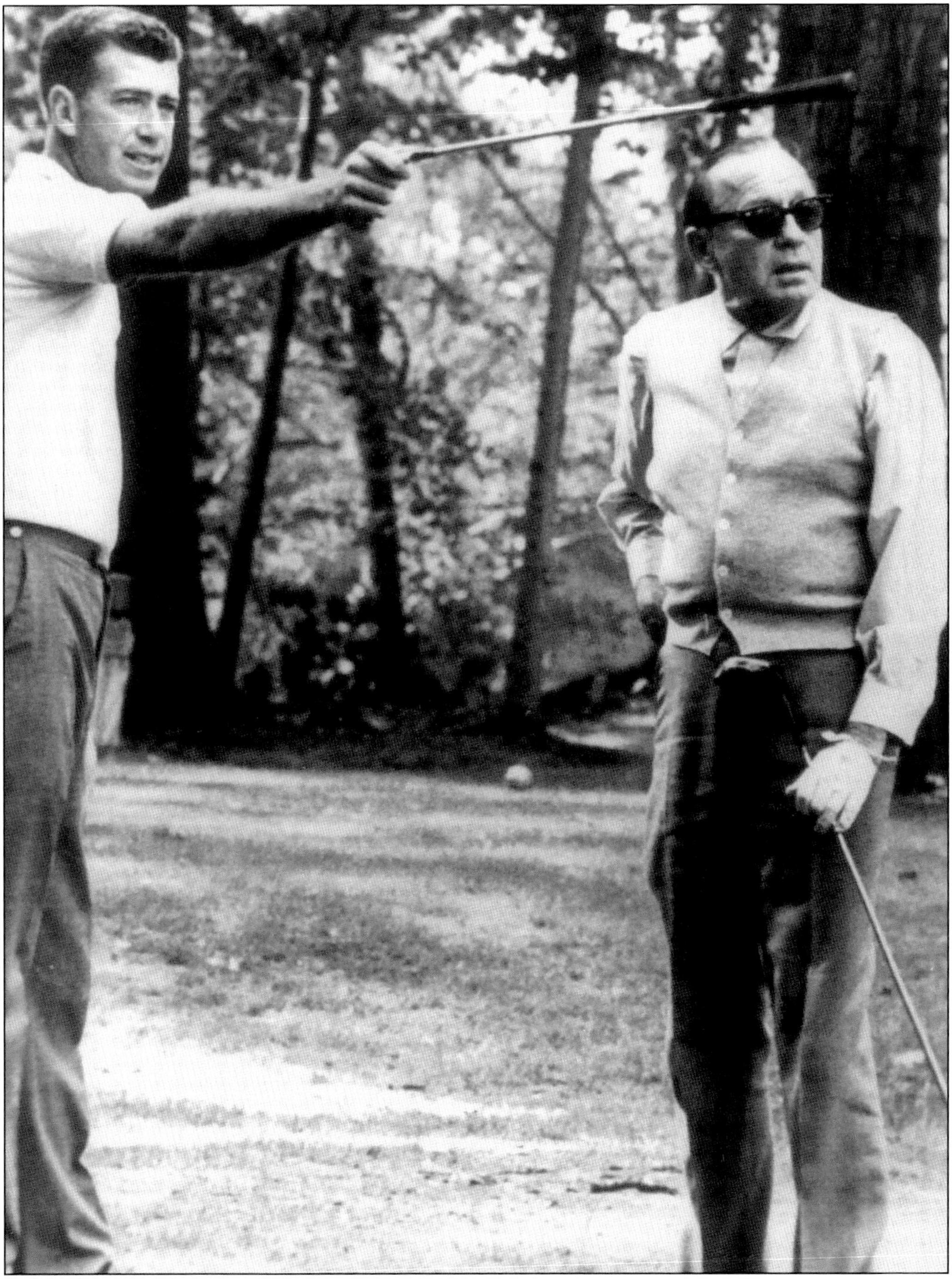

Comedian Jack Benny (right) and resident Dick Mullen take in a round of golf at the Willingboro Country Club in 1967. The 18-hole course on 130 acres of land was constructed in 1965. (Courtesy Willingboro Public Library.)

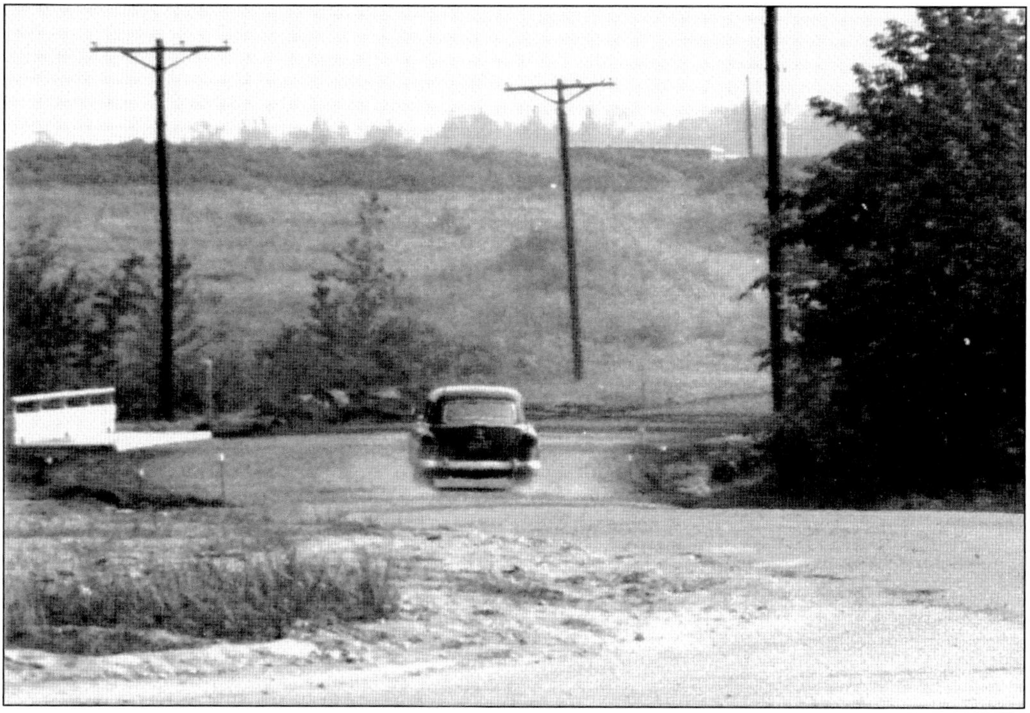

A car kicks up dust as it travels along Park Road (later JFK Way) toward Levitt Parkway c. 1960. Although Levitt began acquiring property in 1954, much of the town remained rural six years later. (Courtesy Dave Retzko)

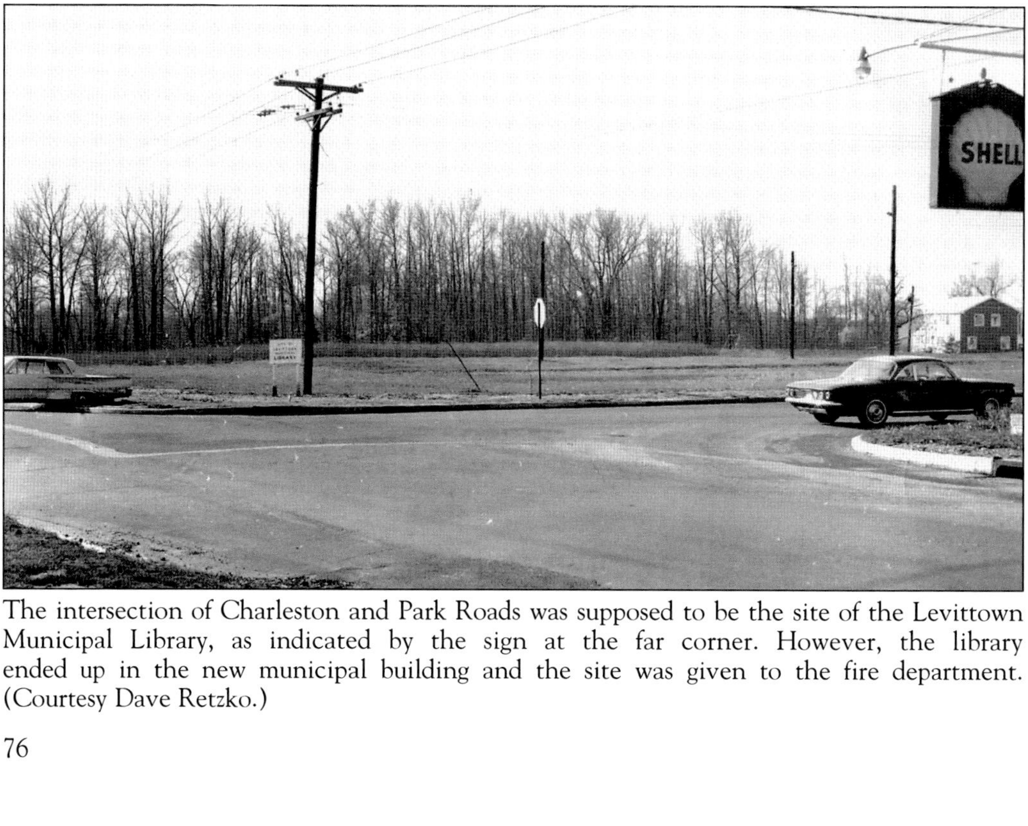

The intersection of Charleston and Park Roads was supposed to be the site of the Levittown Municipal Library, as indicated by the sign at the far corner. However, the library ended up in the new municipal building and the site was given to the fire department. (Courtesy Dave Retzko.)

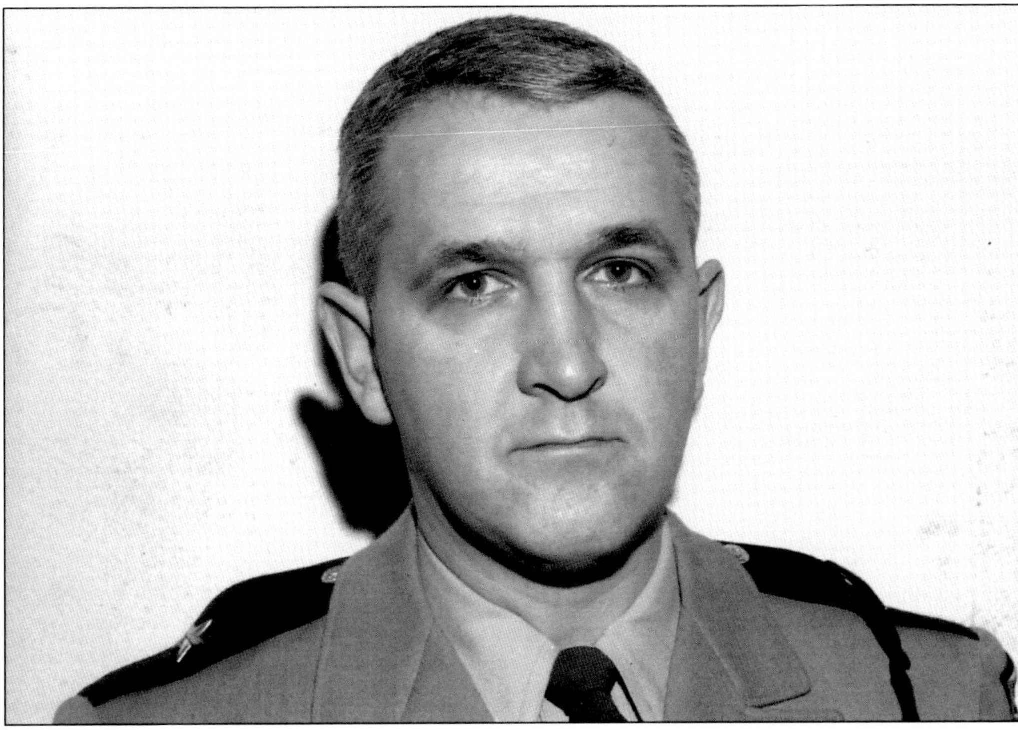

Marshall Roser was Levittown's first police chief, serving from October 1958 to December 1968. Police records show it took Roser only a week before he wrote out the town's first ticket, which went to a Burlington City man involved in a traffic accident. (Courtesy Dave Retzko.)

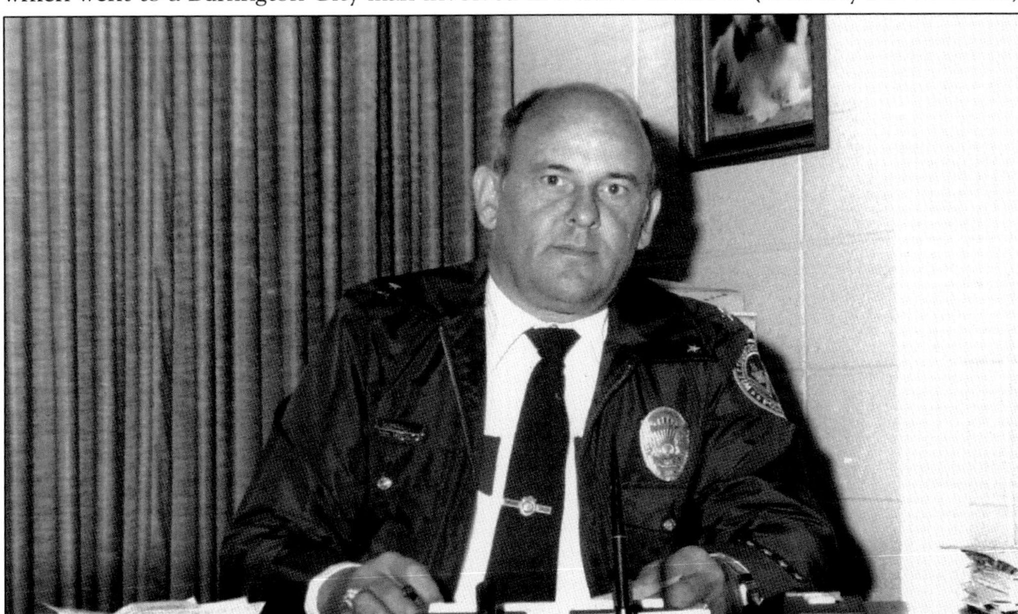

Robert Rossell was the town's second and longest-serving police chief. He joined the force in March 1960 and became chief in December 1968. The photograph on the wall above Rossell's desk shows his dog. (Courtesy Dave Retzko.)

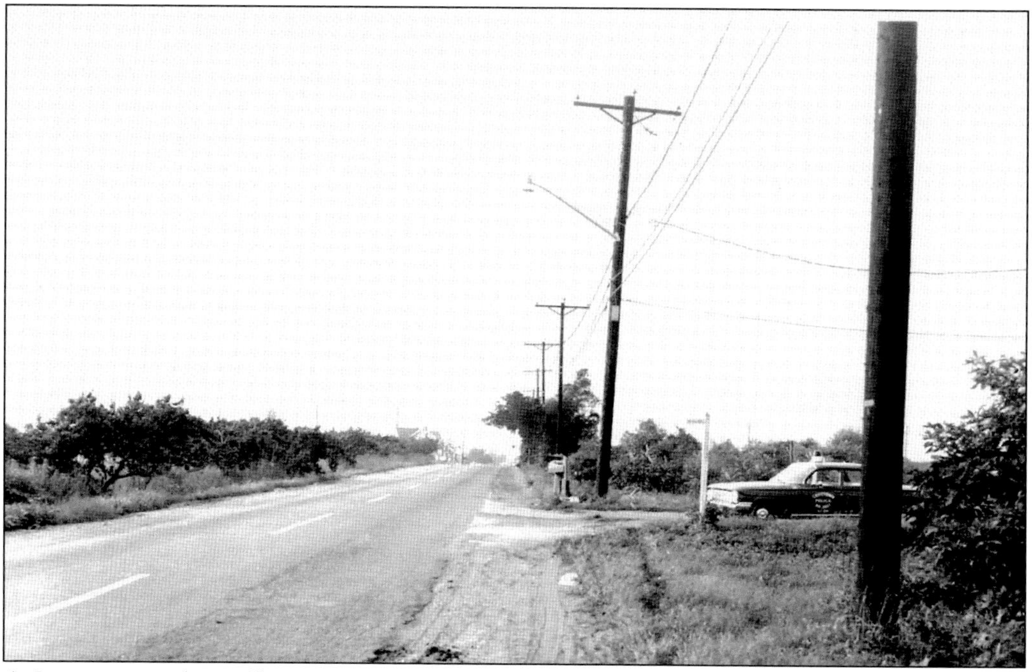

A Levittown police officer waits to trap speeding motorists at Beverly-Rancocas Road and Rose Street in 1961. A large church and a Comcast Cable facility would later be built near the intersection. (Courtesy Dave Retzko.)

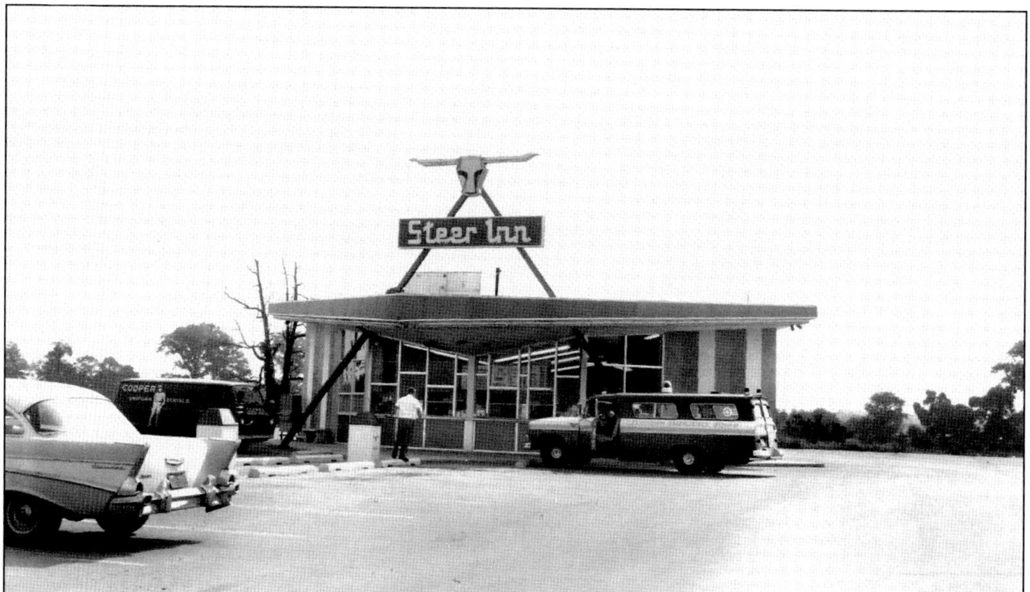

An ambulance belonging to the Levittown Emergency Squad sits in front of the Steer Inn on Route 130 in 1959 or 1960. The Steer Inn was a popular eatery for local residents. (Courtesy Dave Retzko.)

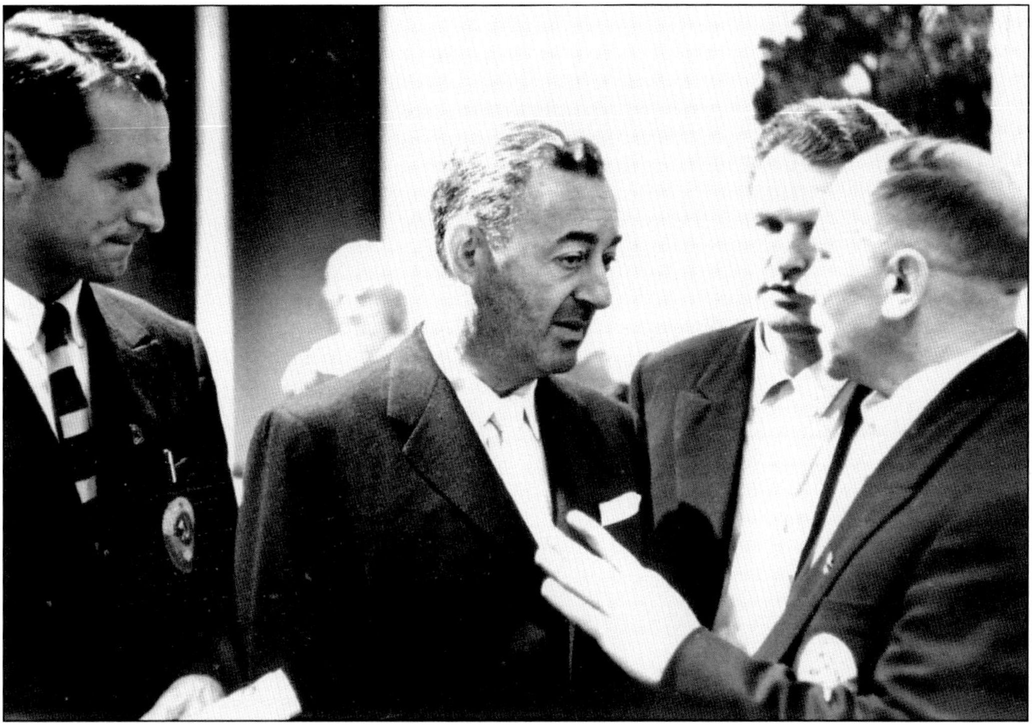

William J. Levitt's pioneering development methods gained international attention. Levitt (center) is shown here with a delegation of Soviet housing officials who visited Willingboro in 1960. (Courtesy Burlington County Times.)

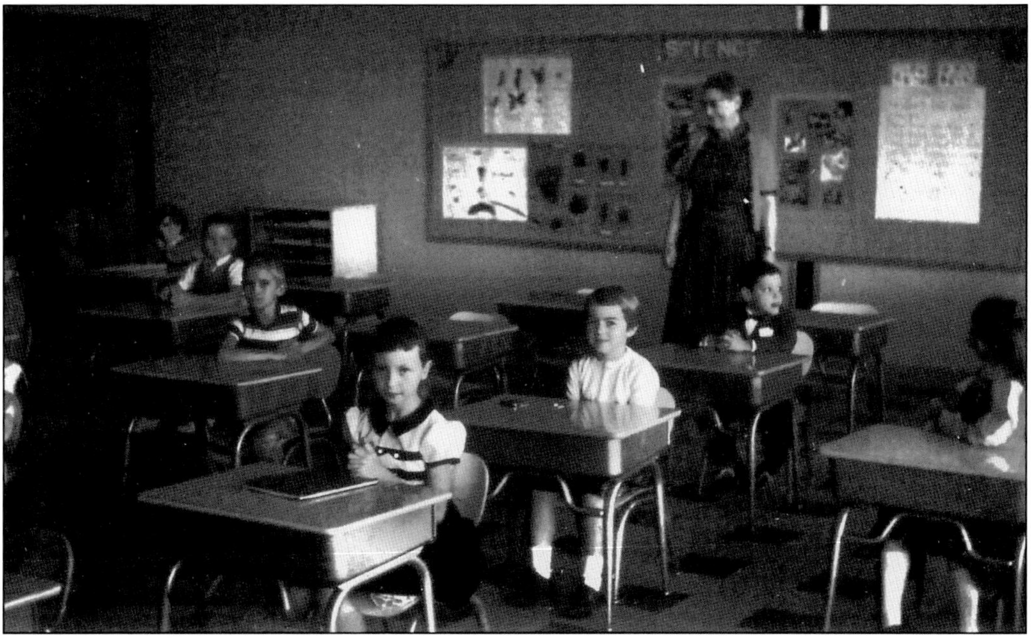

Children, including Jeanne Sever (second row, center), sit in class on their first day at the new J. Cresswell Stuart Elementary School in 1958. The school on Sunset Road was named after one of the town's most prominent farmers and residents. (Courtesy Betty Sever.)

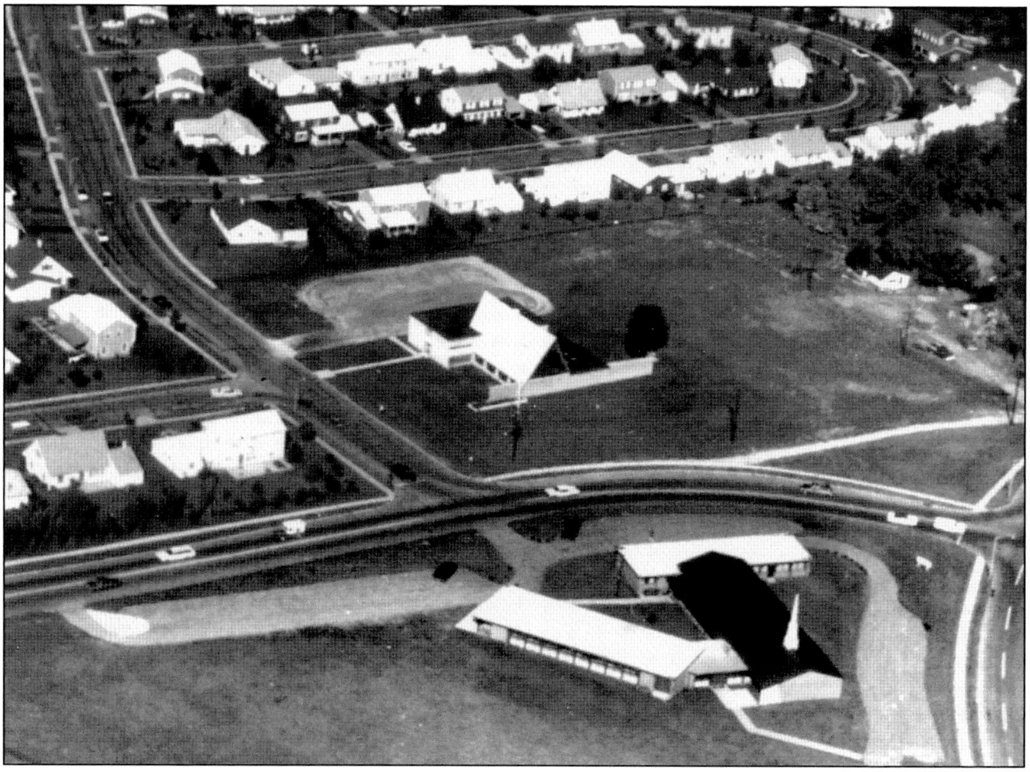

In his new community, Levitt tried to satisfy the spiritual needs of residents by setting aside land for churches and synagogues. In this aerial view of Levitt Parkway and Salem Road, the Parkway Baptist Church is in the background and St. Luke's Lutheran Church is in the foreground. (Courtesy Willingboro Public Library.)

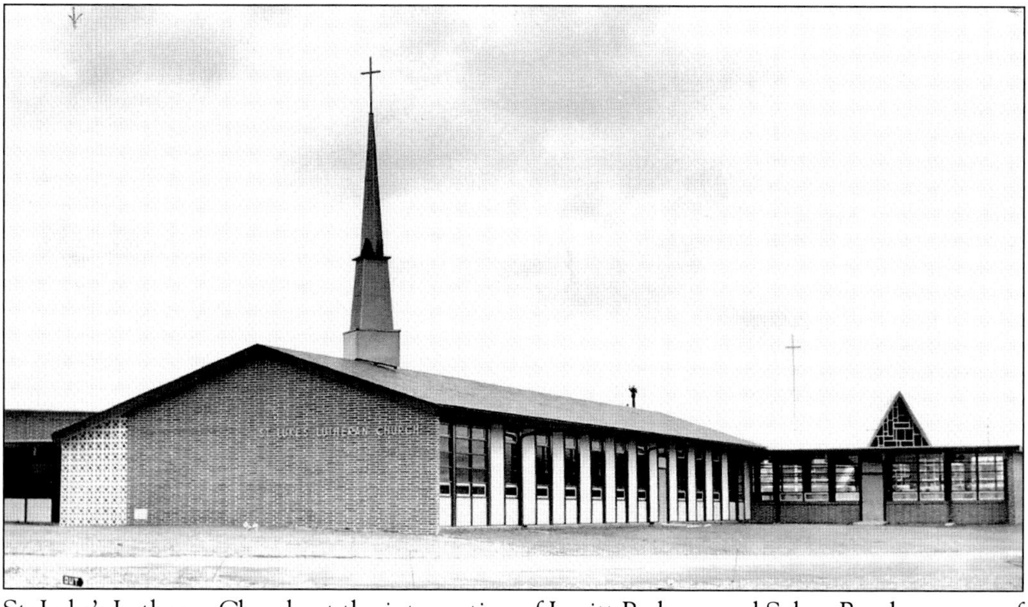

St. Luke's Lutheran Church, at the intersection of Levitt Parkway and Salem Road, was one of the original churches built in the new town. (Courtesy Burlington County Times.)

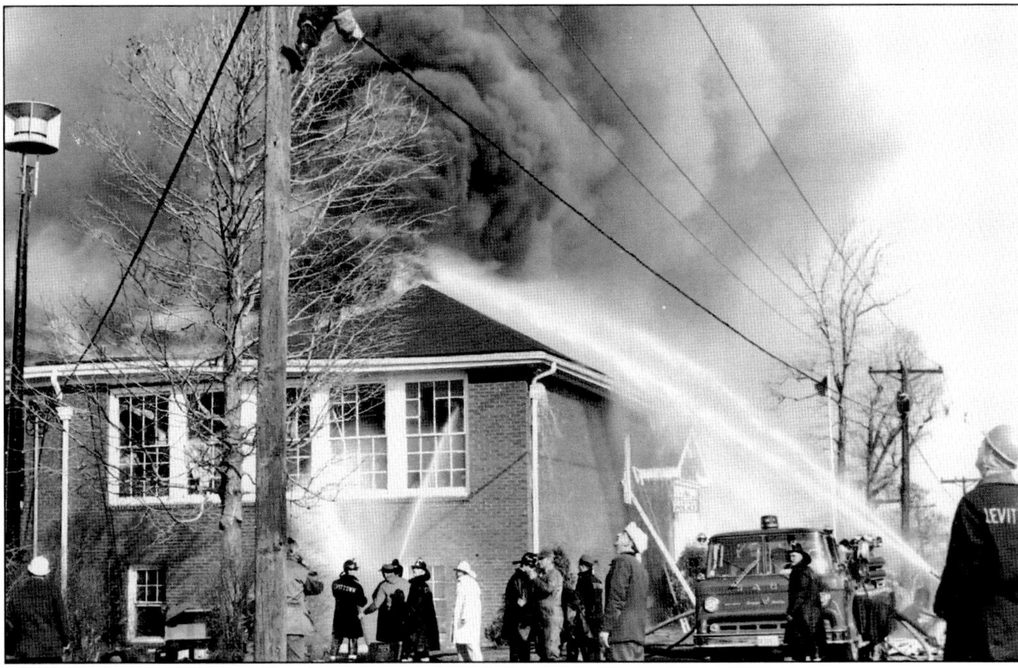

In 1930, the town expanded the Consolidated School. In 1940, the building—which became the municipal building, community center, and library—was refaced with brick. The building burned down in 1964. Locals say firefighters could not get to the fire because it was burning in the wood that was now covered by the brick. (Courtesy Dave Retzko.)

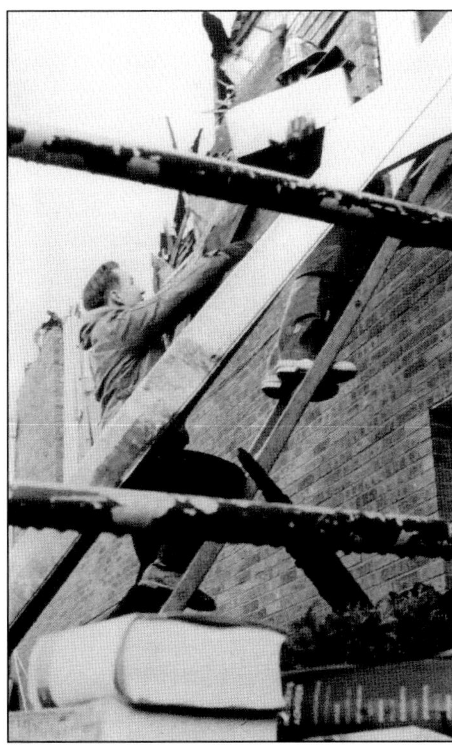

Firefighters and township officials desperately tried to save books and other documents from the burning municipal building. In this photograph, two men poised on a ladder take books out of the building and away from the flames. In the end, however, the inside of the structure was gutted. (Courtesy Willingboro Township Manager's Office.)

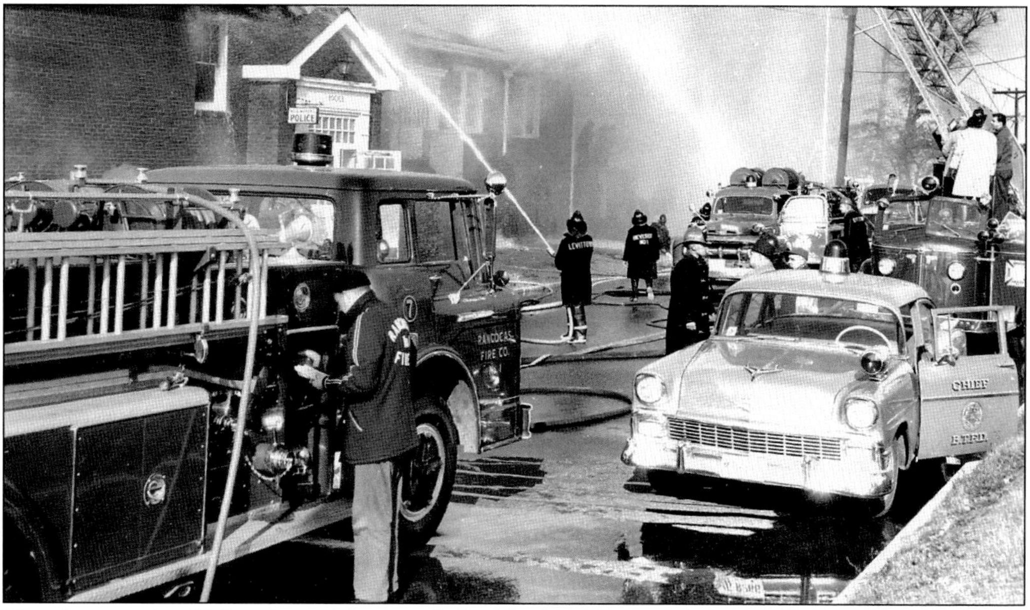

The fire at the Willingboro Municipal Building was one of the most dramatic and most photographed events in town history. In 1965, the township council approved the issuance of $620,000 in bonds to construct a new municipal complex. The building reopened three years after the fire. (Courtesy Willingboro Township Manager's Office.)

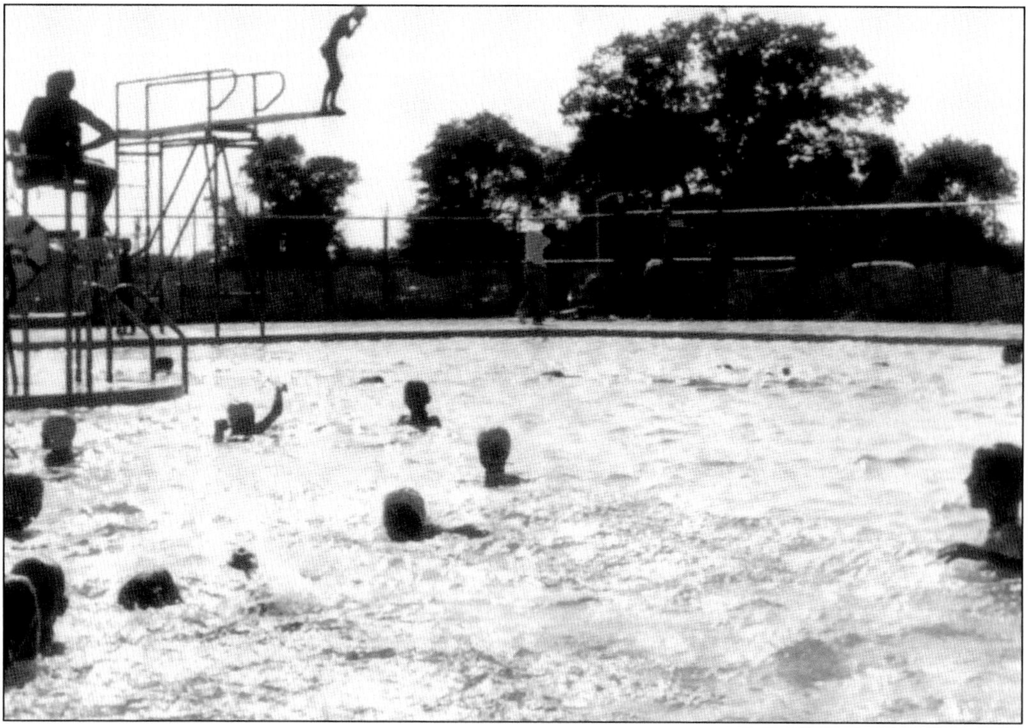

In Levitt's new community, each neighborhood had its own elementary school and adjacent swimming pool. In this photograph, children cool off in one of those pools on a hot summer day. (Courtesy Willingboro Public Library.)

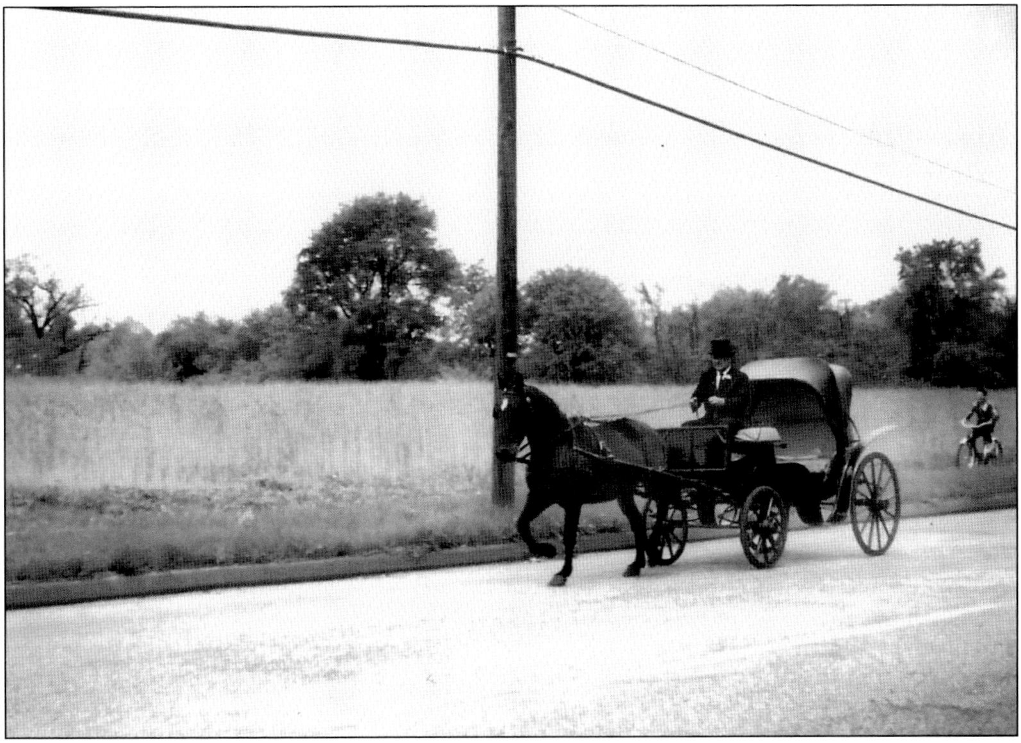

Cars replaced horses as the preferred mode of transportation long before William Levitt came to Willingboro. However, in the early years of the new community, it was still possible to see a horse and buggy around town. (Courtesy Betty Sever.)

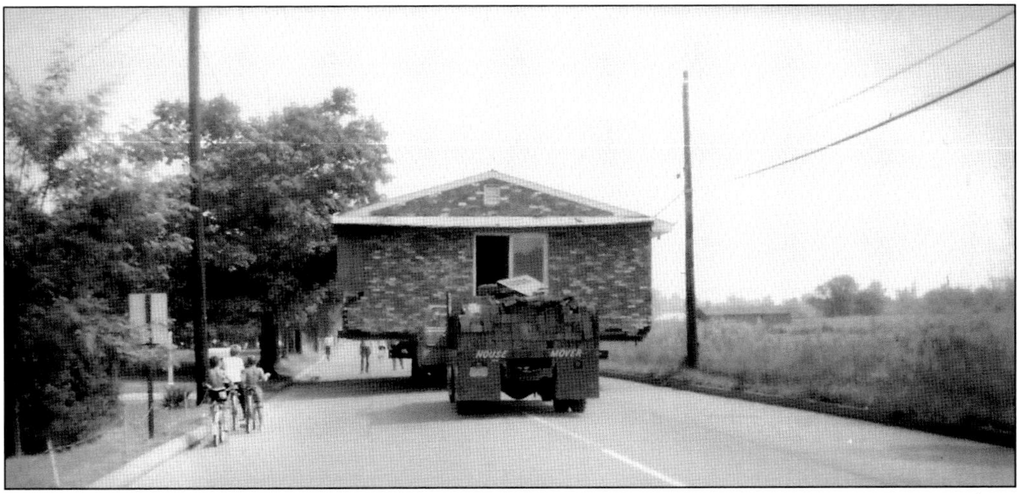

Excited children follow on bicycles as a truck moves a brick house from one location to another. (Courtesy Betty Sever.)

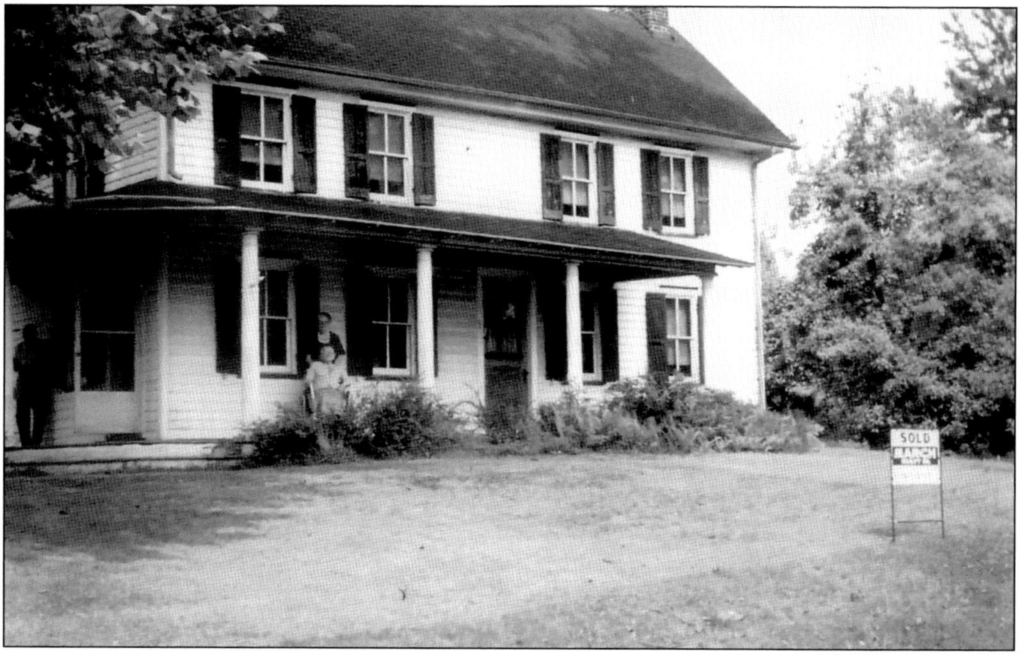

Martha and Alice Bishop sit on the porch of their house off Levitt Parkway before they moved away in the early 1960s. The Bishop family resided in the home for three generations, but the change from peaceful rural life to hectic suburbia was more than they could tolerate. (Courtesy Betty Sever.)

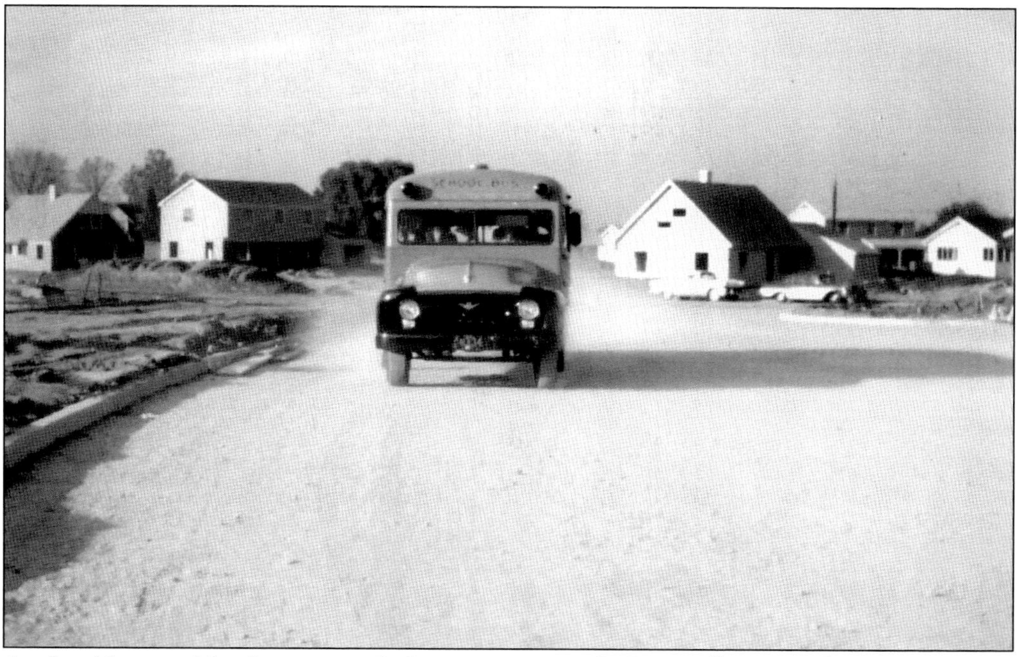

A school bus rumbles down an early Levittown street. J. Cresswell Stuart Elementary School in Somerset Park opened in 1958. Bookbinder Elementary opened to students a year later. (Courtesy Betty Sever.)

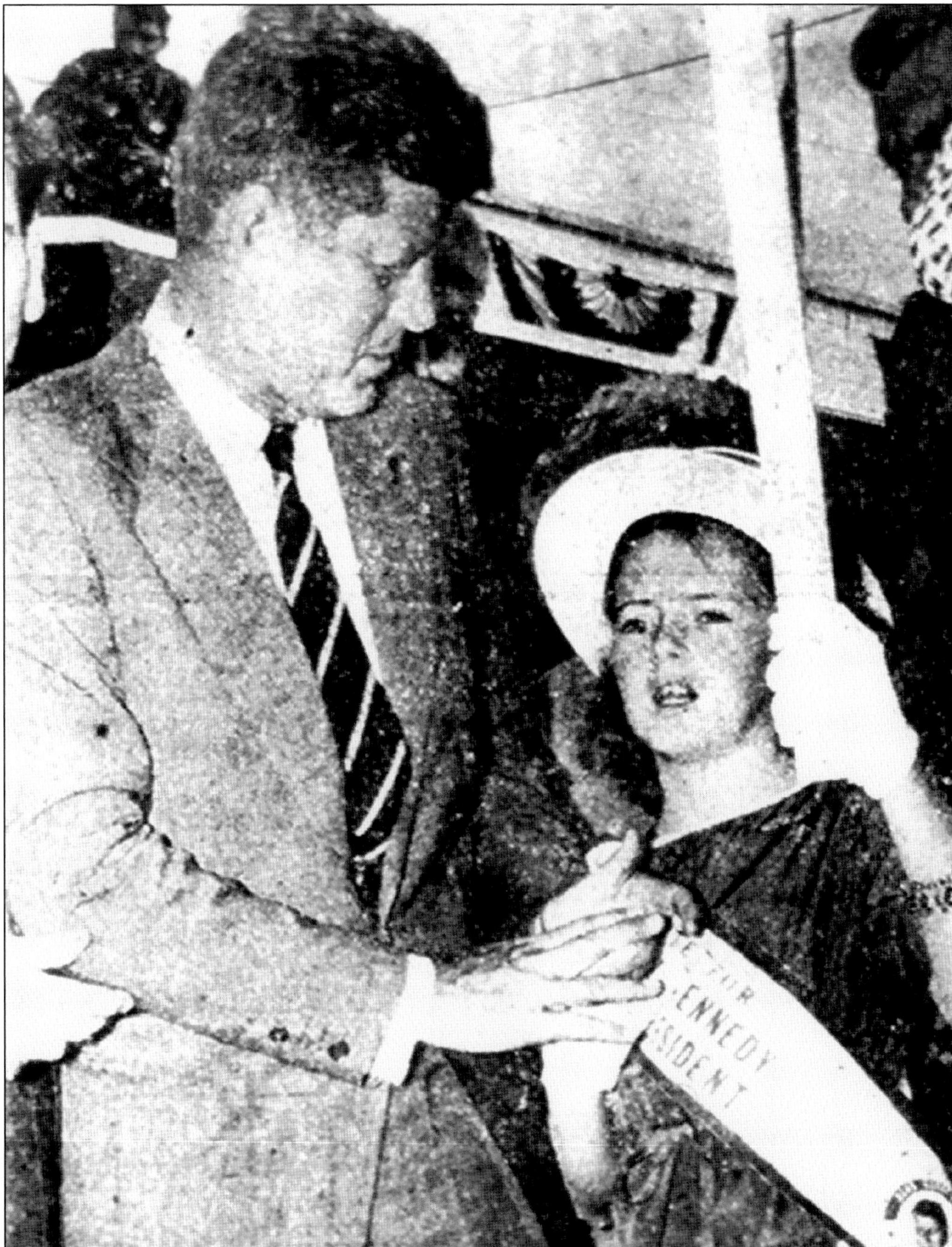

Some 20,000 people came to the Levittown Shopping Plaza (later called the Willingboro Plaza) on October 16, 1960, to see Democratic presidential candidate Sen. John F. Kennedy. The day was special for Connie O'Connor, a 12-year-old from Mount Holly who was chairperson of the Burlington County Junior Citizens for Kennedy. (Courtesy Burlington County Times.)

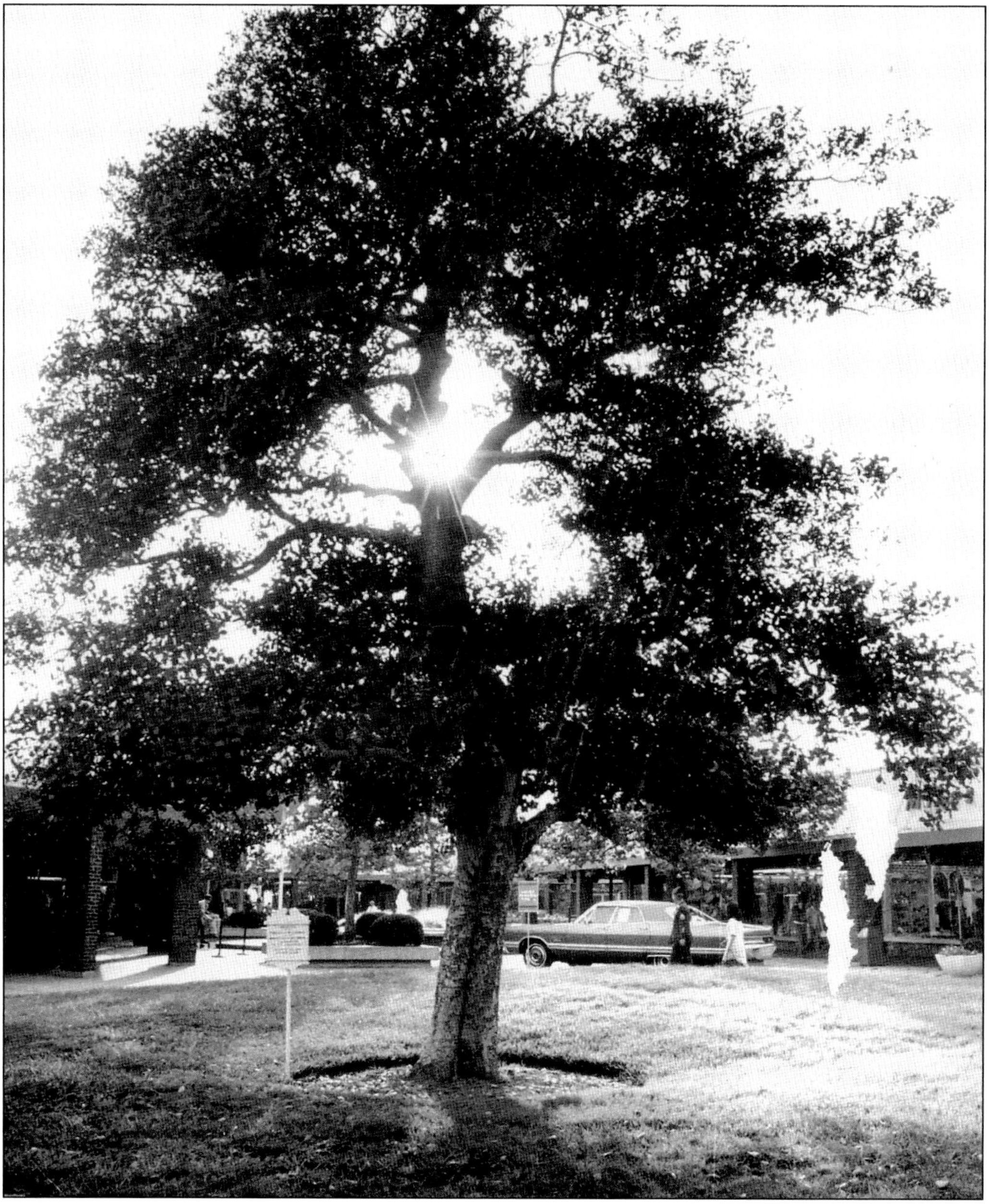

The Willingboro Plaza was more than just a shopping center. The mall contained grassy areas and trees where people could relax and picnic. Old Heavyberry, shown in this 1968 photograph, was a 30-foot-tall, 200-year-old holly tree that, during the winter, displayed red berries and shiny green leaves. Old Heavyberry grew on a tract of land off Kennedy Way until Levitt transplanted it to the Willingboro Plaza. Strong winds blew it down in 1976. (Courtesy Burlington County Times.)

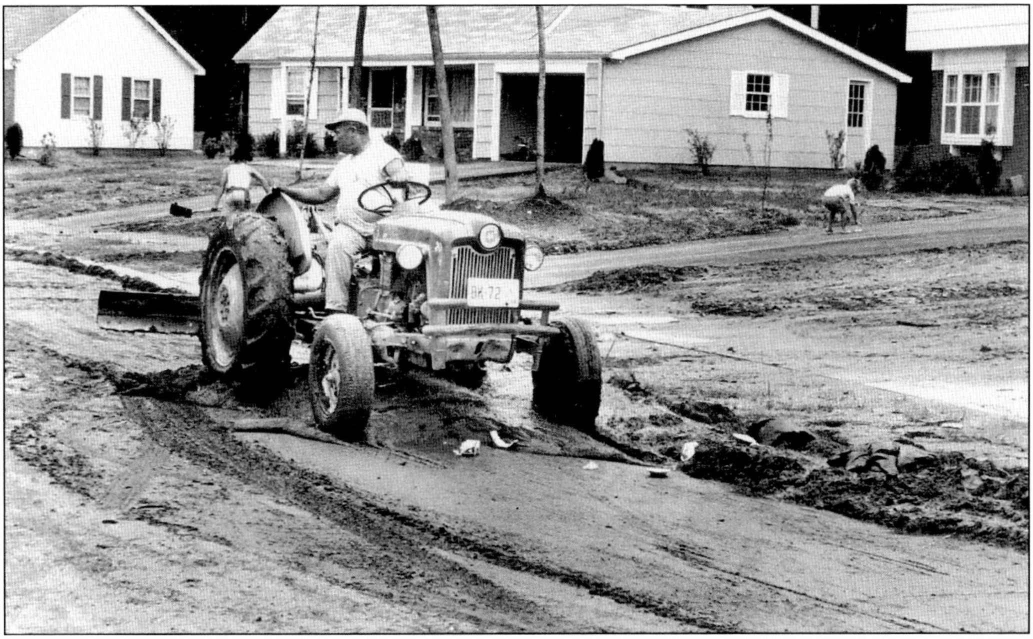

A worker on a tractor prepares a road for paving in the Garfield Park East section in July 1968. Between the late 1950s and early 1970s, Levitt built 13 neighborhoods. (Courtesy Burlington County Times.)

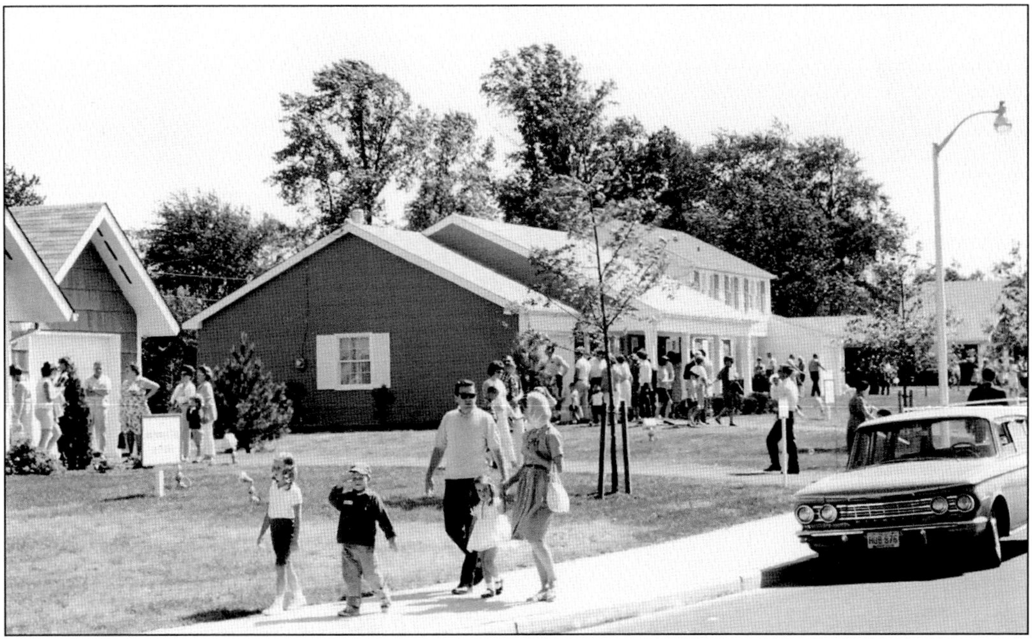

People came to Levittown every time the developer unveiled new model homes, as seen here in 1965. Levitt originally planned to construct 15,000 homes, but only some 11,000 were actually built. (Courtesy Burlington County Times.)

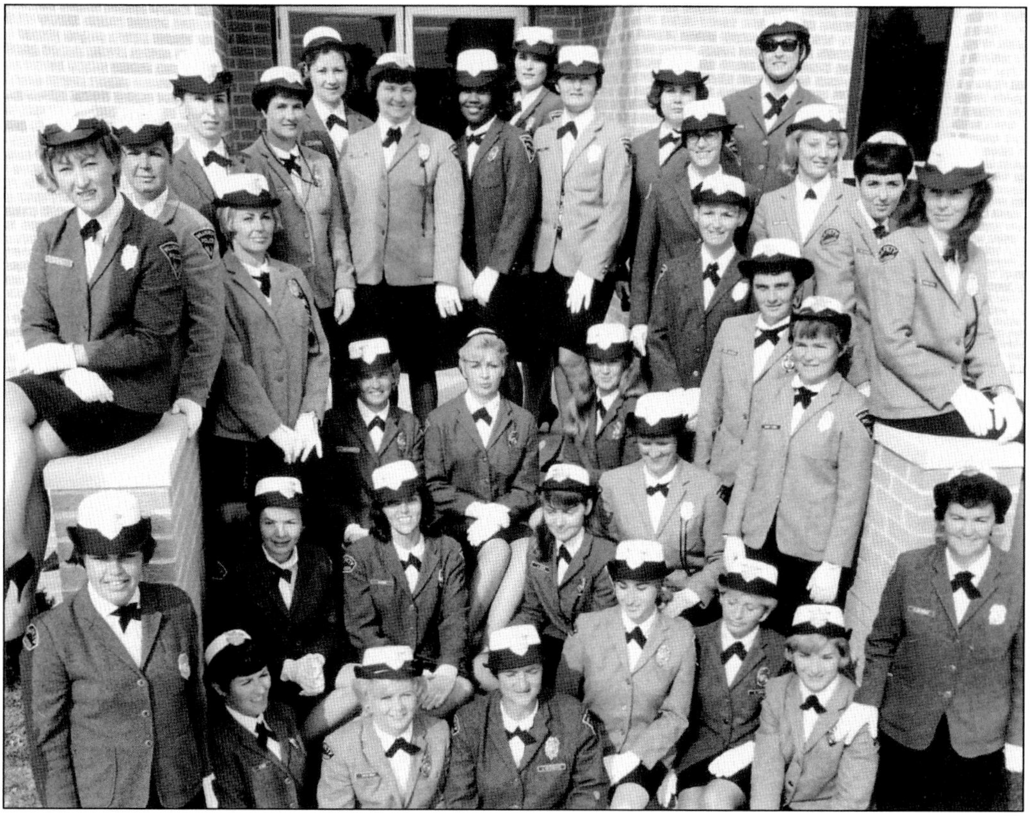

Law enforcement is not just a job for men. A group of female officers who served as crossing guards and had other special duties poses in front of the police department in October 1968. (Courtesy Burlington County Times.)

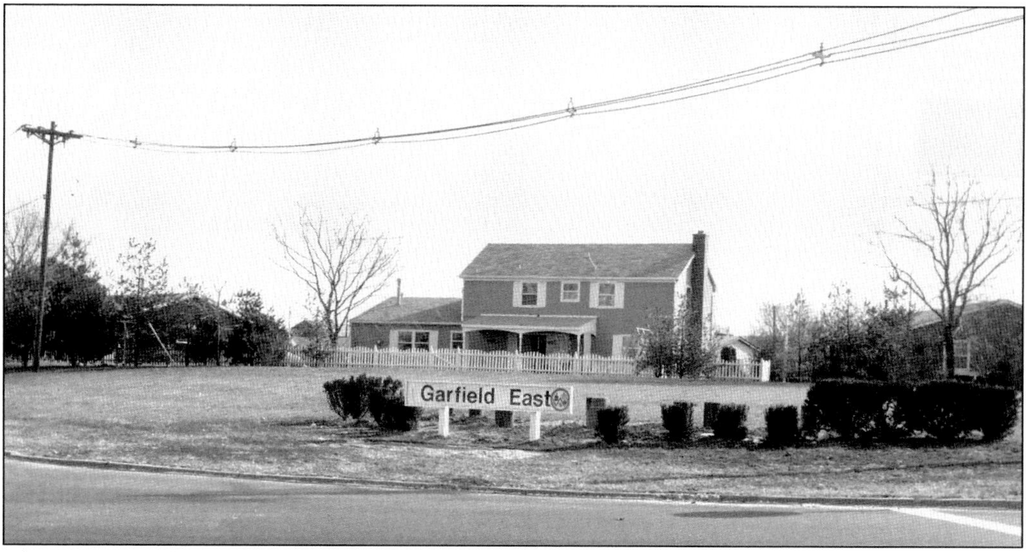

This two-story house stands at the entrance to the section of Willingboro that Levitt called Garfield Park East. The first houses in this neighborhood were built in 1969. (Courtesy Willingboro Township Manager's Office.)

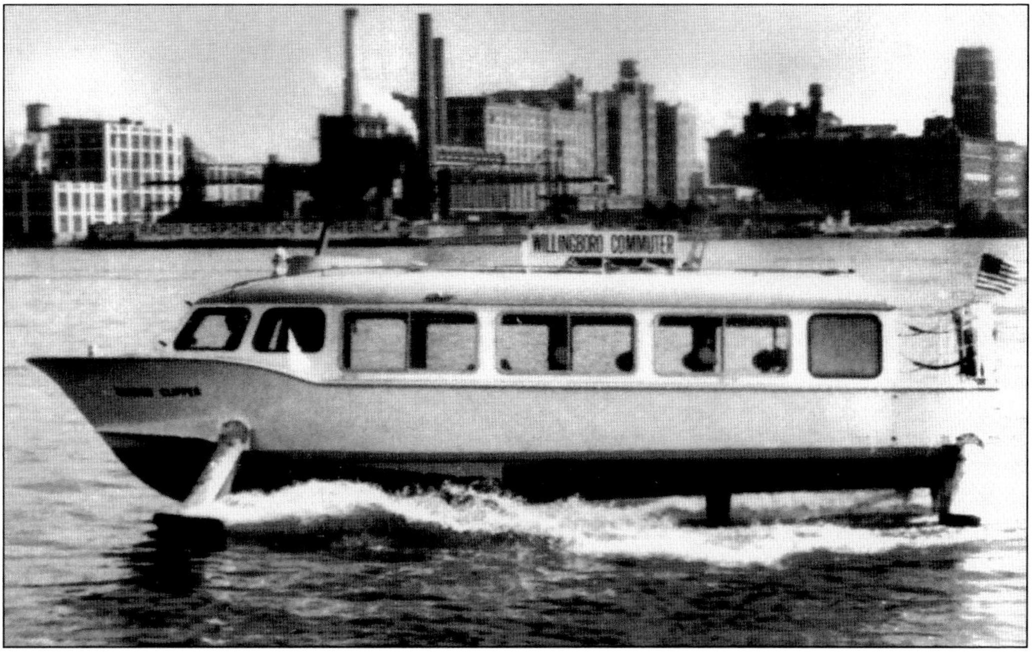

Willingboro's location on the Rancocas Creek near the Delaware River made it a popular destination for travelers and merchants. For a short time during the 1960s, a boat called the *Willingboro Commuter* took local residents to Philadelphia and back. (Courtesy Willingboro Public Library.)

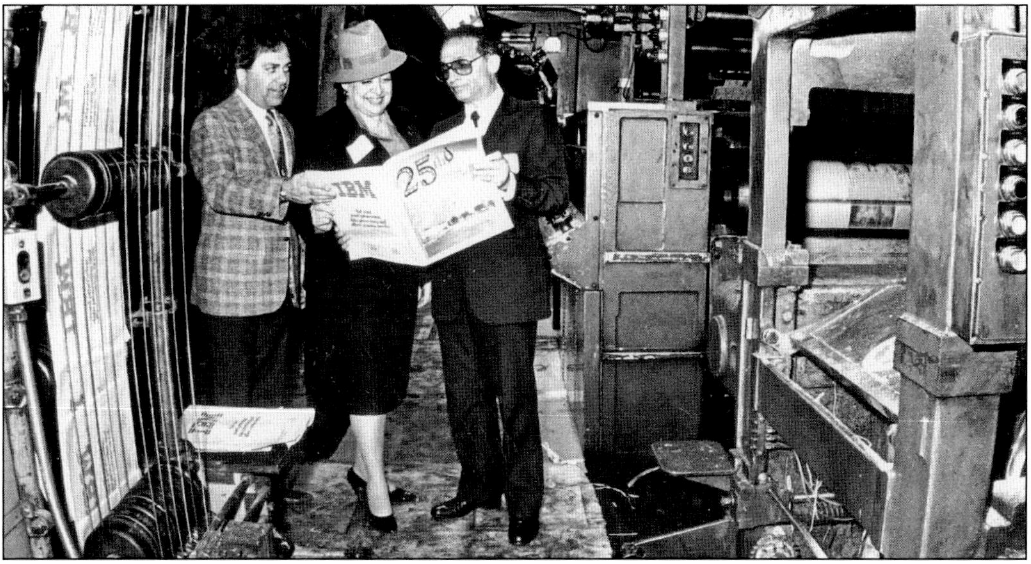

The *Burlington County Times* and the developments of Levitt and Sons are inextricably linked. S.W. Calkins established the *Bucks County Courier Times* as Levitt constructed his second Levittown in Pennsylvania. As the developer built his first homes in rural Burlington County in 1958, Calkins launched the *Levittown Times*. He changed the name to the *Burlington County Times* in 1963 to go along with the residents' decision to call the town Willingboro again. This is a photograph from the newspaper's 25th-anniversary celebration. (Courtesy Burlington County Times.)

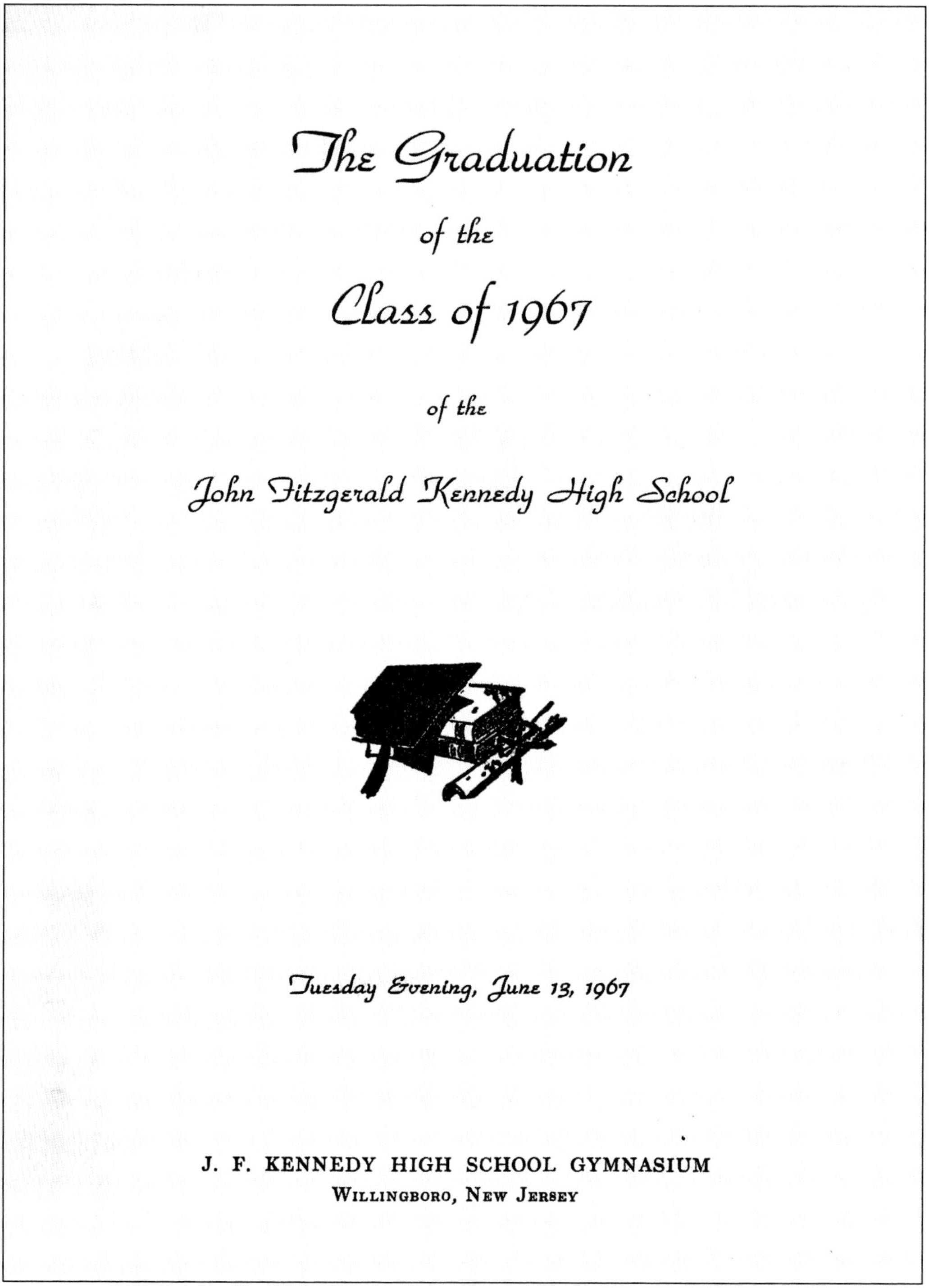

The Graduation

of the

Class of 1967

of the

John Fitzgerald Kennedy High School

Tuesday Evening, June 13, 1967

J. F. KENNEDY HIGH SCHOOL GYMNASIUM

WILLINGBORO, NEW JERSEY

John F. Kennedy High School opened November 12, 1965, close to two years after the president was assassinated. New Jersey Gov. Richard J. Hughes formally dedicated the school. Shown is the cover of the school's graduation program from June 13, 1967. (Courtesy Marion Huddleston.)

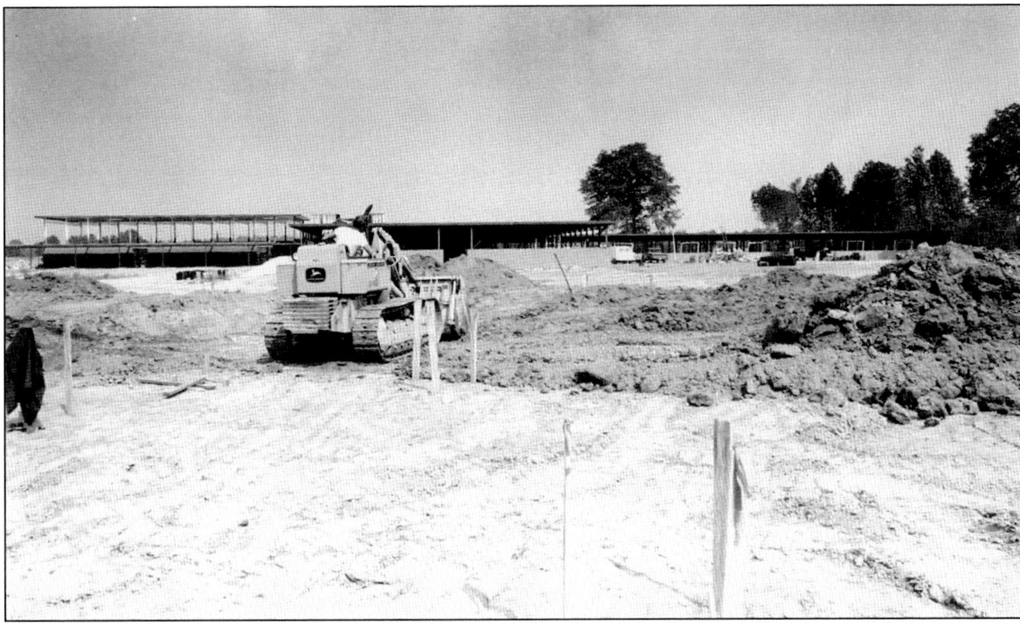

A heavy equipment operator works on the parking lot of the Martin Luther King Jr. Elementary School on Northampton Drive in September 1968. The school opened in 1969. (Courtesy Burlington County Times.)

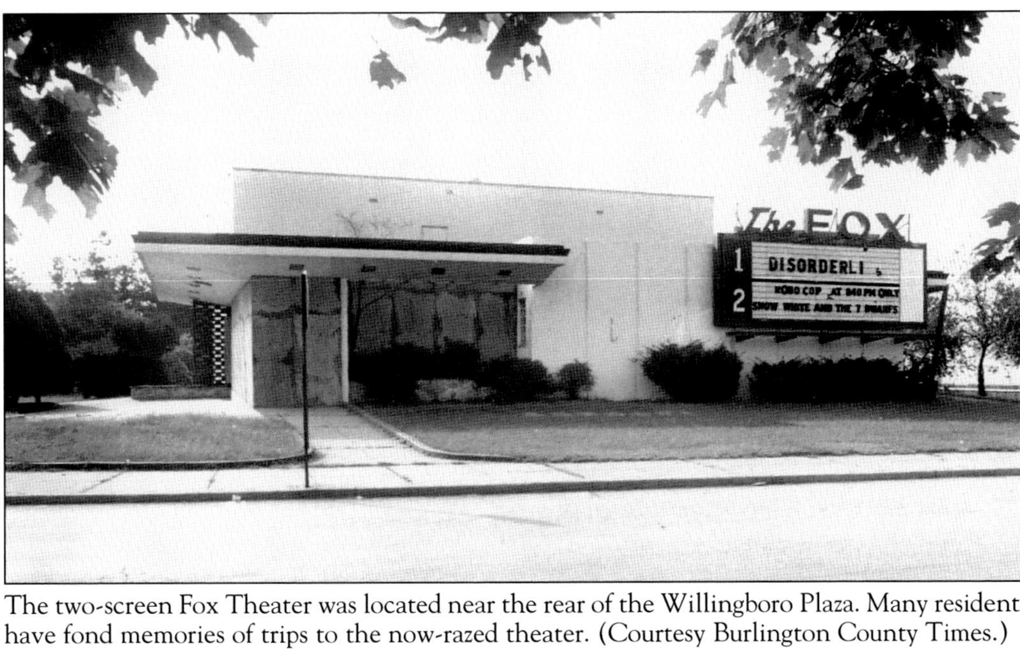

The two-screen Fox Theater was located near the rear of the Willingboro Plaza. Many residents have fond memories of trips to the now-razed theater. (Courtesy Burlington County Times.)

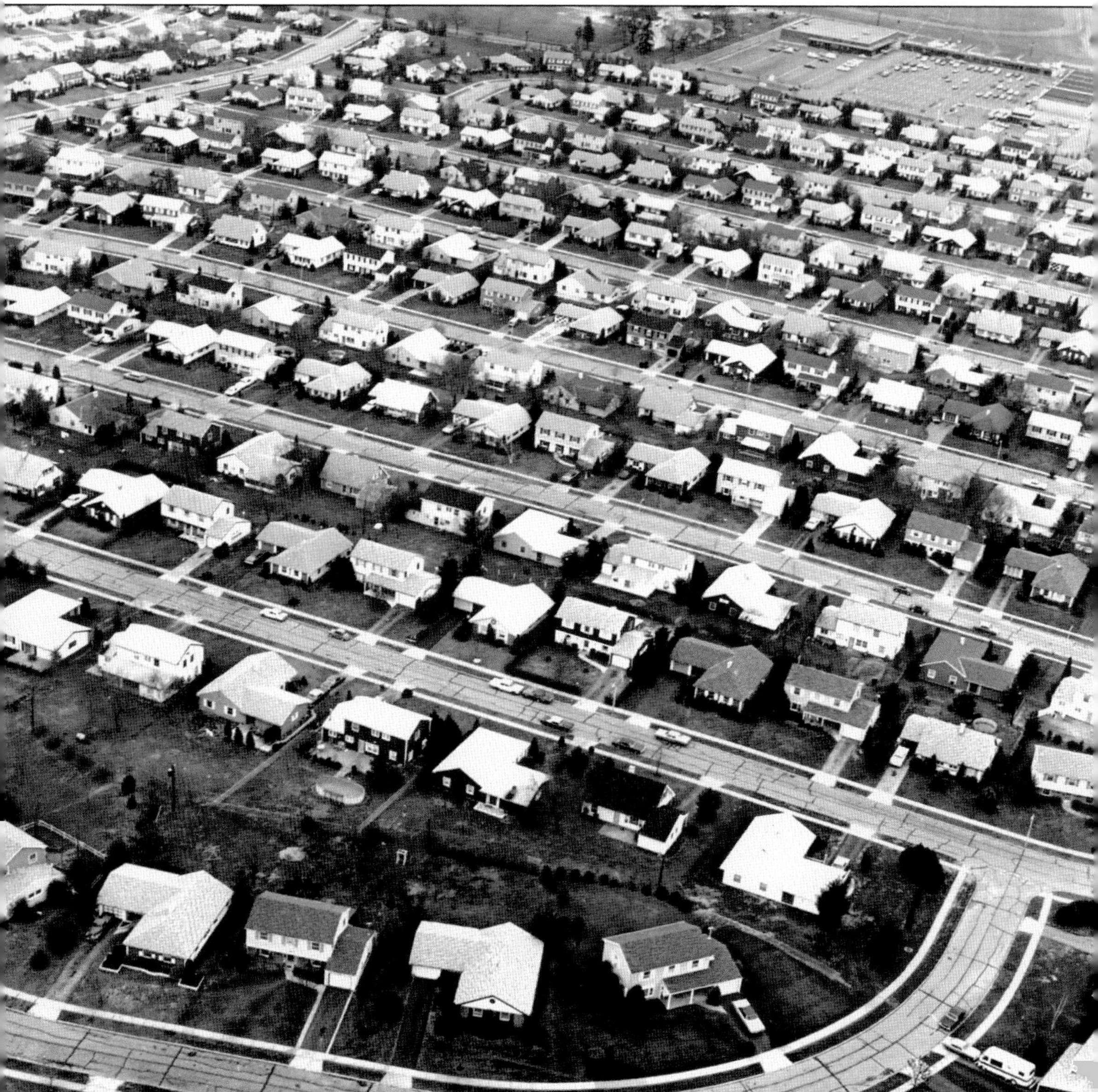

This aerial view shows the Pennypacker Park neighborhood, which Levitt built in 1960. It is easy to see the different models of homes available to residents. (Courtesy Burlington County Times.)

Four

A Community Matures

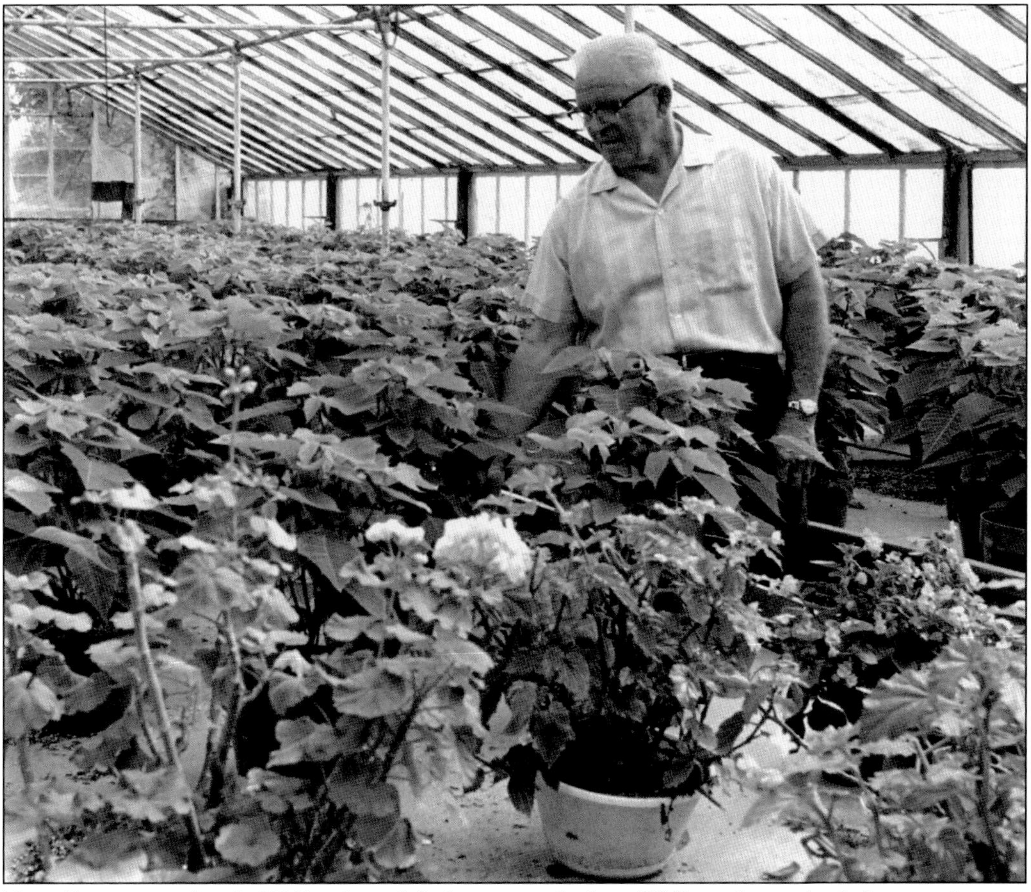

Not all vestiges of early Willingboro life disappeared when William Levitt built his new homes. James Cresswell Stuart, a prominent farmer, maintained his residence and his greenhouse, shown in this 1974 photograph. An elementary school bears Stuart's name. (Courtesy Burlington County Times.)

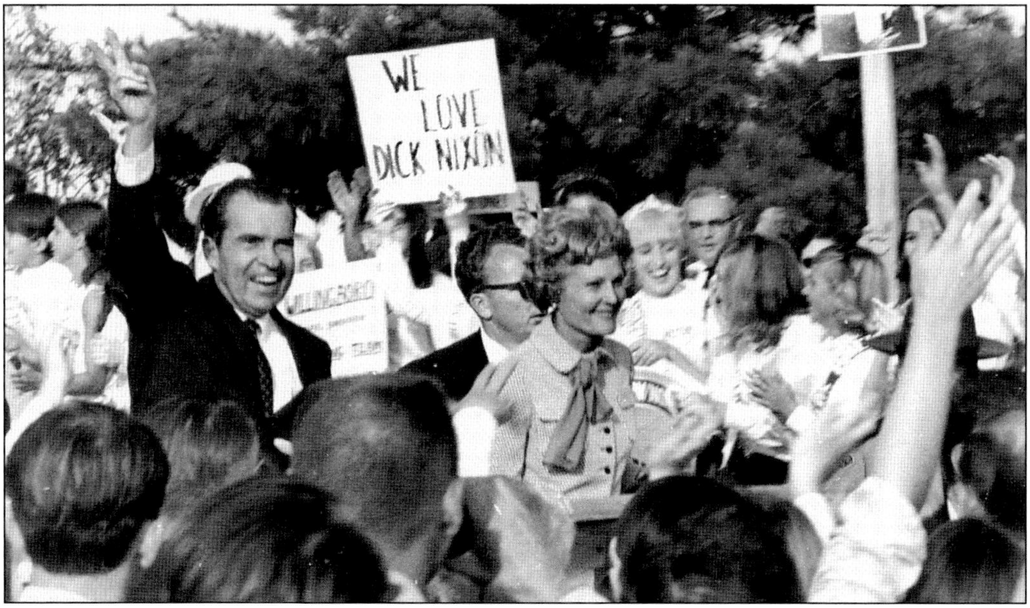

Even though the township later became known as a Democratic stronghold, thousands of cheering people came to the Willingboro Plaza shopping mall in 1968 for a campaign stop by Republican presidential candidate Richard Nixon. (Courtesy Burlington County Times.)

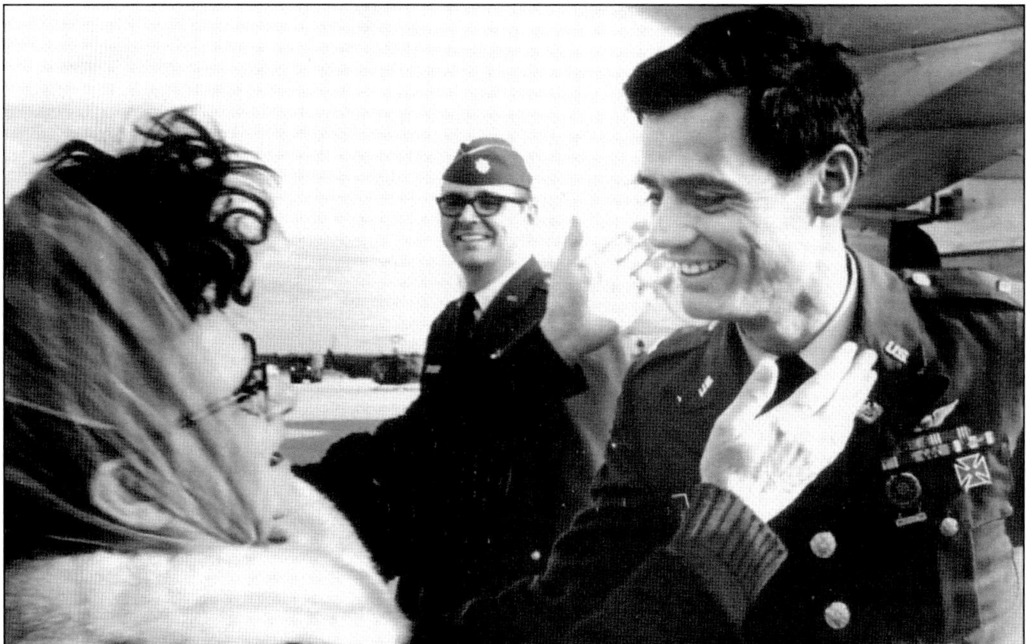

Willingboro resident Frank Anton was a chief warrant officer in the U.S. Army and a member of an Army aviation unit. He was flying a UH-1C Gunship over the Que Son Valley during a combat mission in Vietnam when he was shot down in January 1968. Held as a prisoner of war by the North Vietnamese until April 1973, Anton maintains that the U.S. government knew of his situation but never attempted a rescue. Anton is shown here returning to McGuire Air Force Base. (Courtesy Burlington County Times.)

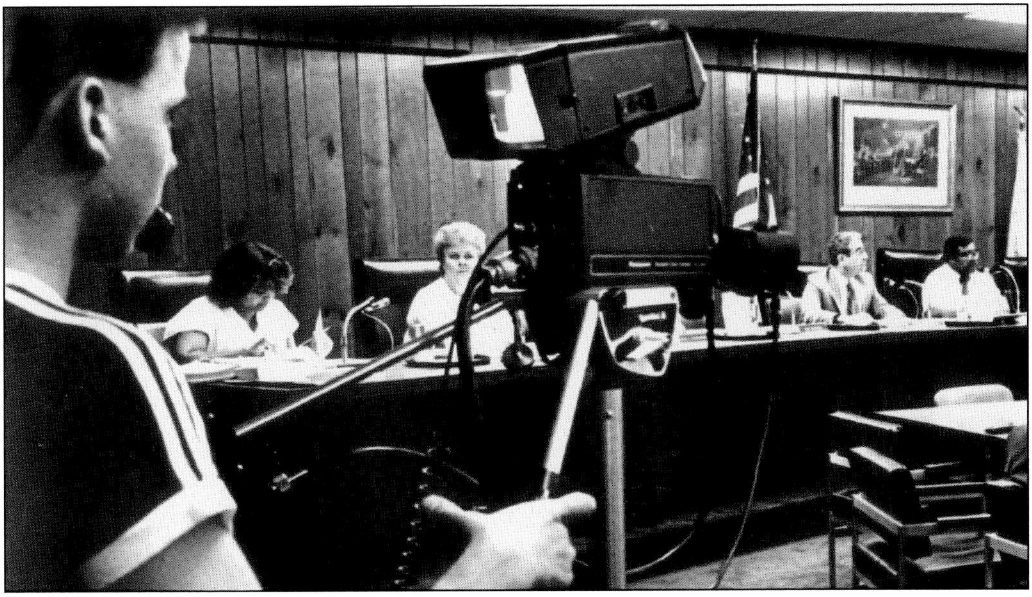

In 1973, the Willingboro Board of Education became the first school board in the nation to televise its meetings. Board members often argued bitterly over even the most minor issues, and the meetings became known as the best show in town. The state commissioner of education forced Willingboro to turn the cameras off in 2000. (Courtesy Burlington County Times.)

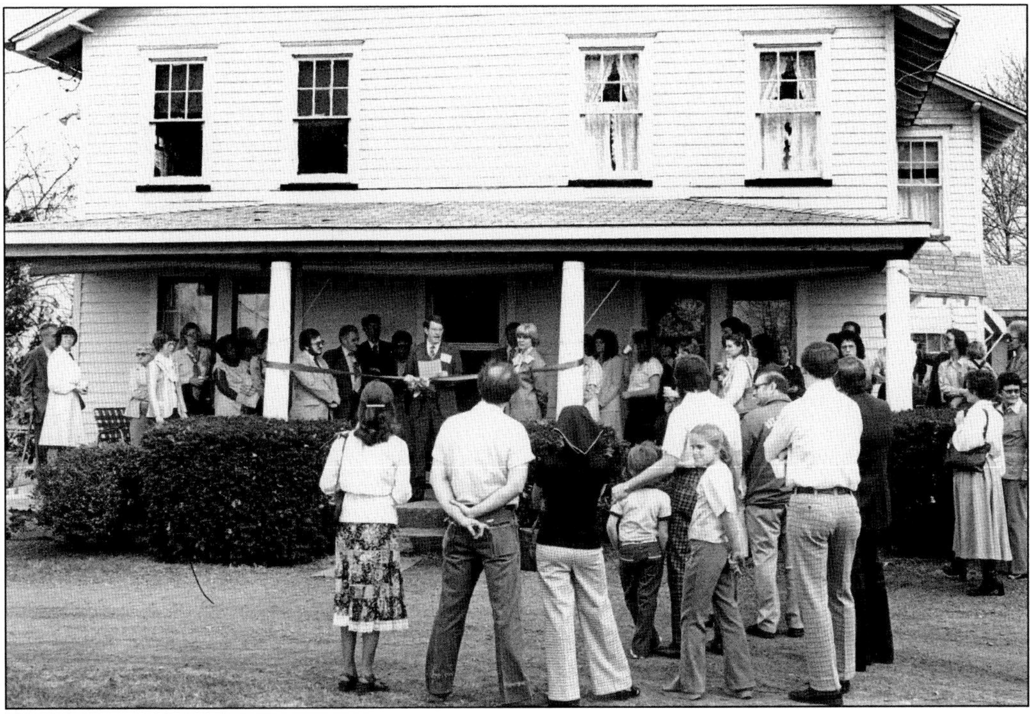

In April 1979, township officials opened Providence House, a shelter for abused women and their children. The shelter was located in a homestead that survived Levitt's penchant for tearing down old homes to make way for his development. (Courtesy Willingboro Township Manager's Office.)

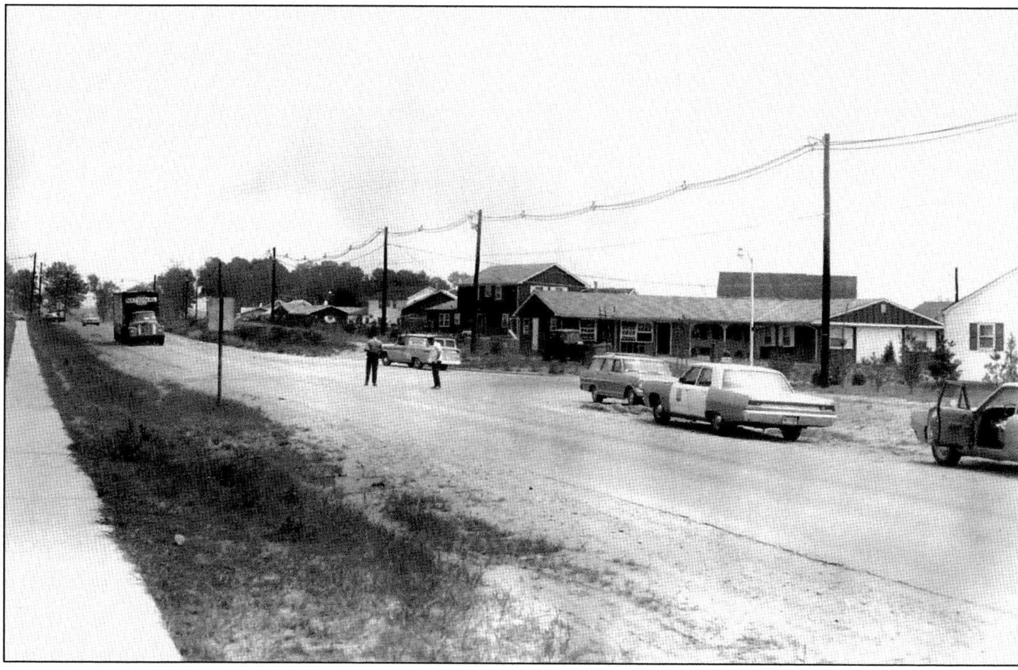

Police officers investigate an accident on Levitt Parkway in July 1968. Even then the street, which coming out of neighboring Westampton was known as Woodlane Road, spanned only one lane in each direction and had no curb. (Courtesy Dave Retzko.)

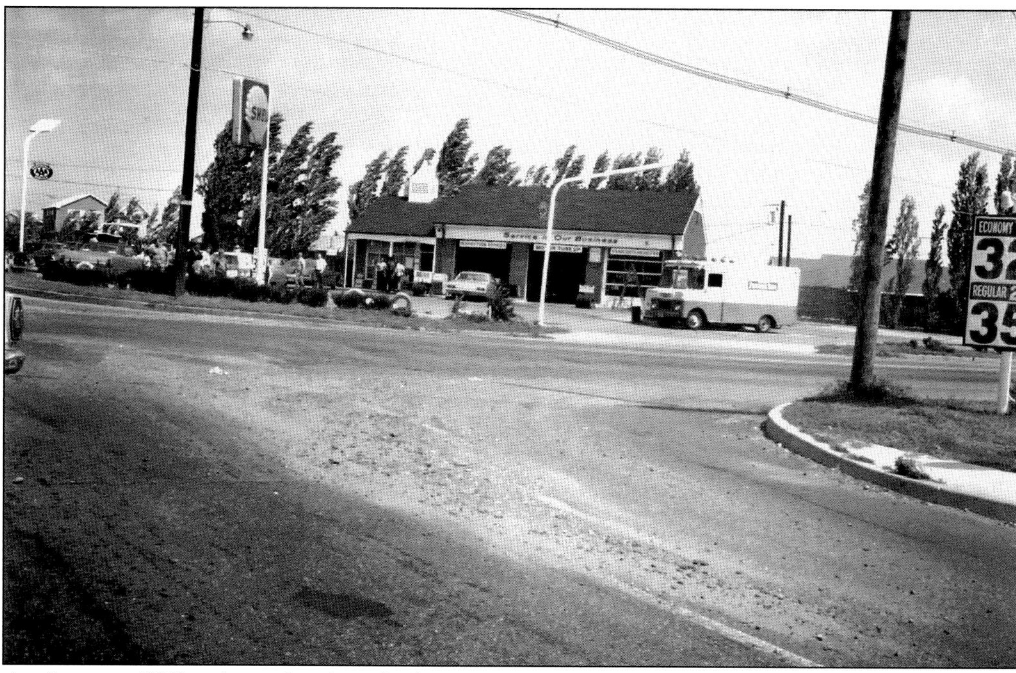

As the new Willingboro developed, the intersection of Beverly-Rancocas Road and John F. Kennedy Way (formerly Park Road) became one of the town's major crossroads. The site had two gas stations, as shown in this 1967 photograph. Gas was much cheaper back then—32¢ to 35¢ per gallon. (Courtesy Dave Retzko.)

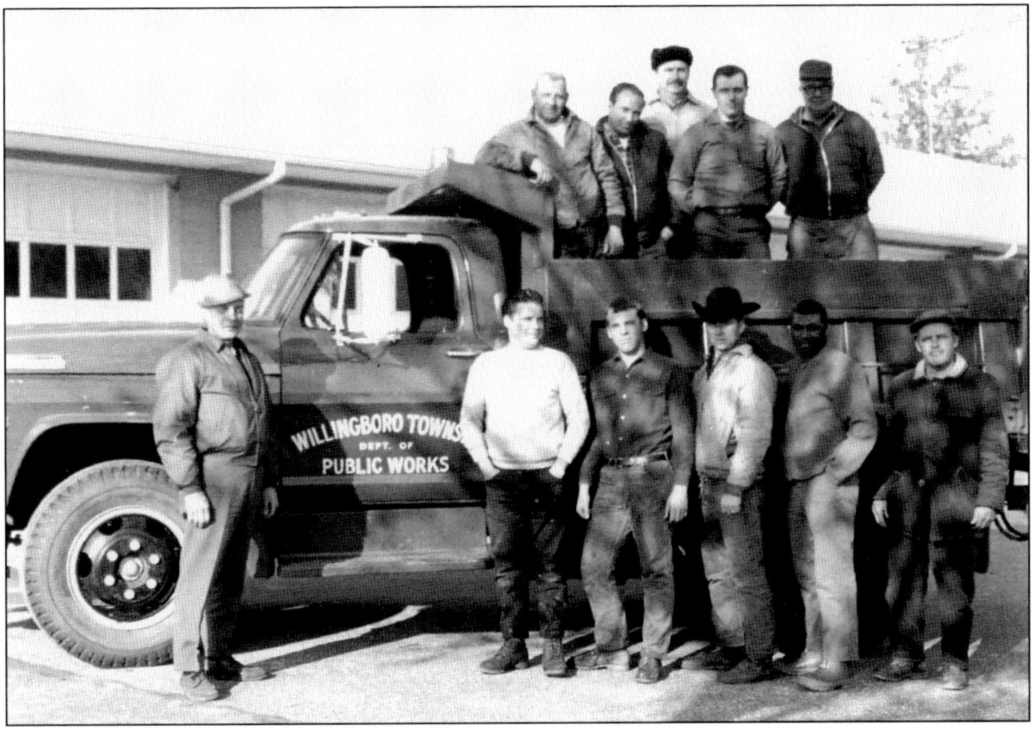

Members of the Willingboro Public Works Department pose in front of a truck in 1971. The department was charged with keeping Willingboro's winding streets and broad parkways clean and free of snow. (Courtesy Willingboro Township Manager's Office.)

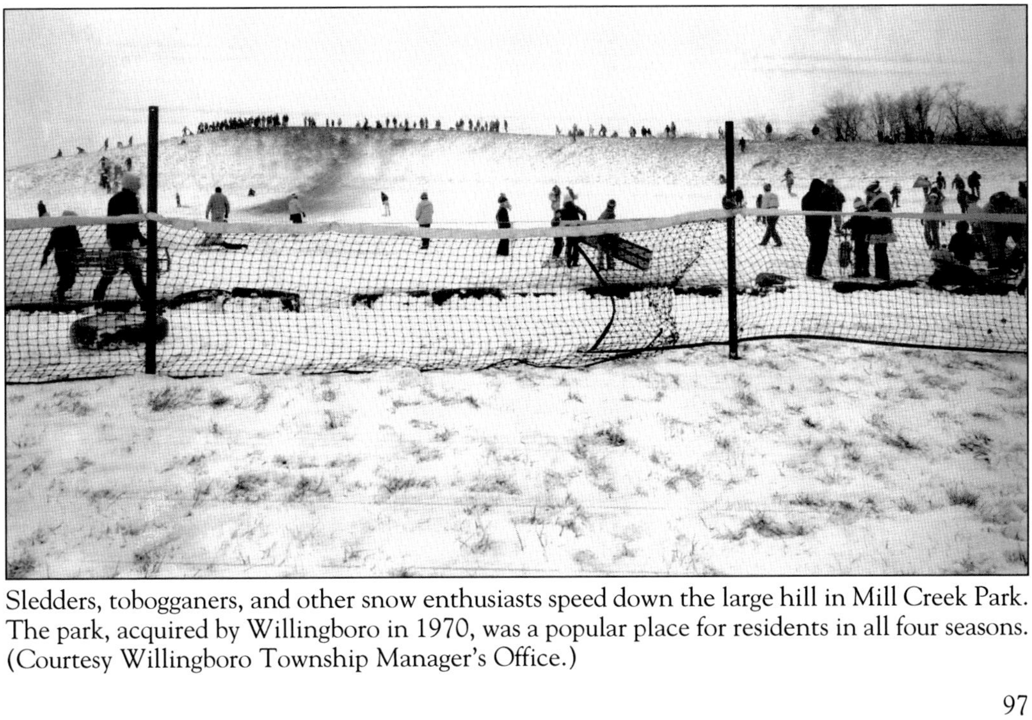

Sledders, tobogganers, and other snow enthusiasts speed down the large hill in Mill Creek Park. The park, acquired by Willingboro in 1970, was a popular place for residents in all four seasons. (Courtesy Willingboro Township Manager's Office.)

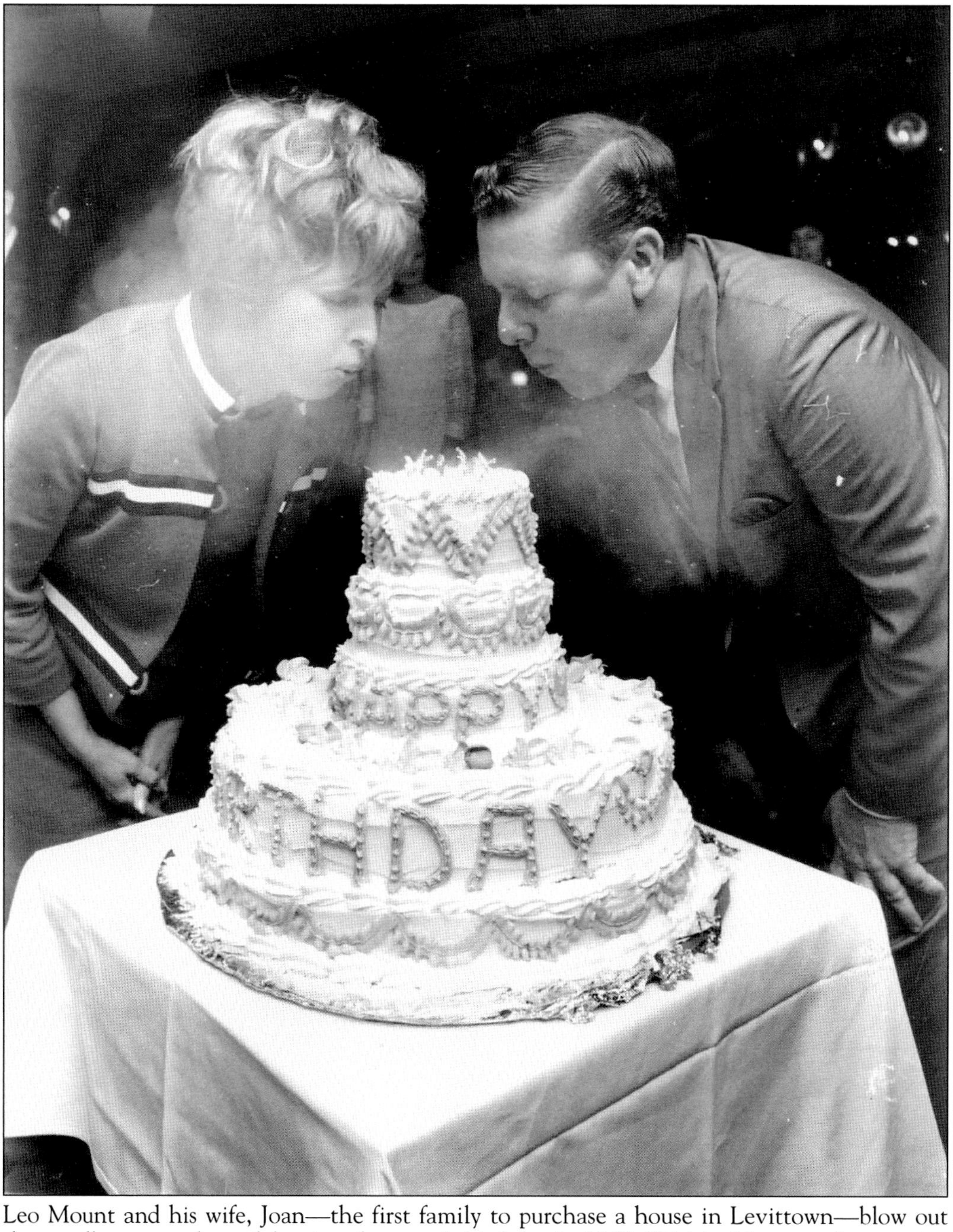

Leo Mount and his wife, Joan—the first family to purchase a house in Levittown—blow out the candles on a cake, celebrating the town's birthday in 1968. Within 10 years of occupying the township's first house on Sussex Drive, the Mounts moved to Millbrook Drive. (Courtesy Burlington County Times.)

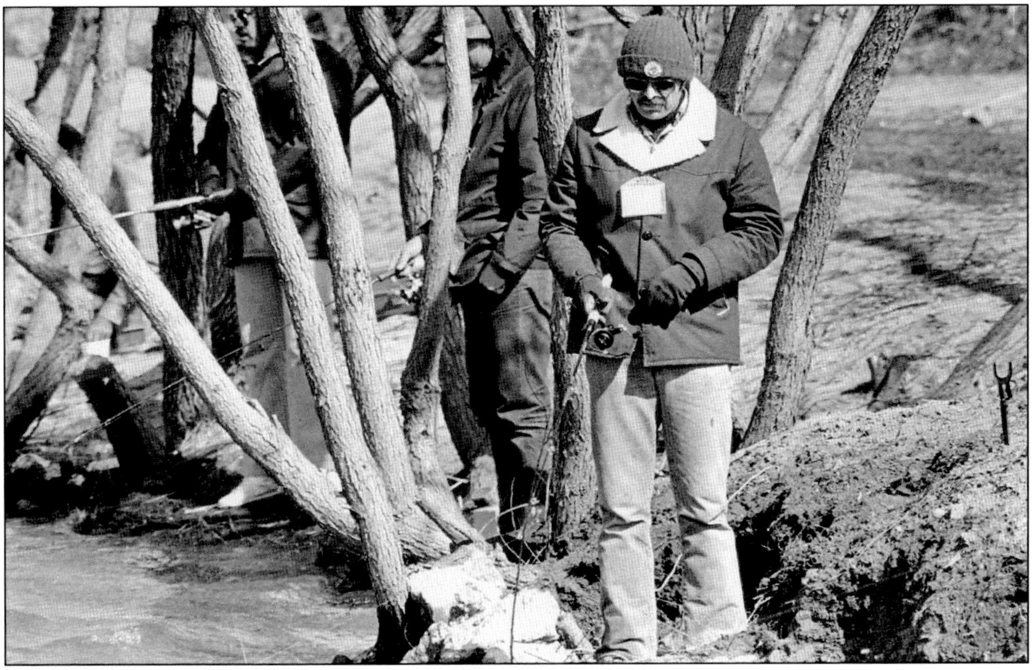

Levitt and Sons donated Crystal Lake, located near the water and sewer plant, to the township in 1972. Every spring, the state stocks the lake with trout, which these three men were hoping to catch in April 1979. (Courtesy Burlington County Times.)

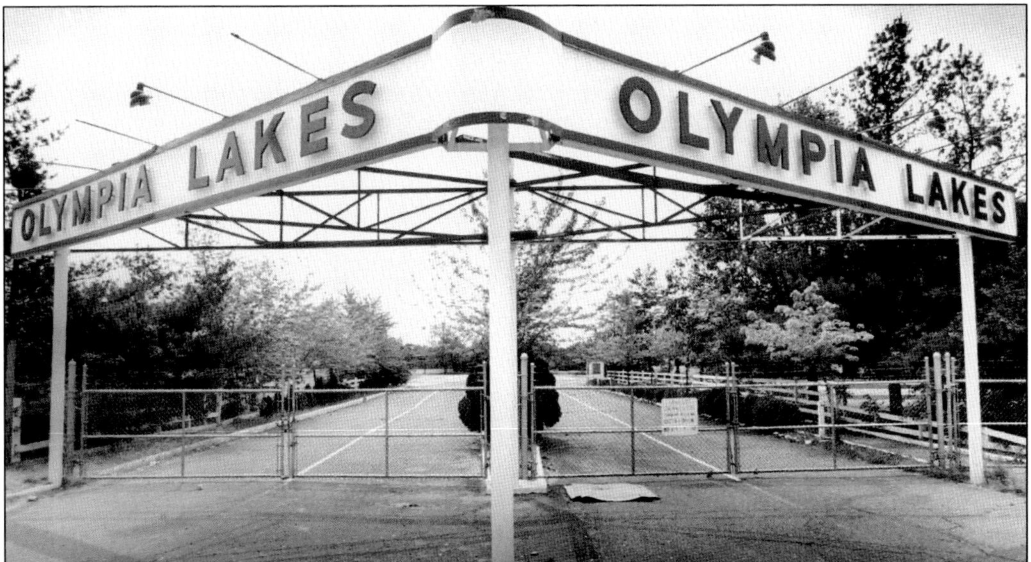

Olympia Lakes, a 105-acre area between Route 130 and Beverly-Rancocas Road, was a popular recreation spot from 1938 until the owners closed it for financial reasons in 1976. The lakes were formed at the beginning of the 20th century when workers building the Philadelphia subway system pumped sand and dirt out of the ground and into rail cars or boats docked on the Rancocas Creek. The two pits then filled with water. The remnants of the rail line still exist, as does a three-story, steel-reinforced concrete gantry used to transport the sand. (Courtesy Burlington County Times.)

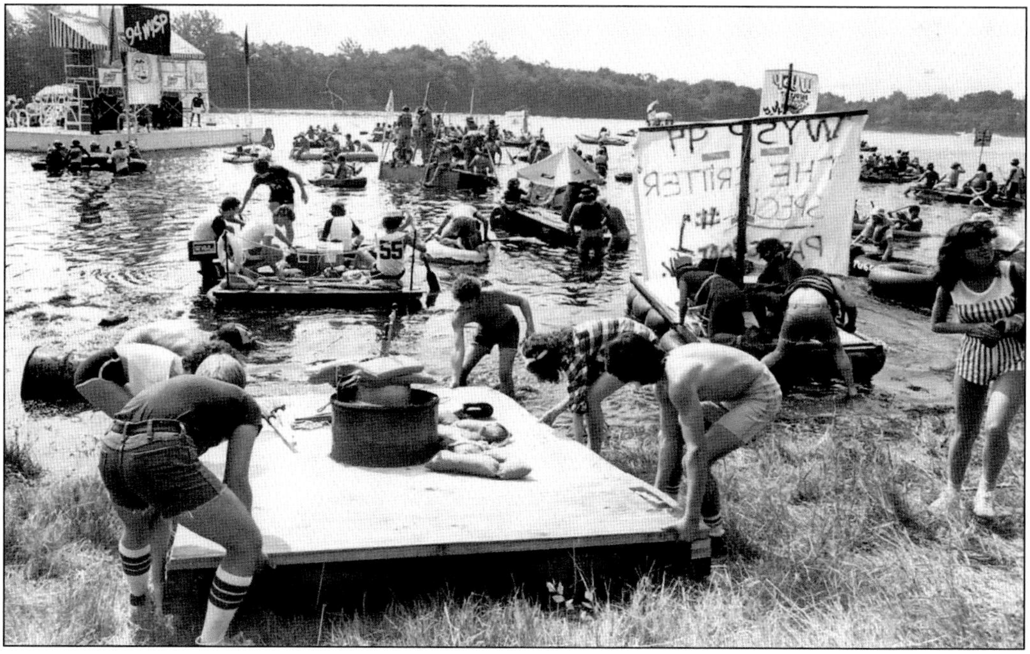

Olympia Lakes, consisting of two man-made bodies of water off Route 130, was a popular recreation spot. In 1982, Philadelphia radio station WYSP hosted a raft race in which participants crossed the lakes on homemade contraptions. (Courtesy Burlington County Times.)

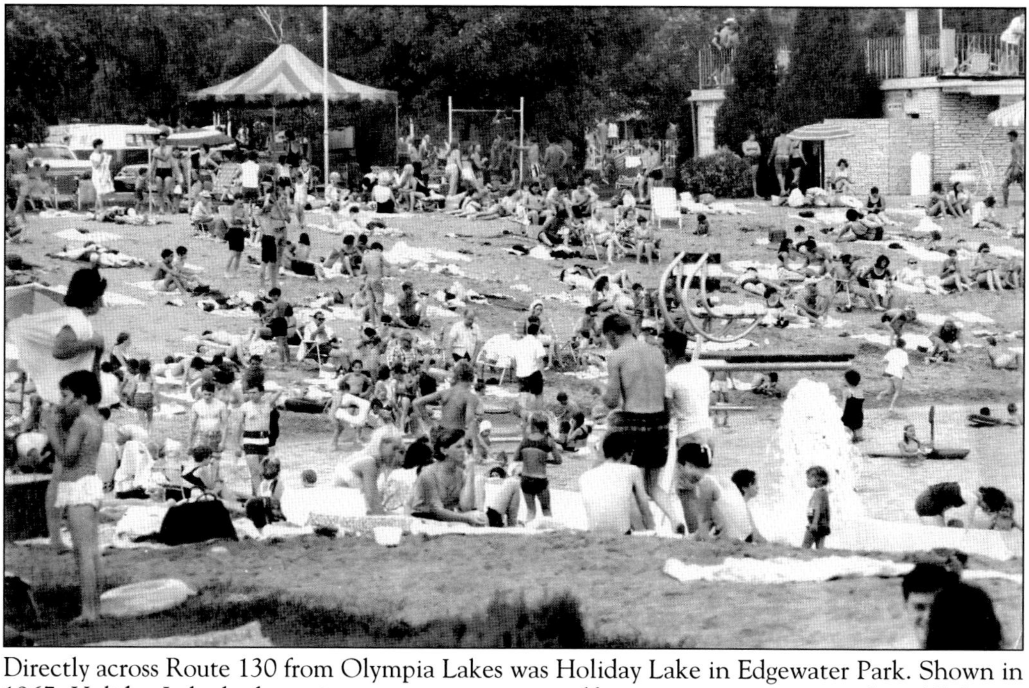

Directly across Route 130 from Olympia Lakes was Holiday Lake in Edgewater Park. Shown in 1967, Holiday Lake had tennis courts, a miniature golf course, a swimming pool, paddleboats, picnic areas, and, of course, a lake. From the 1940s through the 1980s, as many as 8,000 people a day visited the recreation spot. (Courtesy Burlington County Times.)

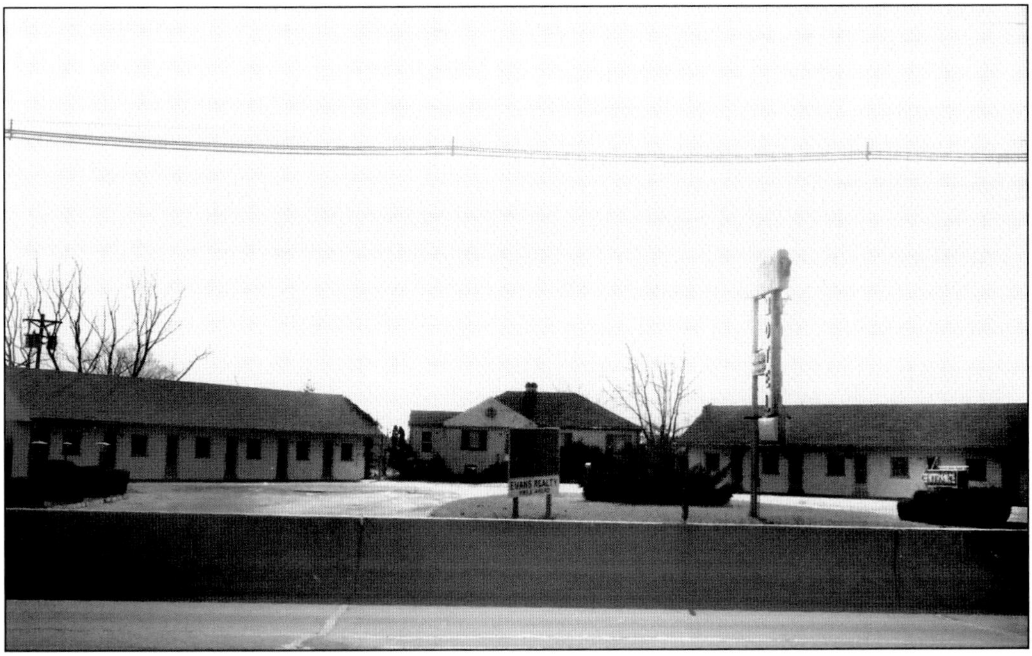

Route 130 became a heavily traveled roadway, and motels popped up all along the corridor to accommodate area visitors and truckers. Willingboro had the three-building Route 130 Motel, shown here before it was razed in 1971. (Courtesy Dave Retzko.)

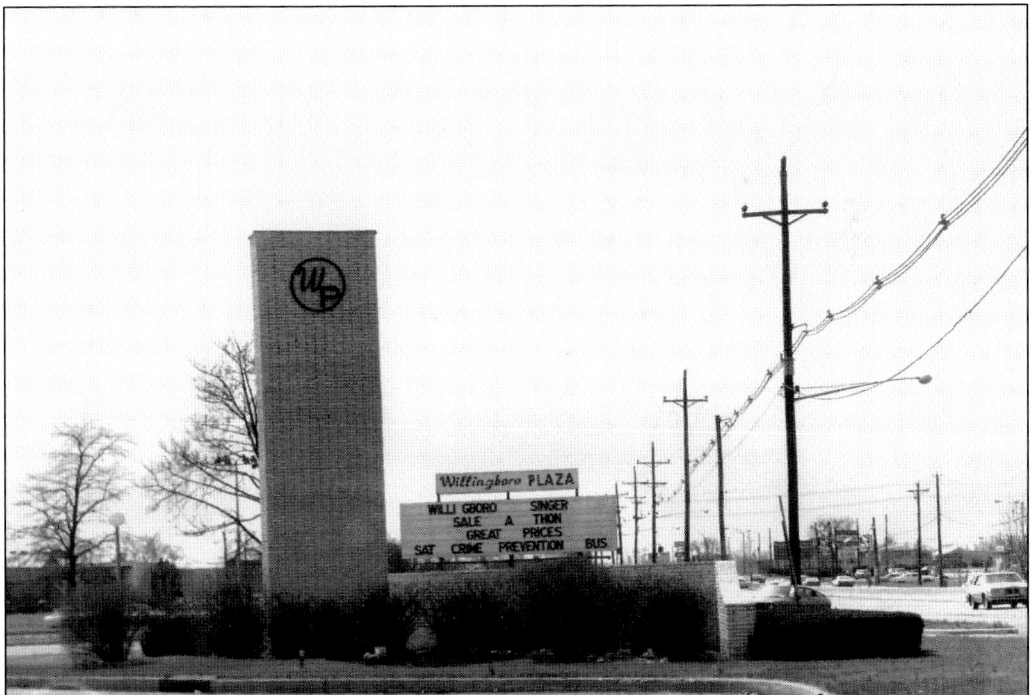

Cars prepare to enter the Willingboro Plaza shopping mall from Route 130 *c.* 1975. The mall was one of the area's premier places to shop or just hang out. However, the person who wrote the sign couldn't spell the town's name. (Courtesy Dave Retzko.)

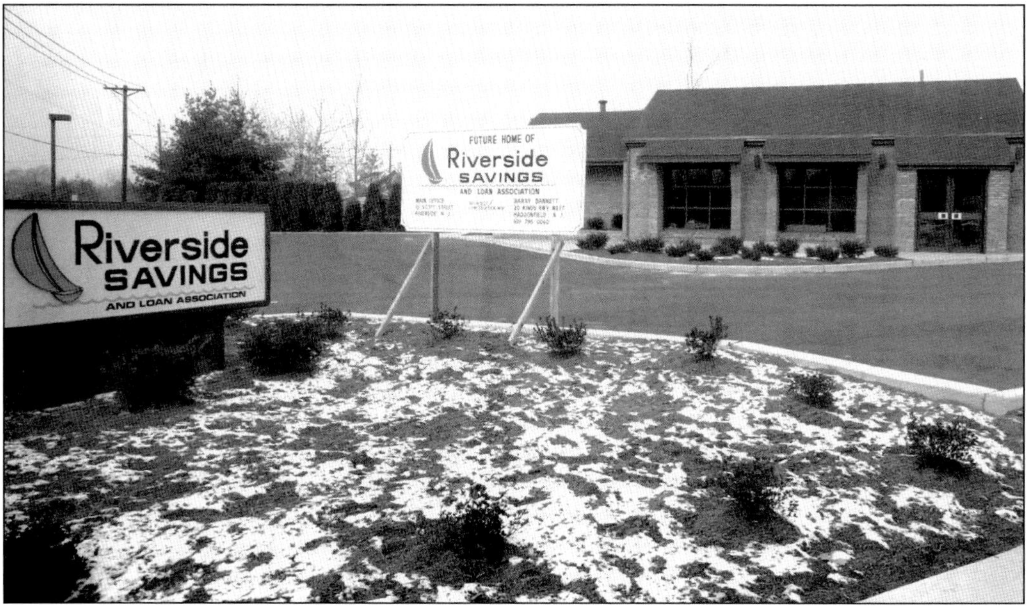

Willingboro not only grew residentially during the 1960s and 1970s but also commercially. Riverside Savings Bank was one of the many banks, supermarkets, and other stores that opened to serve township residents. (Courtesy Willingboro Township Manager's Office.)

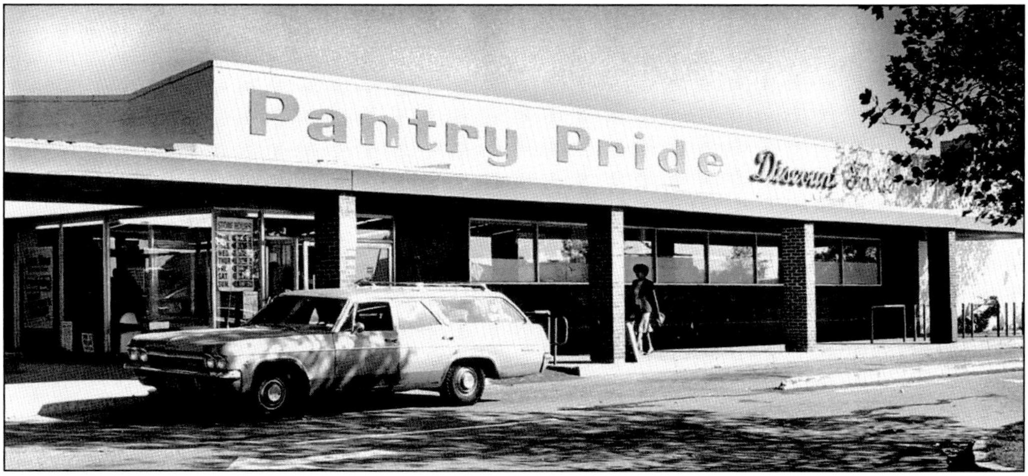

Pantry Pride was one of several supermarket chains that opened food stores in Willingboro. Pantry Pride operated in the Willingboro Plaza from 1959 to 1978. (Courtesy Burlington County Times.)

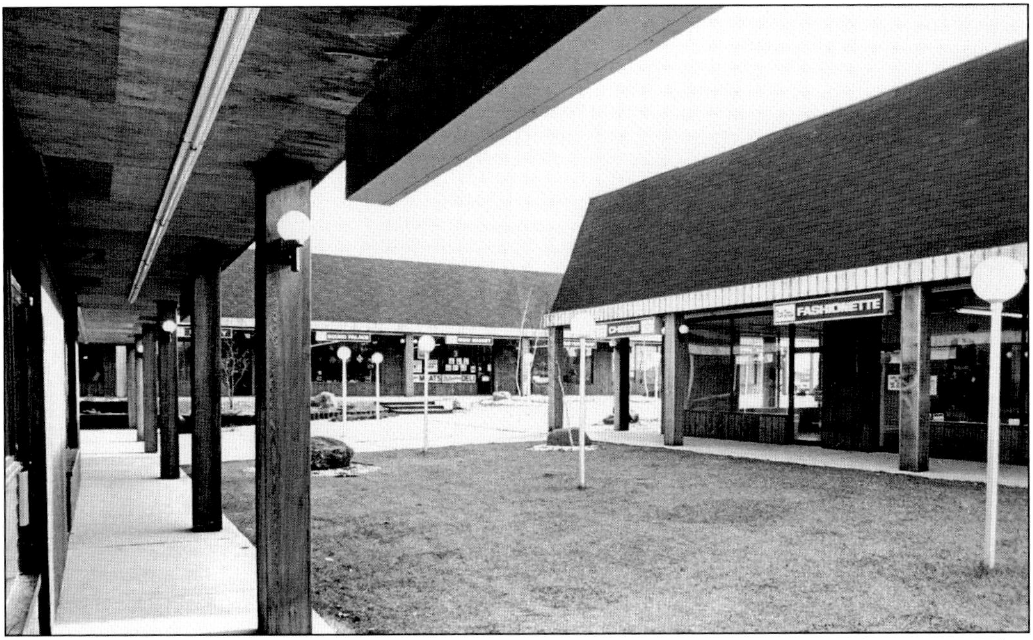

The East Ridge Plaza on Beverly-Rancocas Road near Garfield Drive opened in 1973. This shopping center was open to the air and included many small stores. (Courtesy Burlington County Times.)

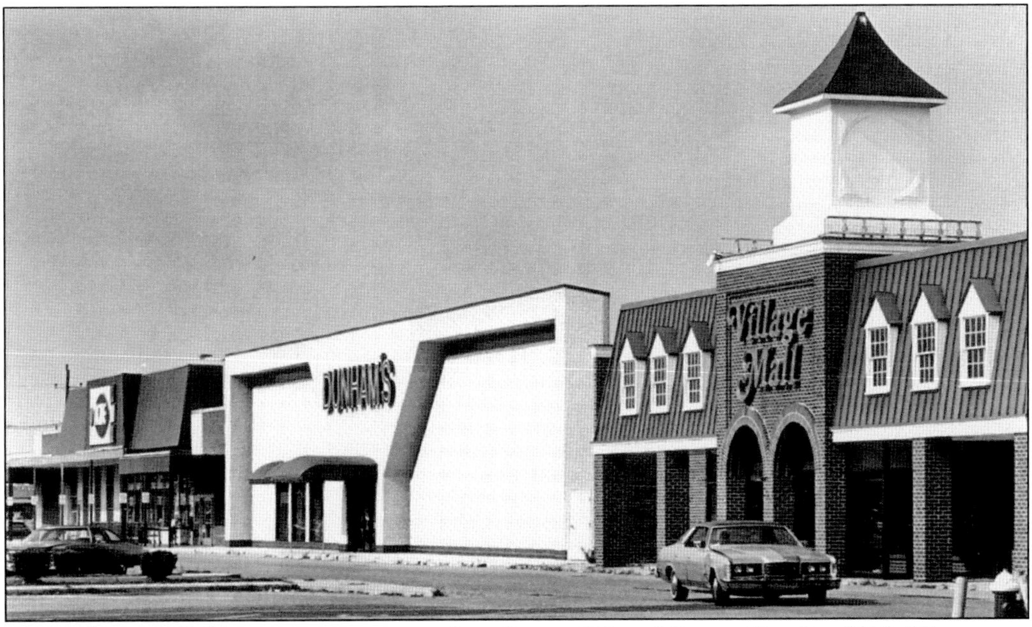

The Village Mall shopping center opened on Route 130 and Sunset Road in 1973. The center had two anchor stores that opened into an enclosed building housing several smaller retailers and a movie theater. Although the mall featured a supermarket, it never attracted a great deal of business. (Courtesy Burlington County Times.)

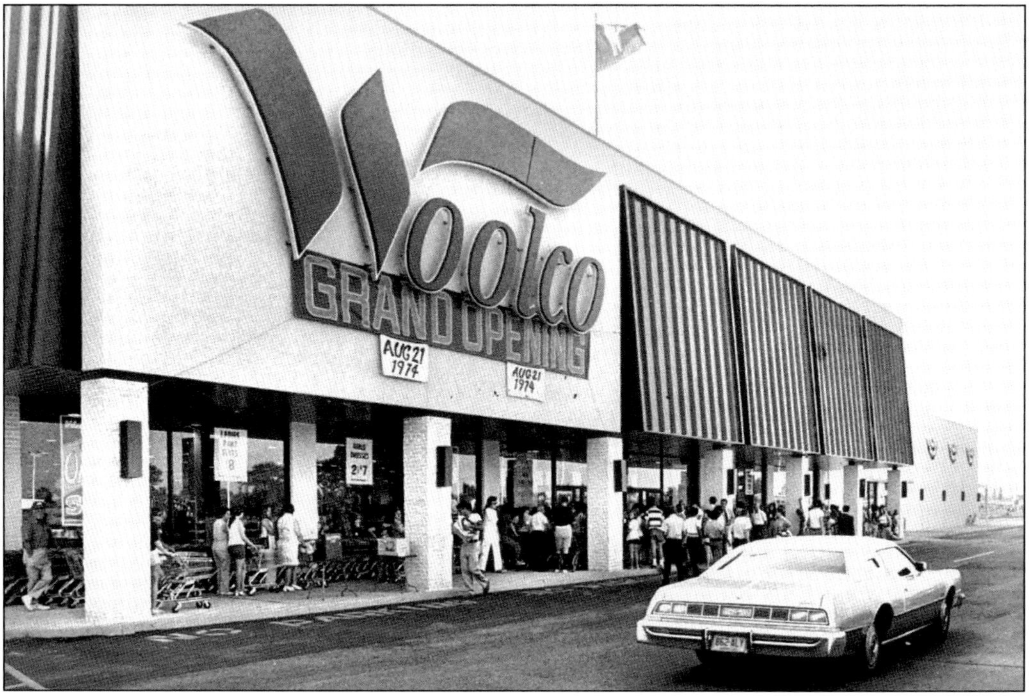

The Woolco discount clothing store debuted at the Village Mall on August 21, 1974. (Courtesy Burlington County Times.)

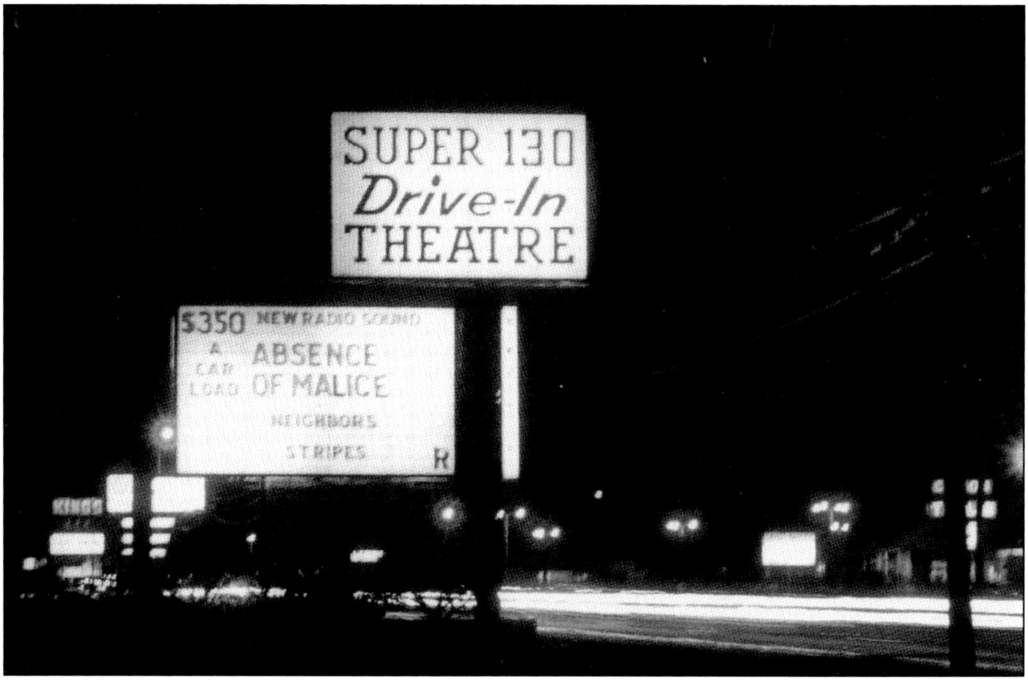

New Jersey was the home of drive-in movie theaters, and Willingboro residents had a convenient place to watch a flick under the stars. The Super 130 Drive-In Theatre, shown here in 1982, operated for years in nearby Edgewater Park. (Courtesy Burlington County Times.)

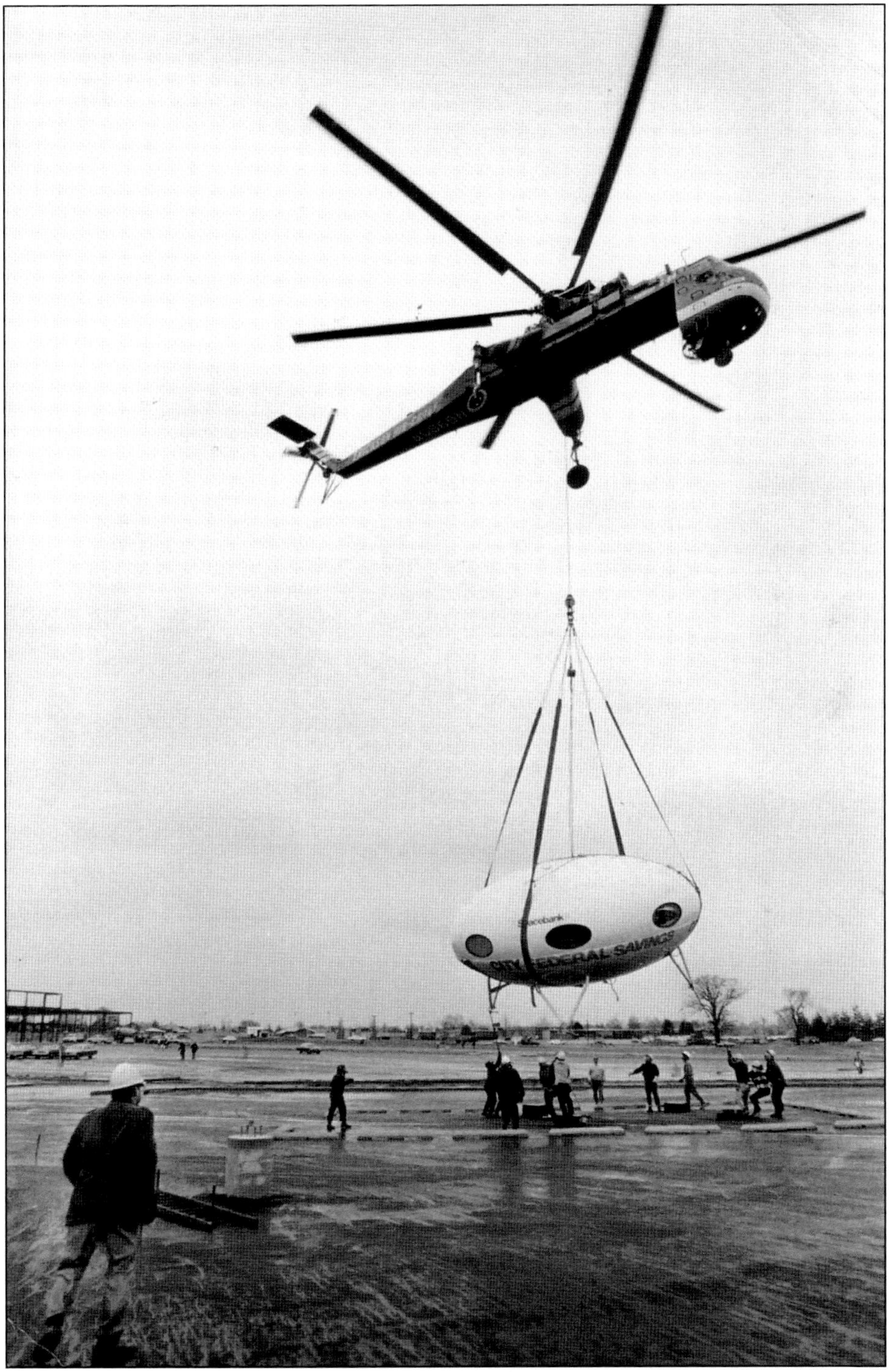

Contrary to some initial reports, a UFO did not land in Willingboro in December 1973. Actually, a helicopter transported the Spacebank, an egg-shaped structure belonging to City Federal Savings, to Mill Creek Park. The township's recreation department used the Spacebank as an office. (Courtesy Burlington County Times.)

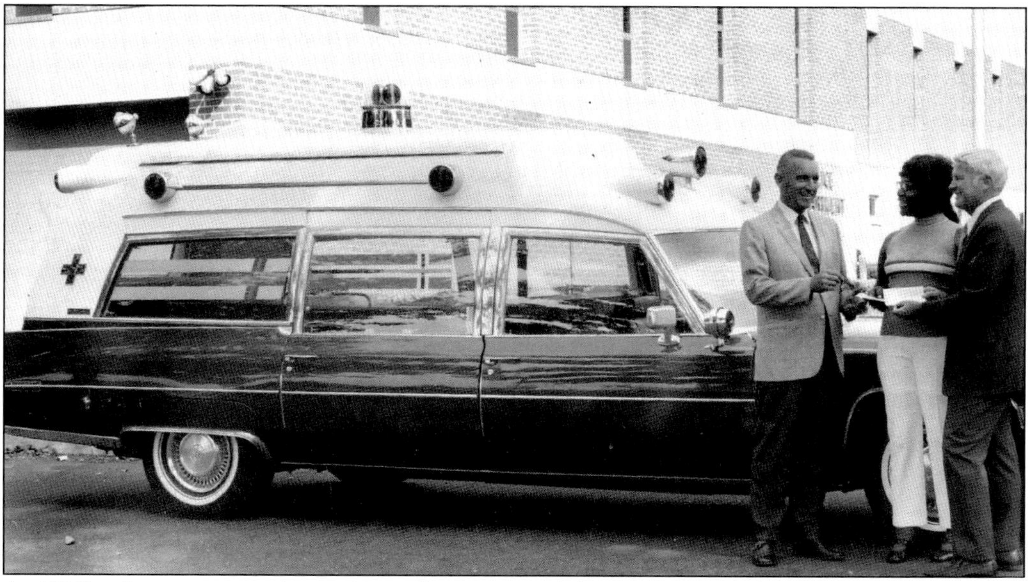

As Willingboro grew in the 1960s and 1970s, so did its need for police, fire, and emergency medical protection. In 1973, the emergency squad received a new ambulance—a specially outfitted station wagon. (Courtesy Willingboro Township Manager's Office.)

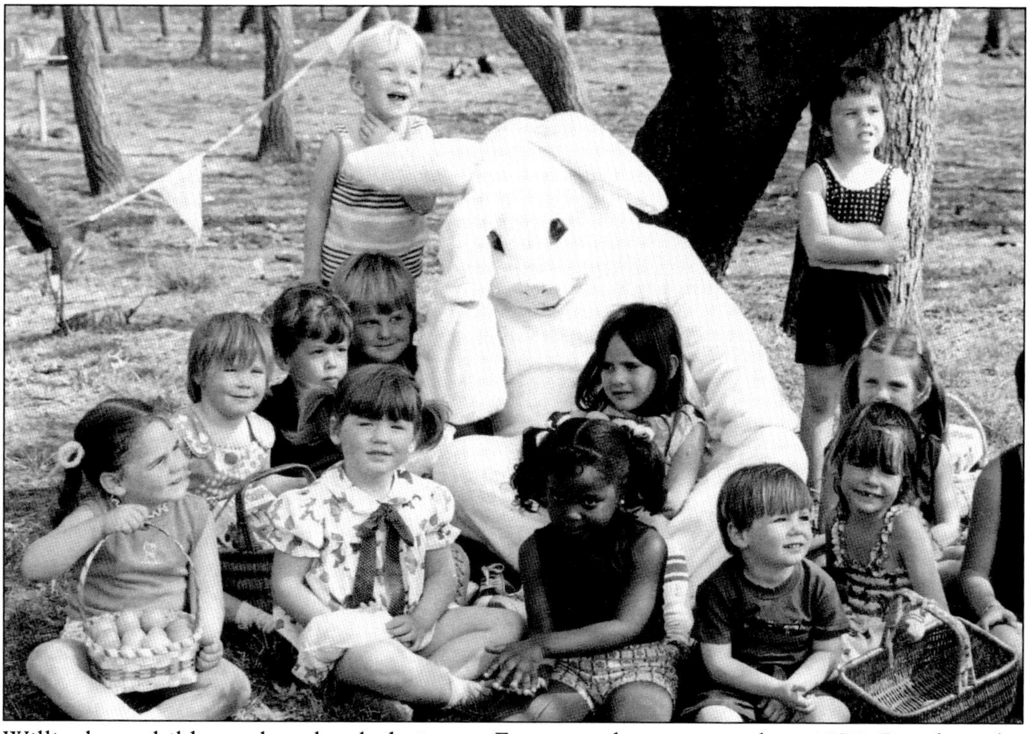

Willingboro children take a break during an Easter egg hunt at a park in 1978. Based on the contents of the baskets in this photograph, some of the children were better at finding the eggs than others. (Courtesy Willingboro Township Manager's Office.)

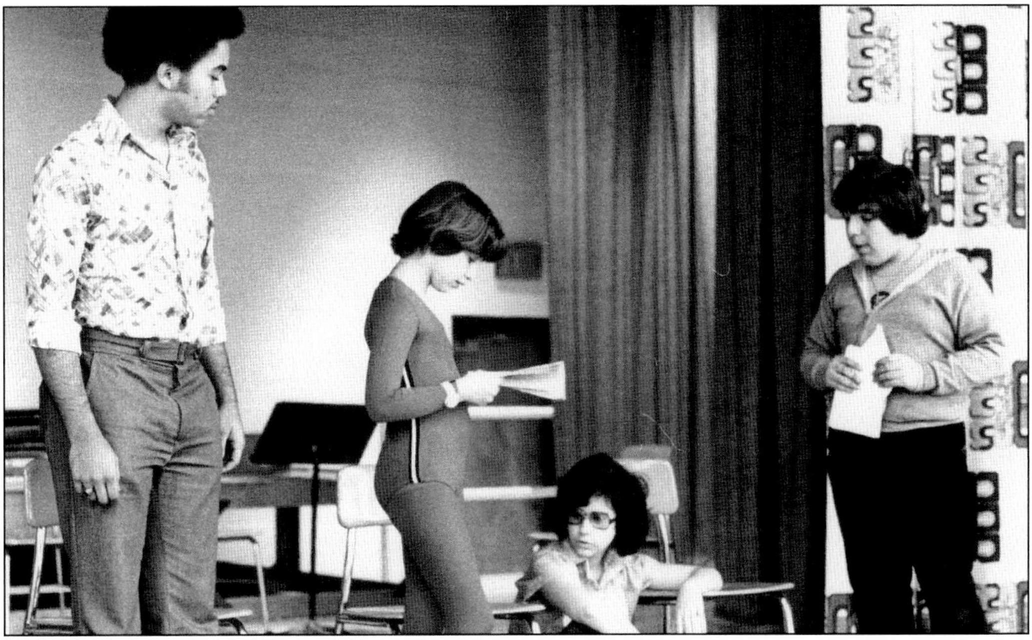

Township residents participated not only in outdoor activities but also in indoor ones. In April 1978, a group put on the theatrical production *The Owl and the Pussycat* at John F. Kennedy High School. (Courtesy Willingboro Township Manager's Office.)

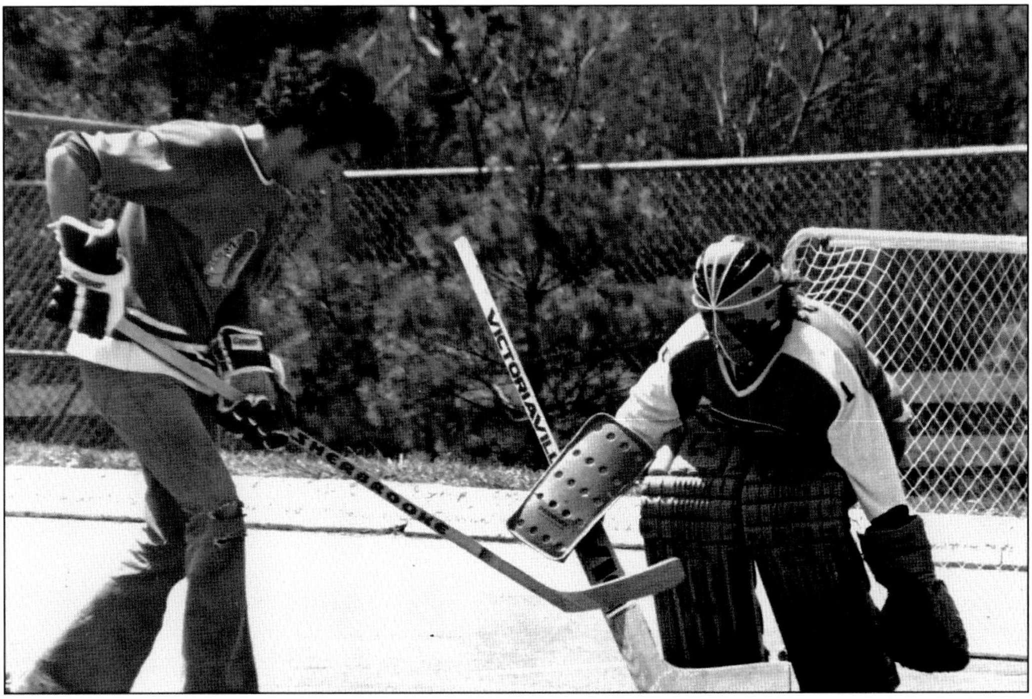

A teenager prepares to take a shot on a goal in the department's street hockey league during the summer of 1975. Teens practiced year-round to become the next Philadelphia Flyers star. (Courtesy Willingboro Township Manager's Office.)

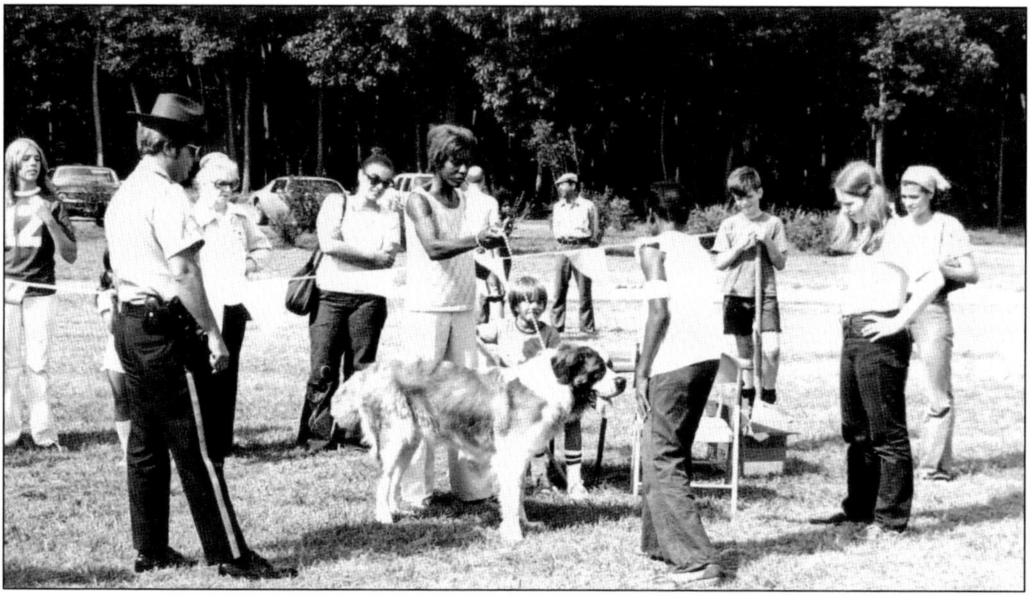

This dog was the center of attention in the township's first pet show at Mill Creek Park, off Beverly-Rancocas Road, in July 1975. The land where the park sits was owned by the Kimble family before being purchased by the township. (Courtesy Willingboro Township Manager's Office.)

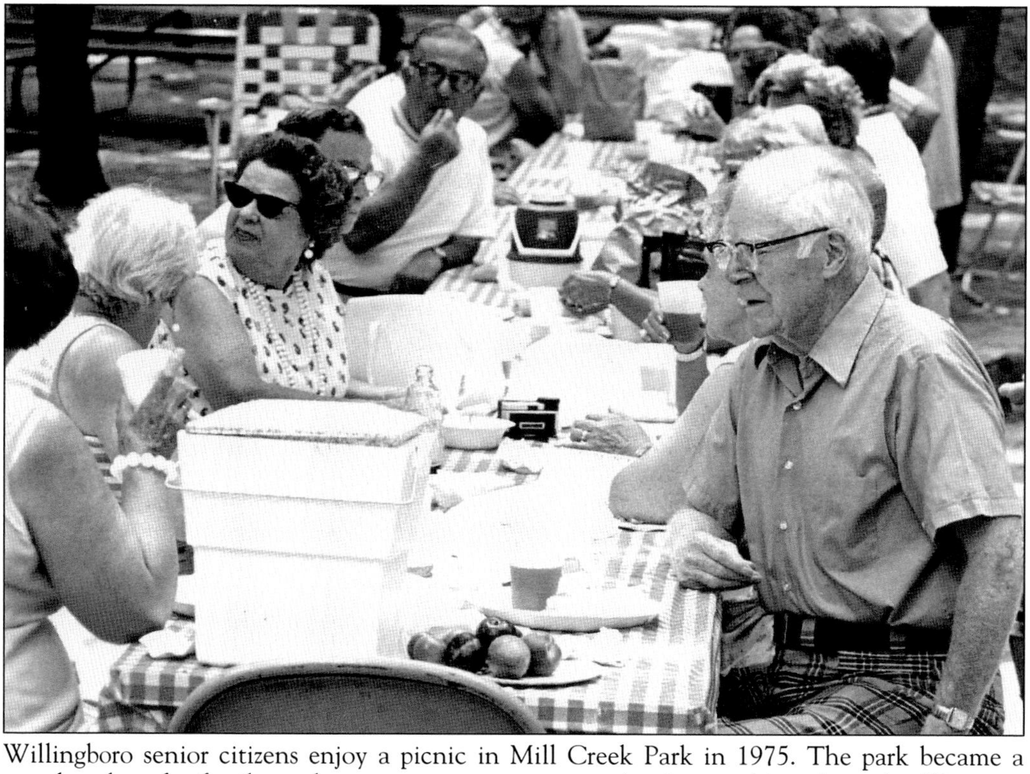

Willingboro senior citizens enjoy a picnic in Mill Creek Park in 1975. The park became a popular place for family cookouts, soccer tournaments, jogging, and jazz festivals. (Courtesy Willingboro Township Manager's Office.)

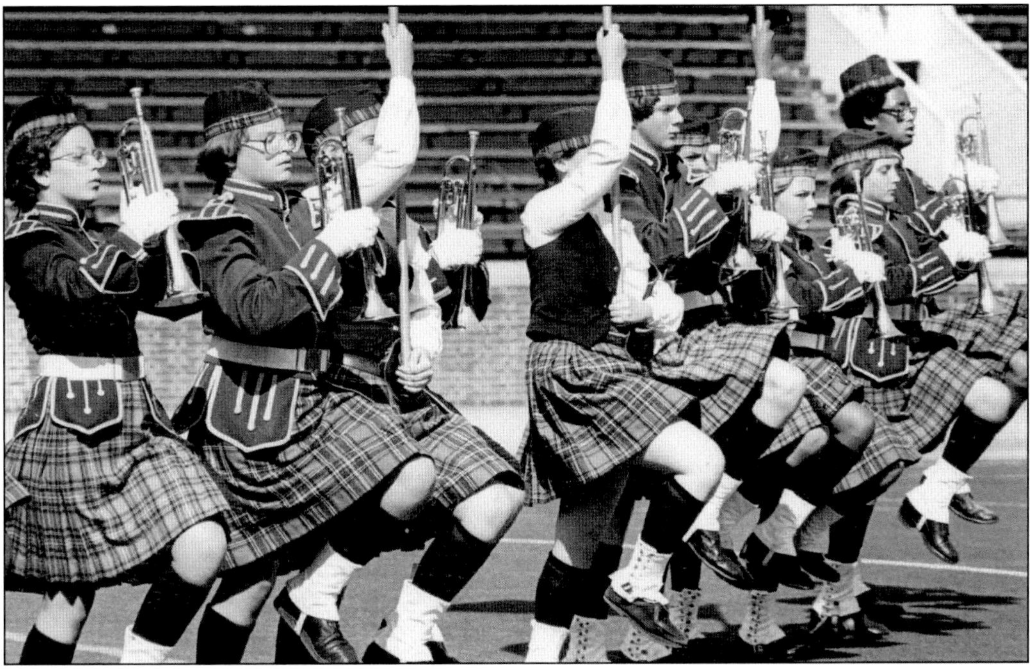

Most teenagers would never be caught dead wearing a kilt. However, it was a regular part of the uniform for members of the Black Watch, a Scottish-inspired drum and bugle corps. This performance occurred in 1976. (Courtesy Burlington County Times.)

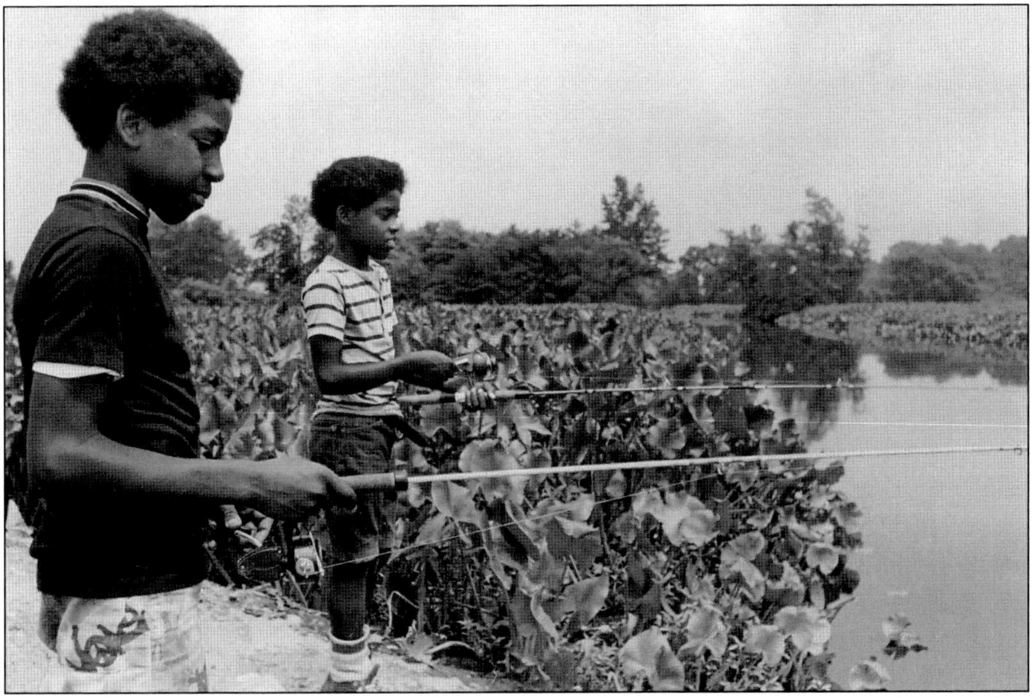

Two children take a shot at catching fish in Mill Creek in August 1972. Willingboro anglers had several places to fish, including Olympia Lakes, Crystal Lake, and the Rancocas Creek. (Courtesy Burlington County Times.)

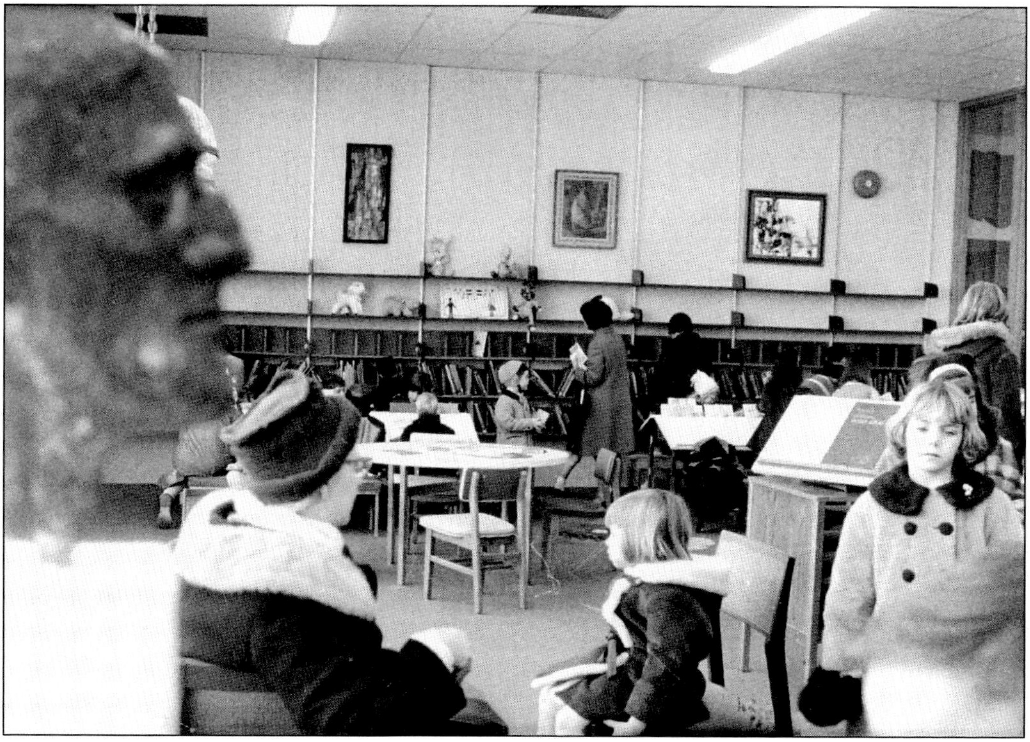

The new residents of Levittown were eager to bring culture into their new community. The Levittown Civic Association established a public library in 1959. The library had its first home in a church and then moved into the old municipal building. After the municipal building burned in 1964, the library found temporary quarters in the Willingboro Plaza. In 1968, the year of this photograph, the library moved into the new municipal building. (Courtesy Burlington County Times.)

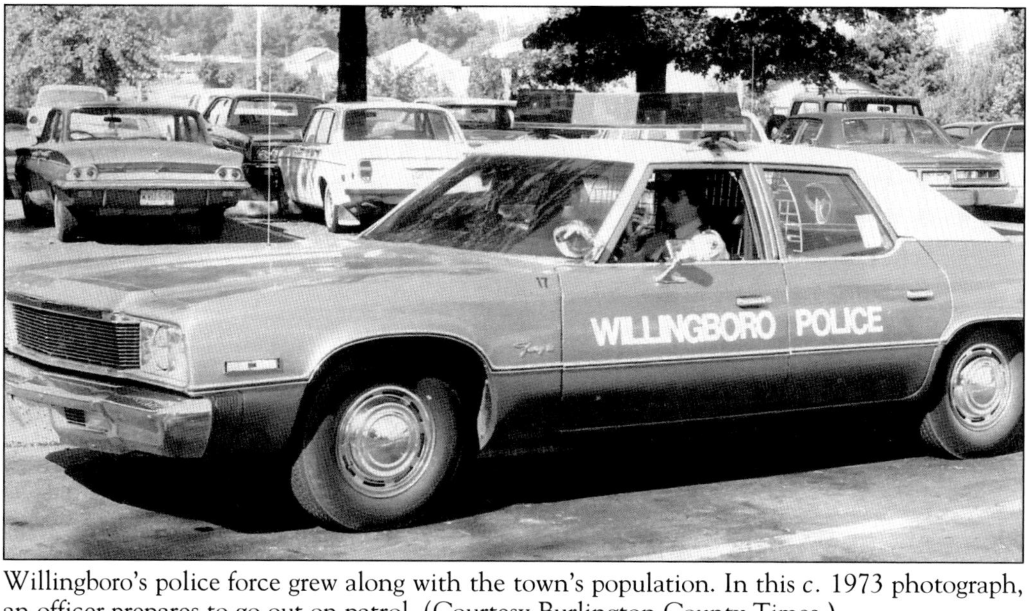

Willingboro's police force grew along with the town's population. In this c. 1973 photograph, an officer prepares to go out on patrol. (Courtesy Burlington County Times.)

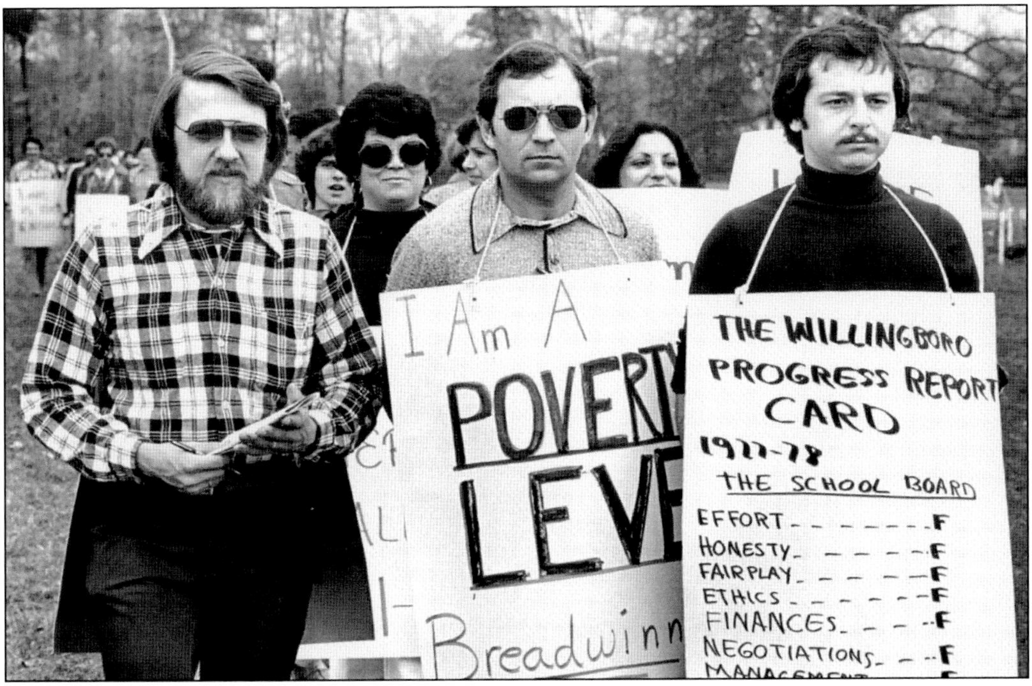

In 1977, the Willingboro Board of Education and the teachers union reached an impasse in contract talks. State mediators were unable to help, and the union went out on strike for the first time in Willingboro history. The walkout lasted 42 days and tore apart many relationships among teachers and residents. (Courtesy Burlington County Times.)

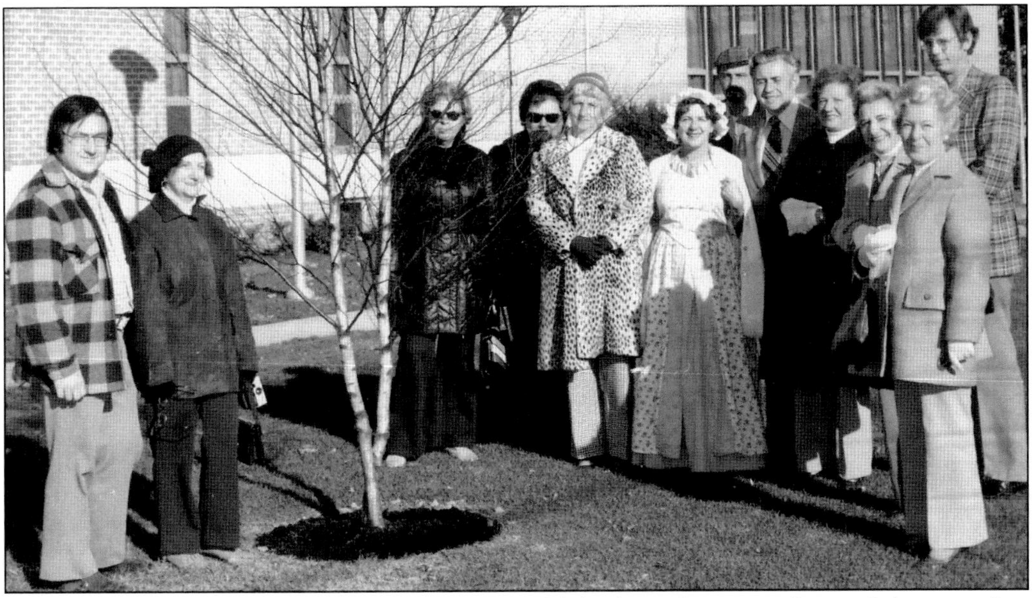

In November 1975, the Willingboro Women's Club planted trees in front of the township municipal building on Salem Road. From left to right are William Kearns Jr. (councilman), Ruth Lang, Emily Myhr, Henrietta Rinderer, Dorothy Daggett, Edith Cain, William McGrath (councilman), Paul Krane (mayor), Helen Keown, Ellen Decker, Ethel Palmer, and John Tegley (township manager). (Courtesy Willingboro Township Manager's Office.)

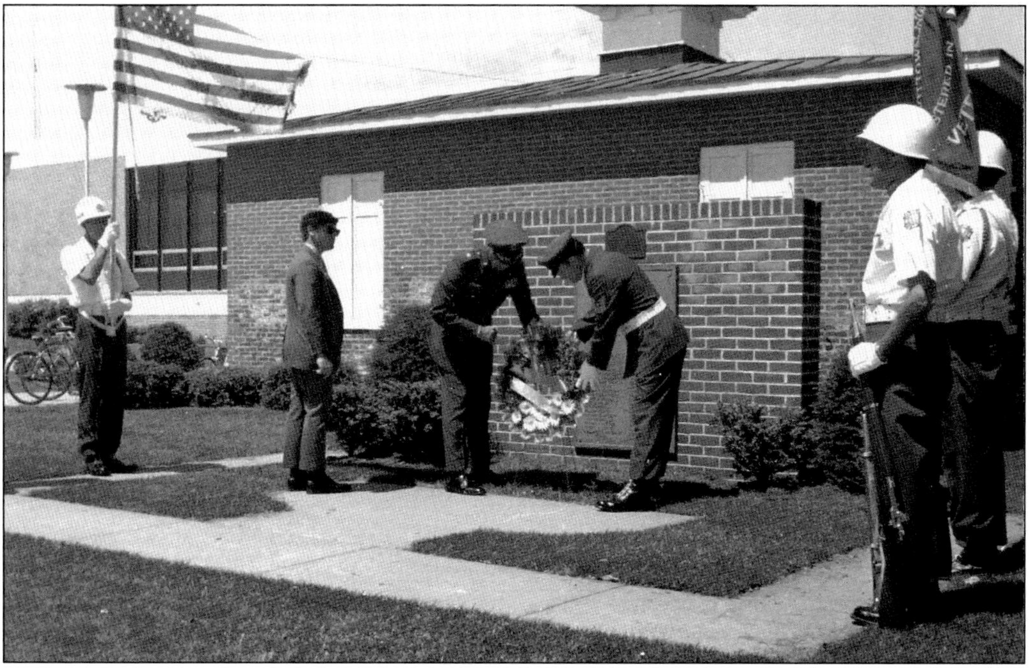

In the township's early Levitt years, nearly half of the new residents were military personnel from nearby Fort Dix and McGuire Air Force Base. With such a significant military presence, ceremonies such as the placing of a wreath in front of the municipal building on Memorial Day 1972 held great significance in the community. (Courtesy Willingboro Township Manager's Office.)

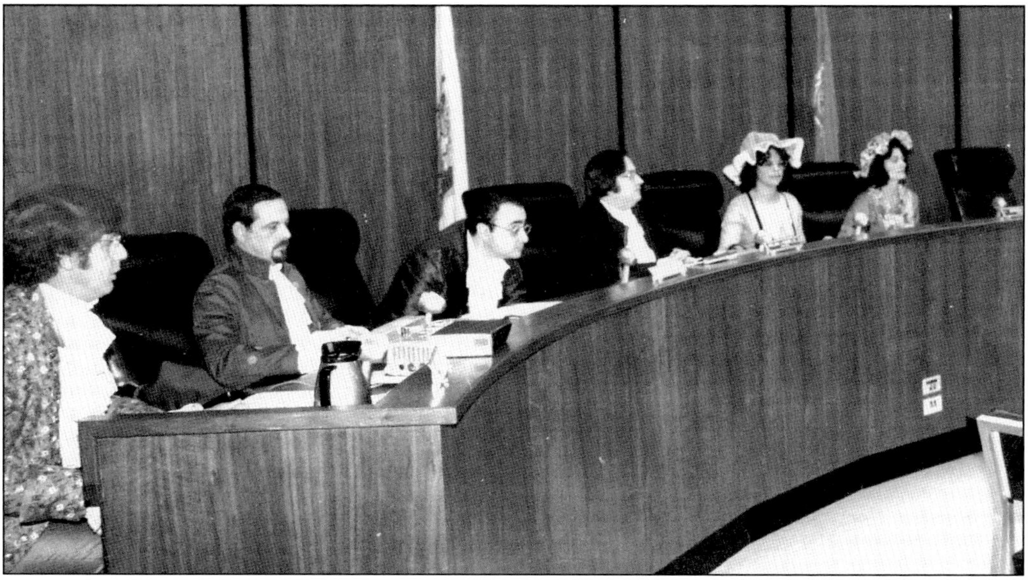

The Willingboro Township Council welcomed the nation's bicentennial by dressing up in Colonial-era costumes for its January 1976 reorganization meeting. From left to right are John Tegley, township manager; William McGrath, mayor; Myron H. Gottlieb, solicitor; William Kearns Jr., councilman; Lenore Stern, township clerk; and Barbara Kalik, councilwoman. (Courtesy Willingboro Township Manager's Office.)

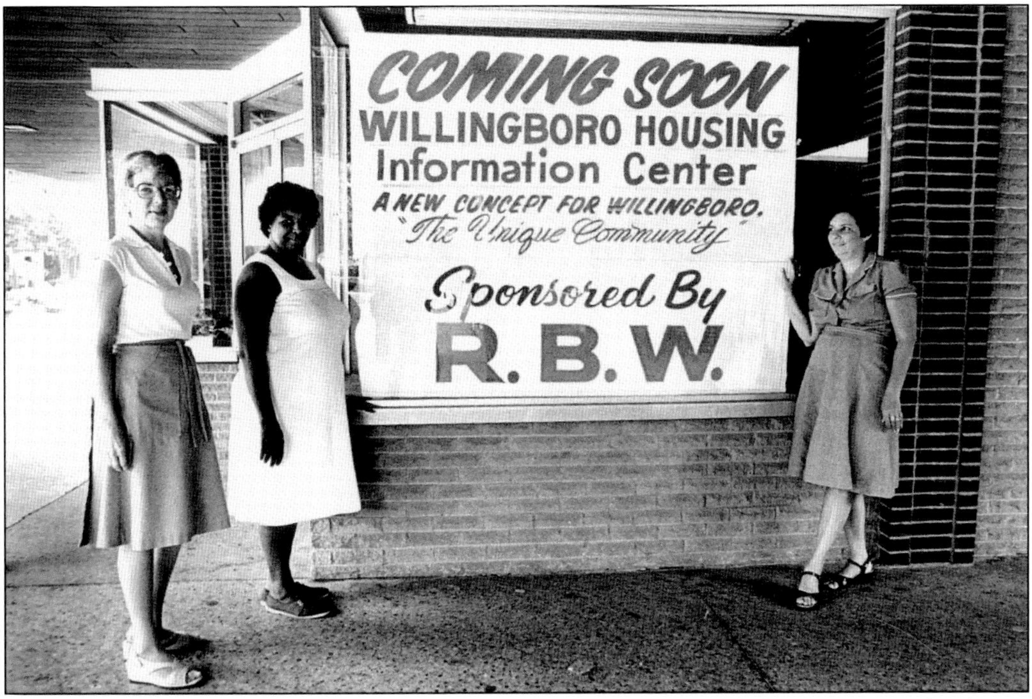

Residents for a Better Willingboro was a civic group that voiced the concerns of ordinary individuals to the township council. From left to right are members Clara Mitchell, Barbara Brown, and Carol Gold, posing in front of the housing information center at the Willingboro Plaza in 1980. (Courtesy Burlington County Times.)

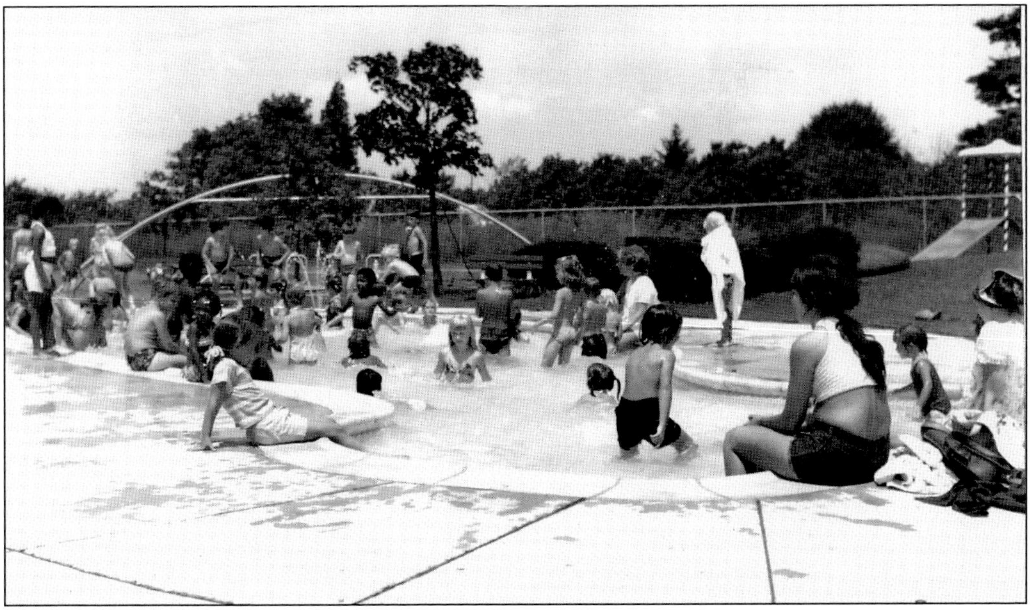

Little ones who could not yet swim were still included in summer fun. Each school also had a smaller wading pool, as shown in this picture from 1975. For anyone who did not like the water at all, there was always the playground. (Courtesy Willingboro Township Manager's Office.)

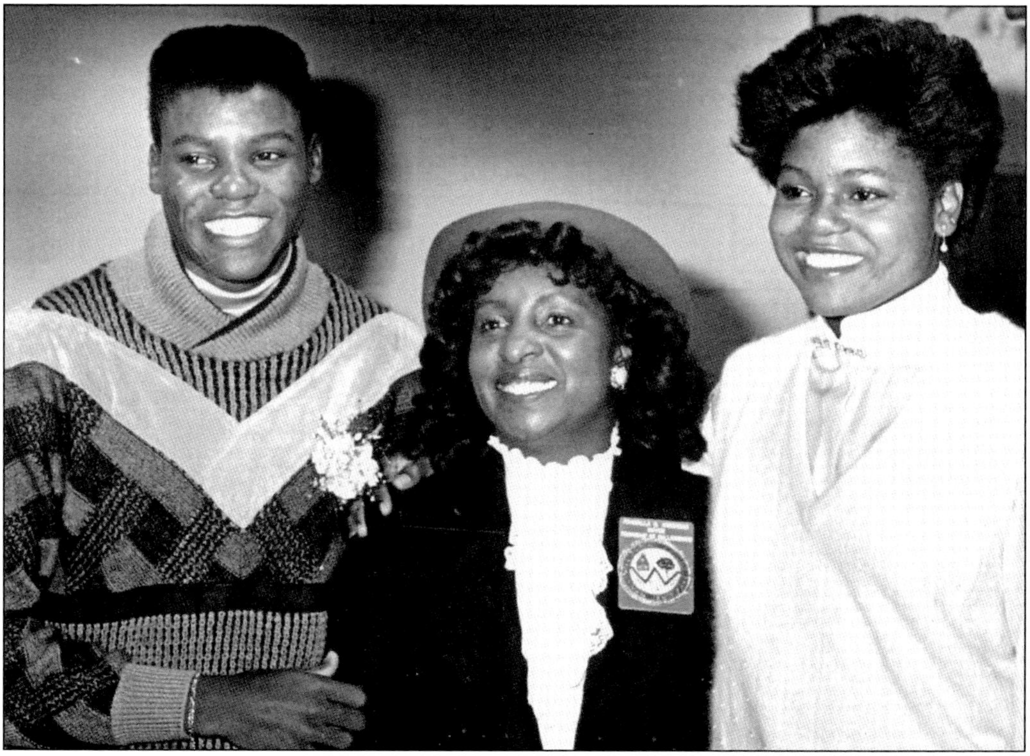

By far, Willingboro's most famous native son is Carl Lewis. A graduate of Willingboro High School, Lewis won eight Olympic gold medals in track and field and is considered one of the top athletes of the 20th century. He poses in this 1984 photograph with his sister Carol (right), also an Olympian, and Mayor Priscilla Anderson. (Courtesy Burlington County Times.)

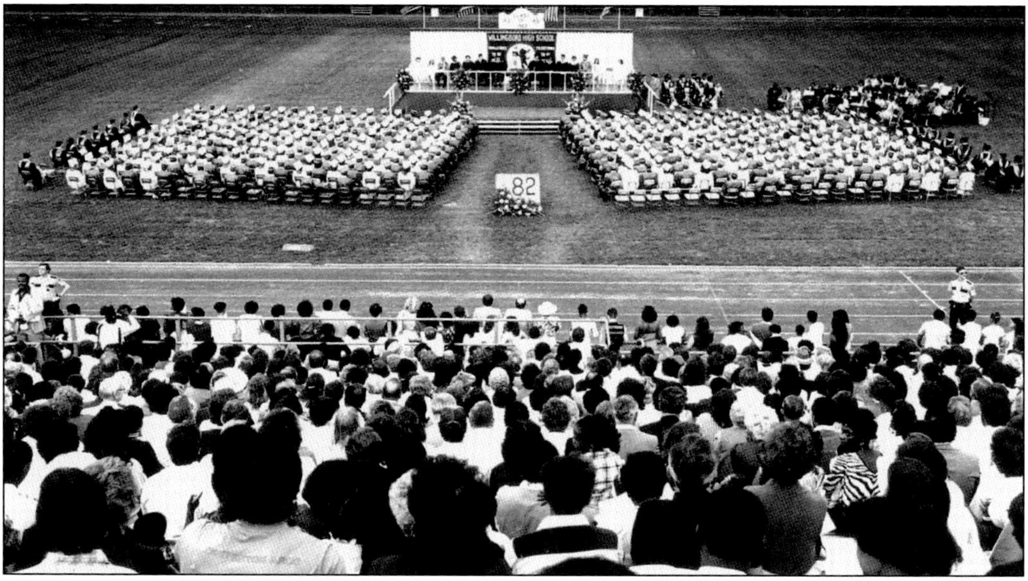

Willingboro High School opened in 1975, helping to relieve overcrowding at John F. Kennedy High School. The latter school eventually closed. In this photograph from June 1982, thousands of people watch the Willingboro High seniors graduate. (Courtesy Burlington County Times.)

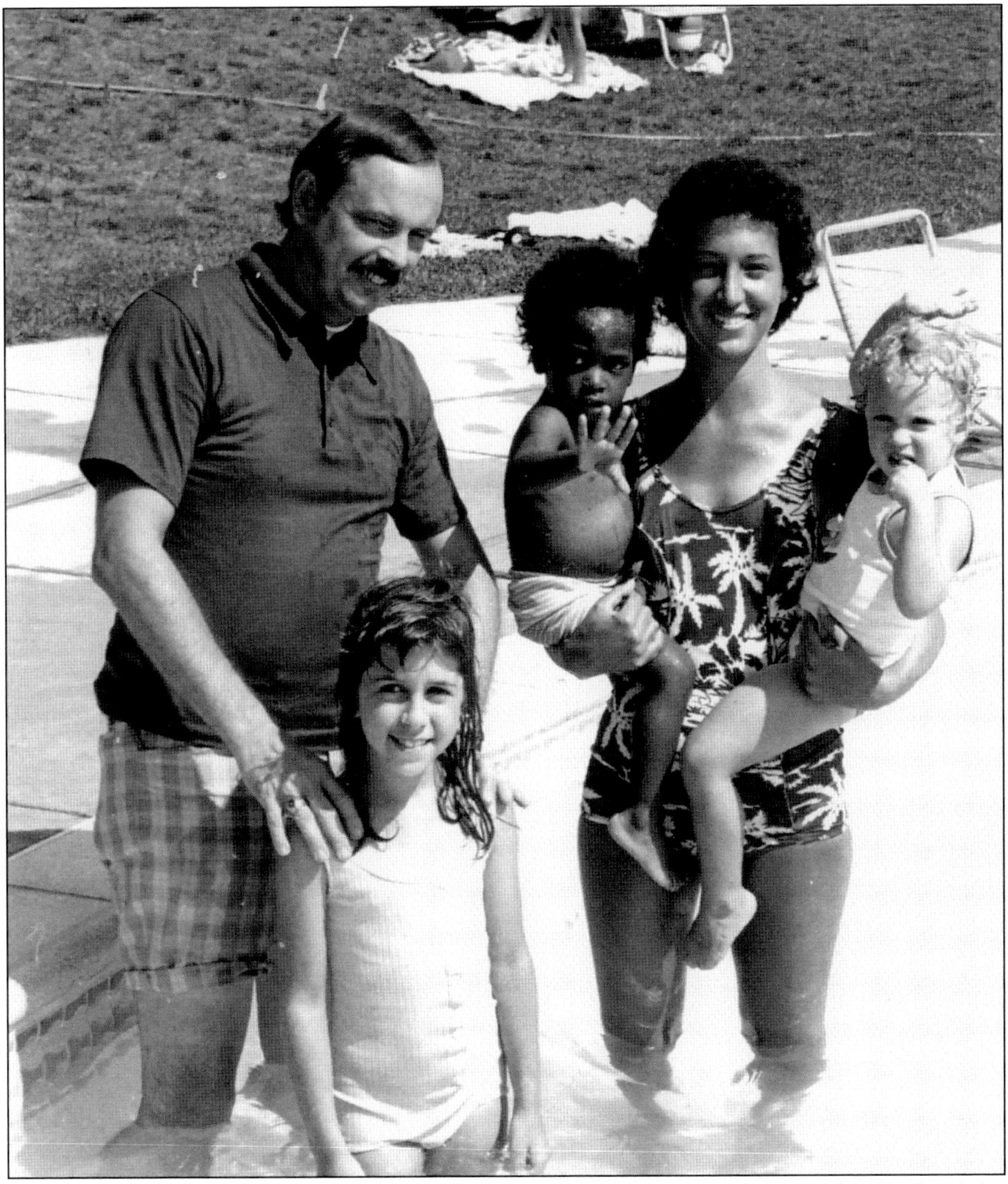

Willingboro's pools were the place to cool off during the hot summer months. Each of the township's 10 elementary schools had a pool, making relaxation within walking distance of nearly every resident. In this 1976 photograph, Mayor William McGrath "crowned" this little girl a bathing beauty winner. (Courtesy Willingboro Township Manager's Office.)

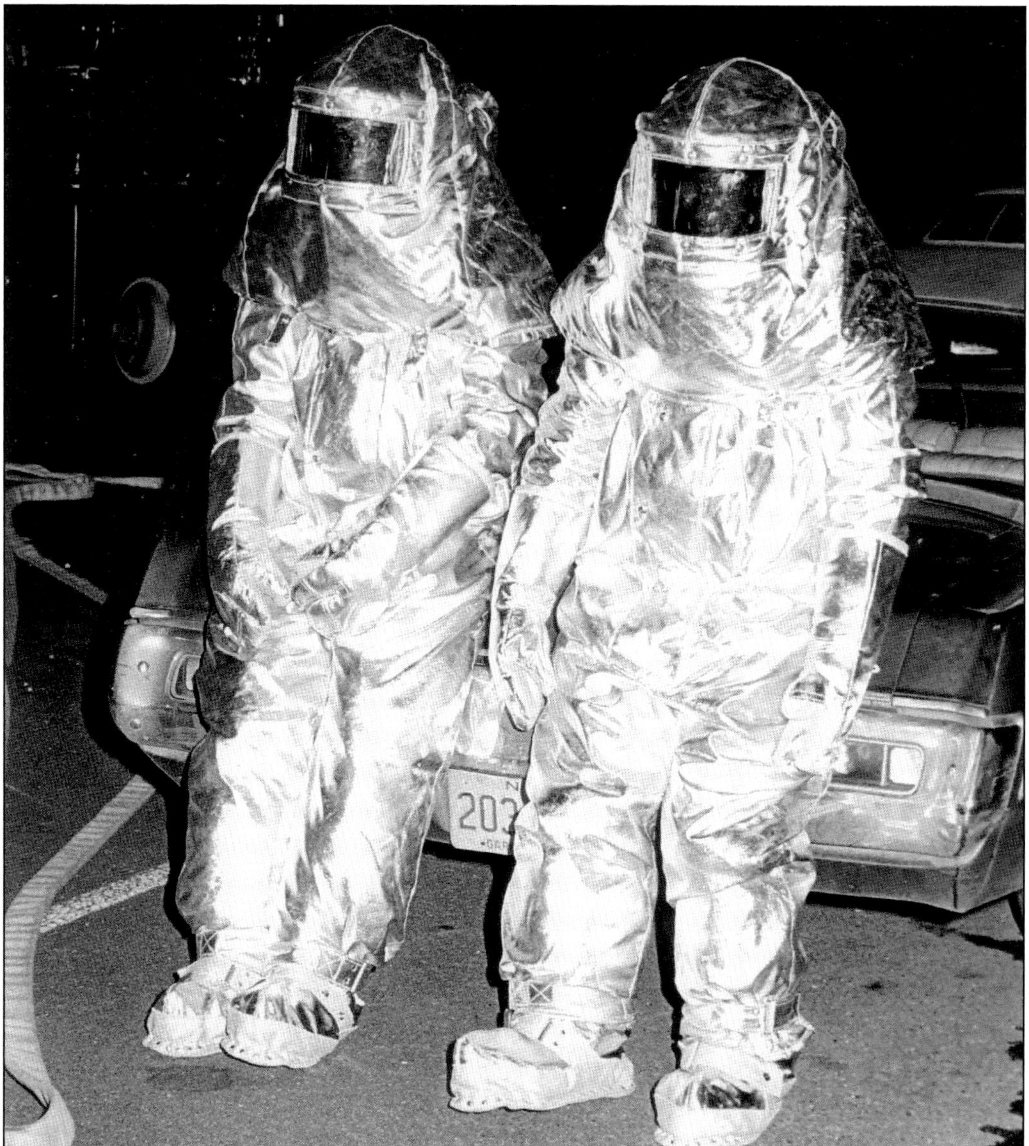

These two men are not astronauts or alien invaders. They are actually Willingboro firefighters wearing protective suits during a visit by New Jersey Gov. Brendan Byrne to the township in May 1977. (Courtesy Burlington County Times.)

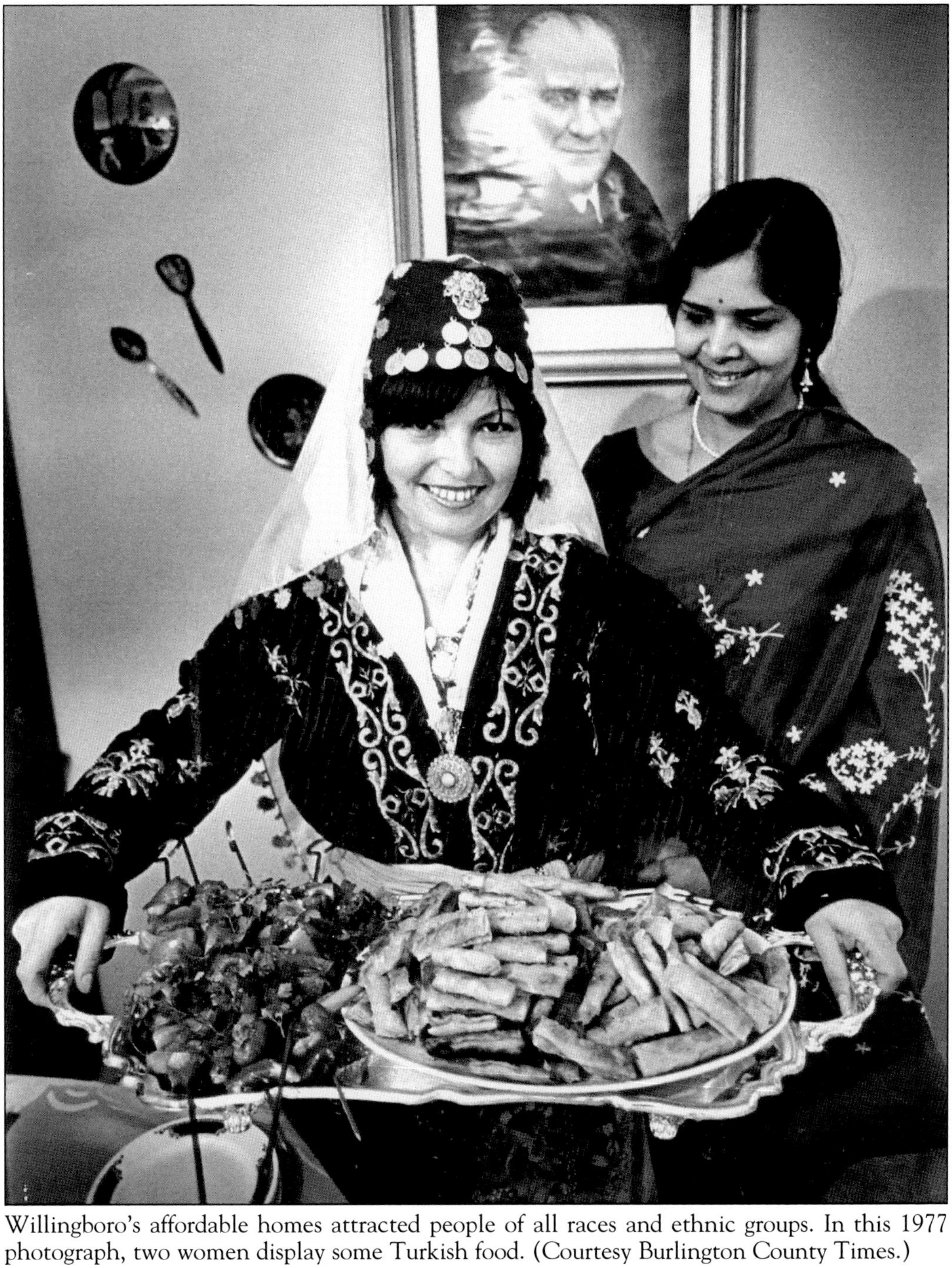

Willingboro's affordable homes attracted people of all races and ethnic groups. In this 1977 photograph, two women display some Turkish food. (Courtesy Burlington County Times.)

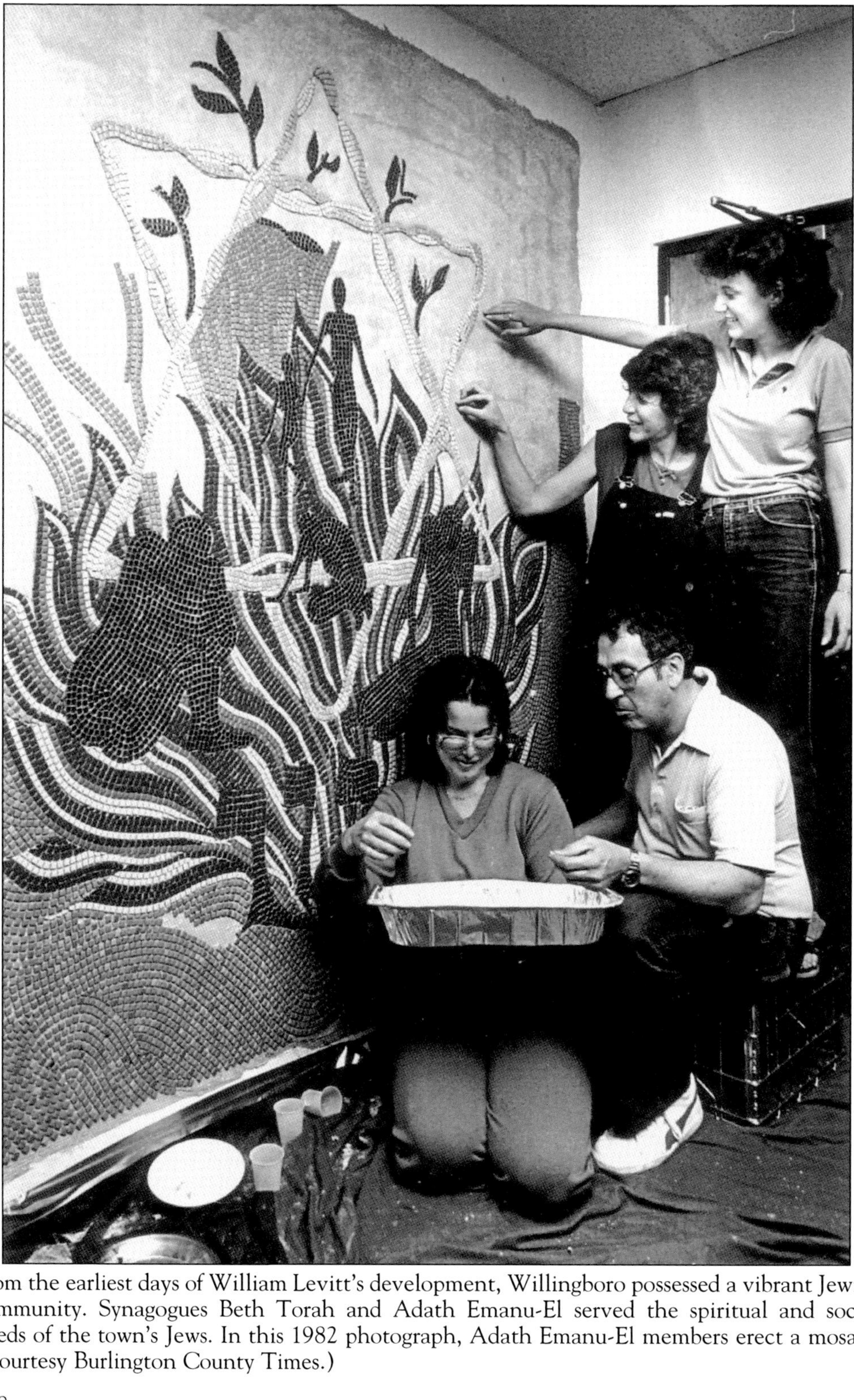

From the earliest days of William Levitt's development, Willingboro possessed a vibrant Jewish community. Synagogues Beth Torah and Adath Emanu-El served the spiritual and social needs of the town's Jews. In this 1982 photograph, Adath Emanu-El members erect a mosaic. (Courtesy Burlington County Times.)

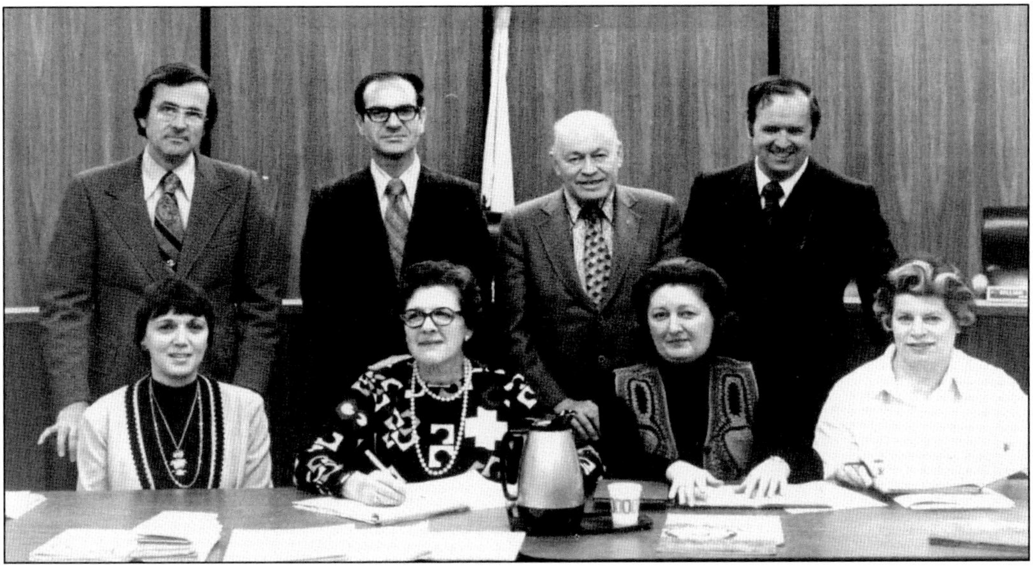

Like other towns, Willingboro planned events to celebrate the nation's bicentennial. Pictured in 1976, from left to right, are members of the township's Bicentennial and Heritage Commission: (front row) Jean Dunn, Edith Cain, Holly Olivares, and Eileen Foy; (back row) Hal Reeves, Murray Goldman, Jack Adams, and Edward A. Kelly Jr. (Courtesy Willingboro Township Manager's Office.)

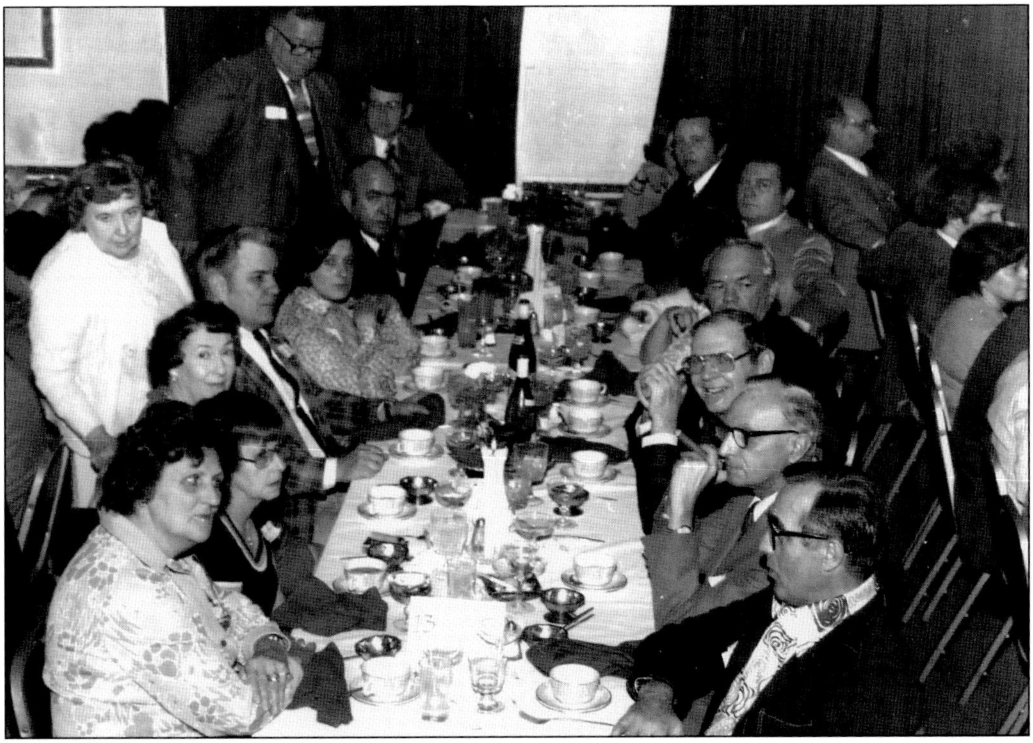

Members of Willingboro's volunteer emergency squad enjoy cups of coffee in 1978. The township held annual dinners for people who served as volunteers on the emergency squad, fire department, and other advisory boards. (Courtesy Willingboro Township Manager's Office.)

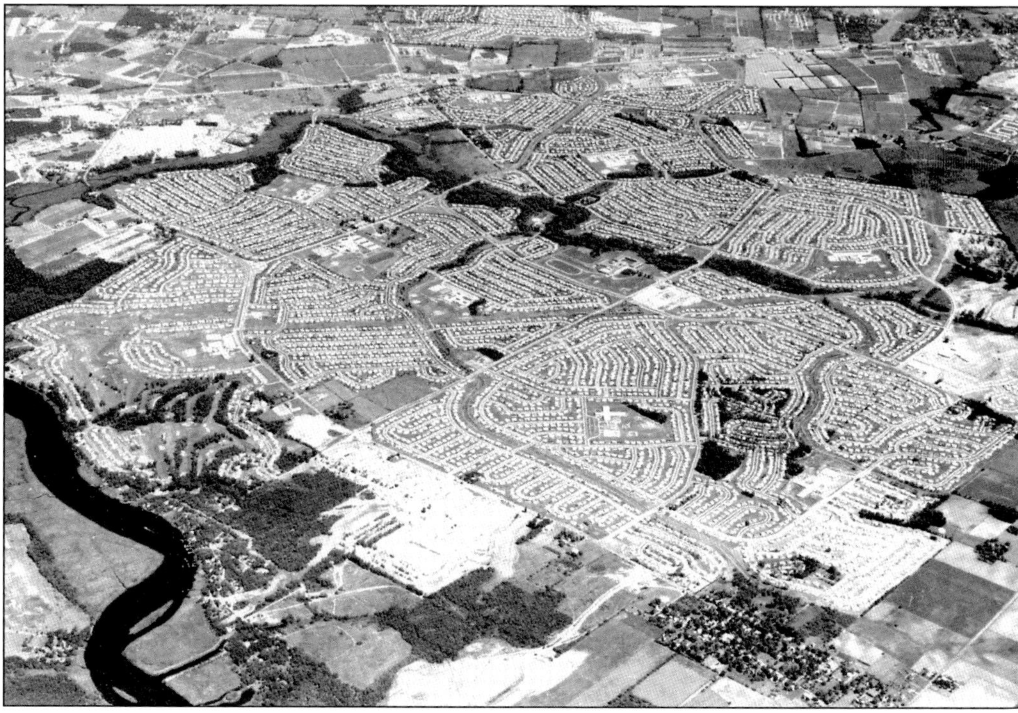

In this aerial photograph from 1973, it is easy to see Levitt and Sons' development plans. Each neighborhood, called a park, contained a school and a swimming pool. Curving streets, each with the same first letter of the name of the park, emptied onto broad, well-landscaped parkways. (Courtesy Burlington County Times.)

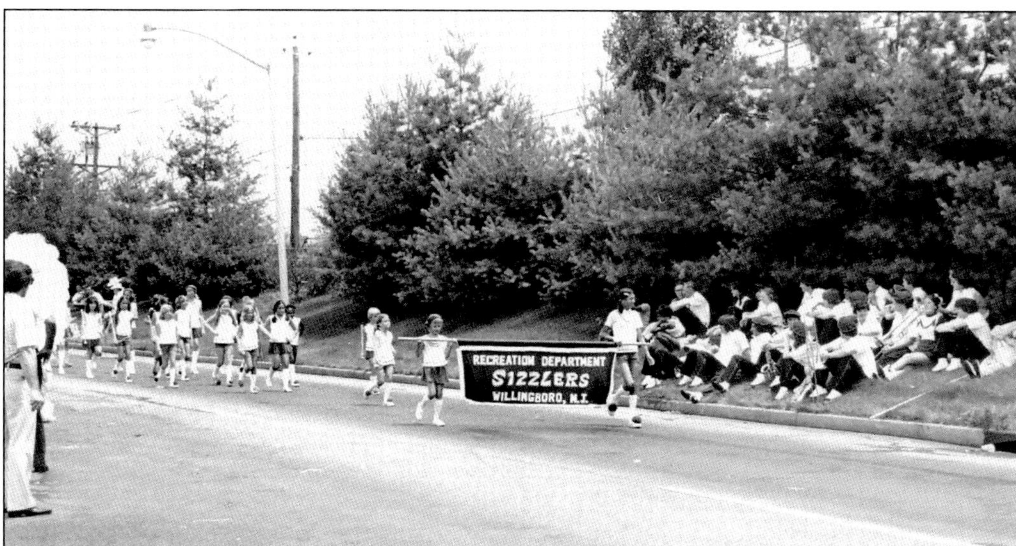

Members of the Sizzlers, a marching group sponsored by the recreation department, twirl their batons in the township's 1976 Fourth of July parade. (Courtesy Willingboro Township Manager's Office.)

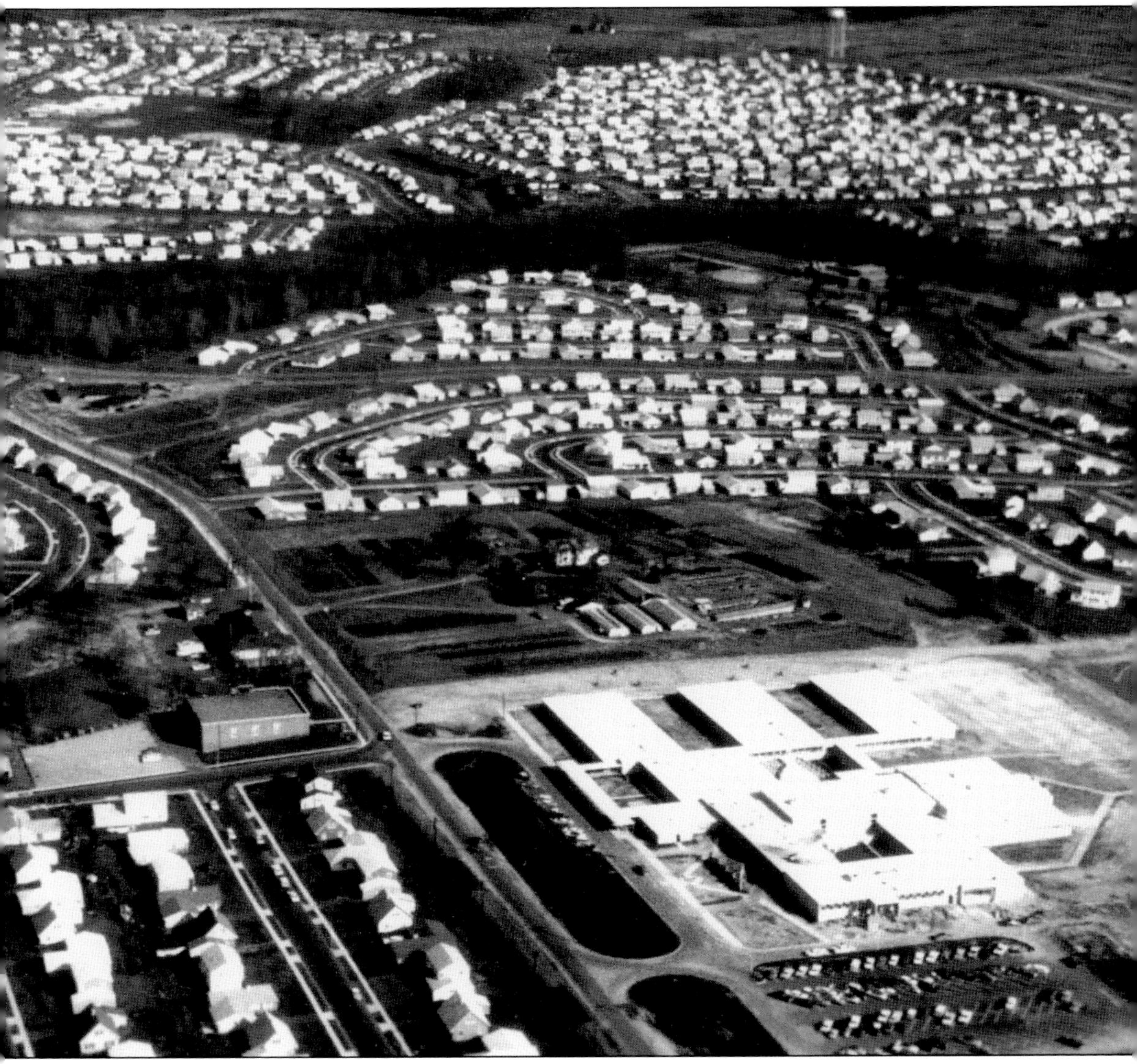

Willingboro High School, in the foreground, was built in 1975. Between 1958 and 1971, 13 schools were built here, and for a while Levitt and Sons both donated the schools and financially subsidized the district's operations. (Courtesy Willingboro Public Library.)

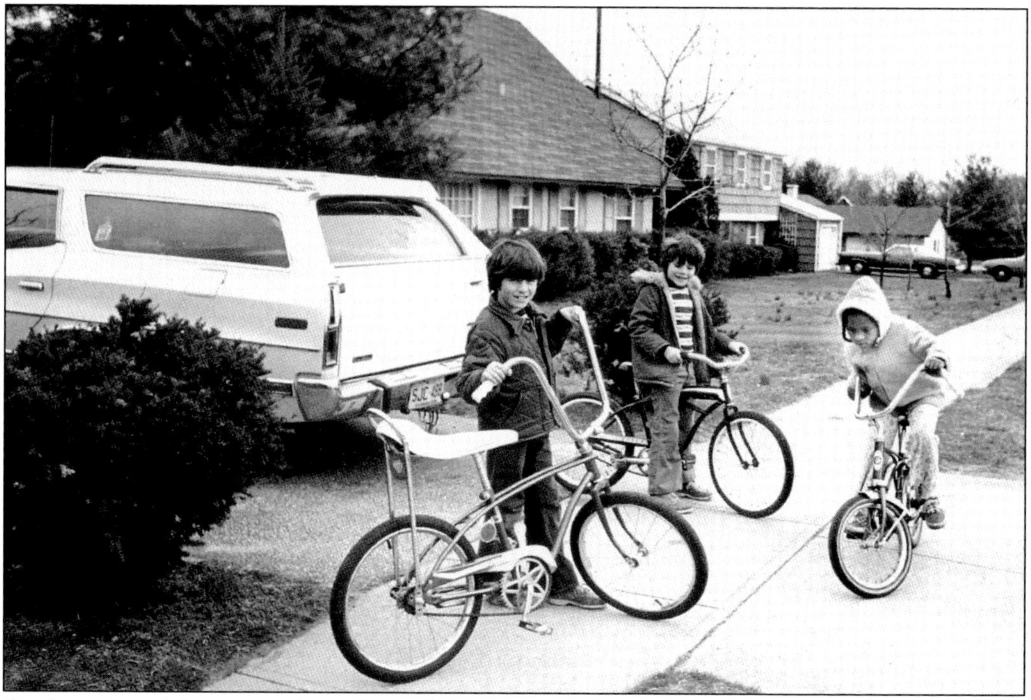

Cool weather did not stop these three children from riding bicycles around their neighborhood in April 1976. (Courtesy Burlington County Times.)

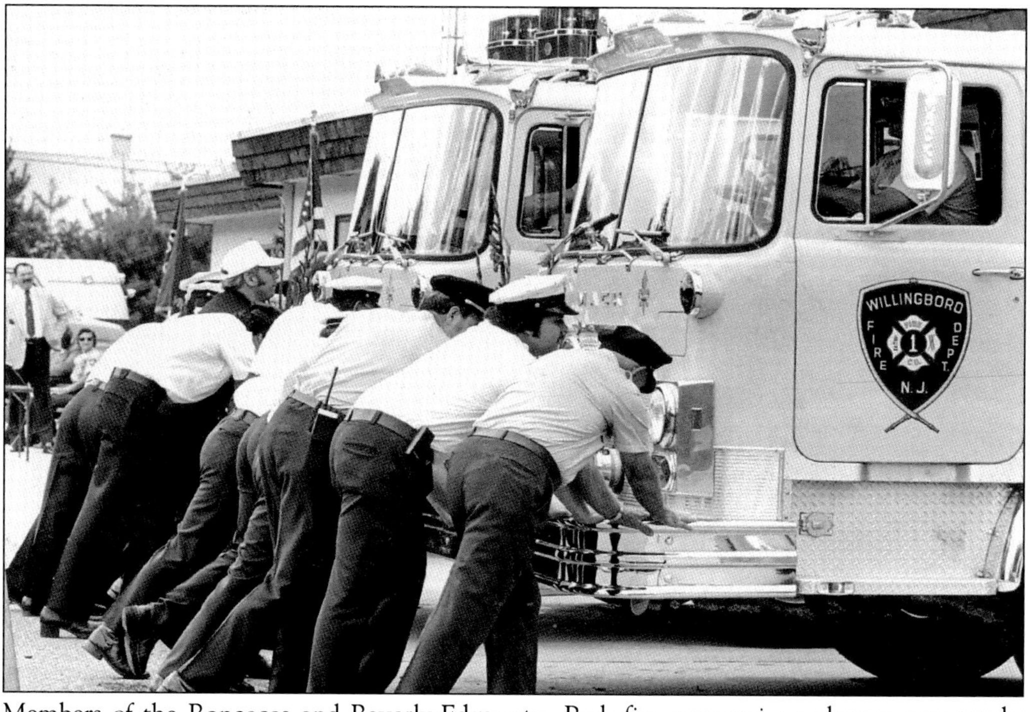

Members of the Rancocas and Beverly-Edgewater Park fire companies welcome new trucks into Willingboro's firefighting corps by pushing them into the firehouse in 1978. (Courtesy Burlington County Times.)

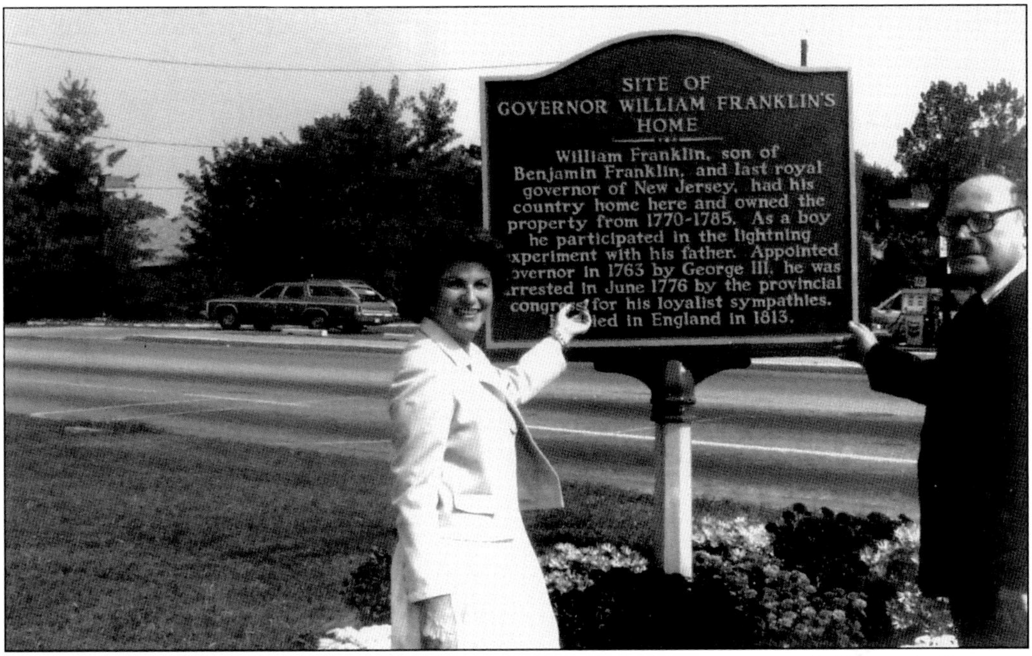

In November 1983, Catherine Costa, New Jersey assemblywoman, and Bernard Sharrow, Willingboro Historical Society chairman, dedicate a sign at the intersection of Beverly-Rancocas Road and John F. Kennedy Way, marking the site of William Franklin's home. (Courtesy Burlington County Times.)

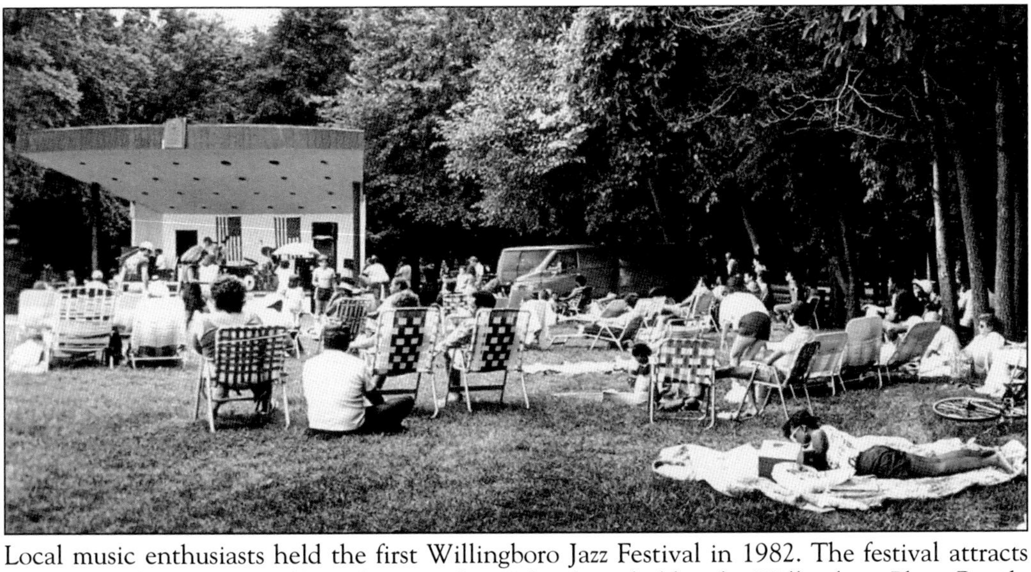

Local music enthusiasts held the first Willingboro Jazz Festival in 1982. The festival attracts thousands of people annually to the township. It has been held at the Willingboro Plaza, Broido Park (as here in 1986), and Mill Creek Park. (Courtesy Burlington County Times.)

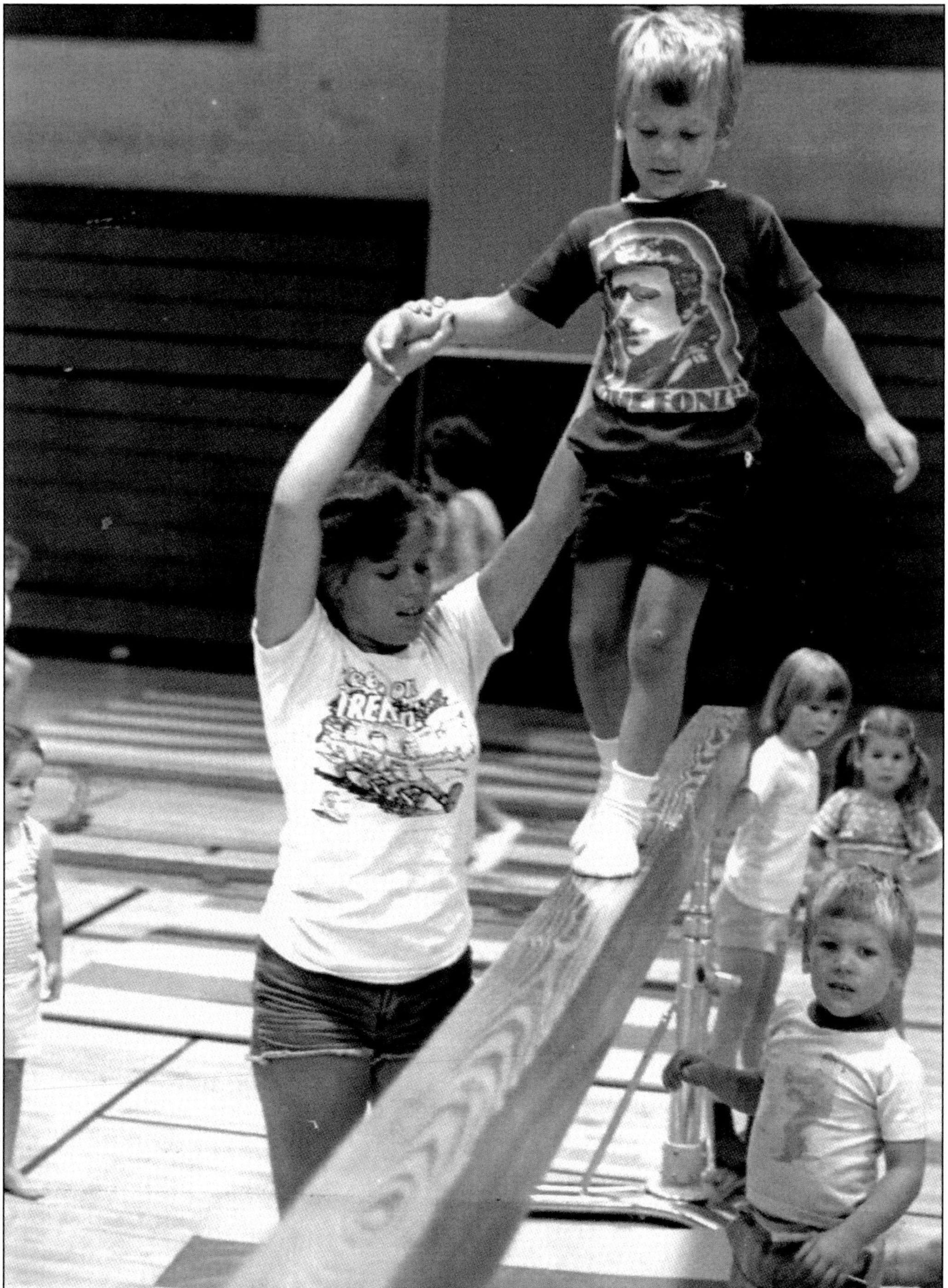

A preschool-aged boy learns how to walk on the balance beam at a session run by the recreation department in 1976. At its height during the 1970s, Willingboro had 1,100 children in its gymnastics program, one of the largest in the country. (Courtesy Willingboro Township Manager's Office.)

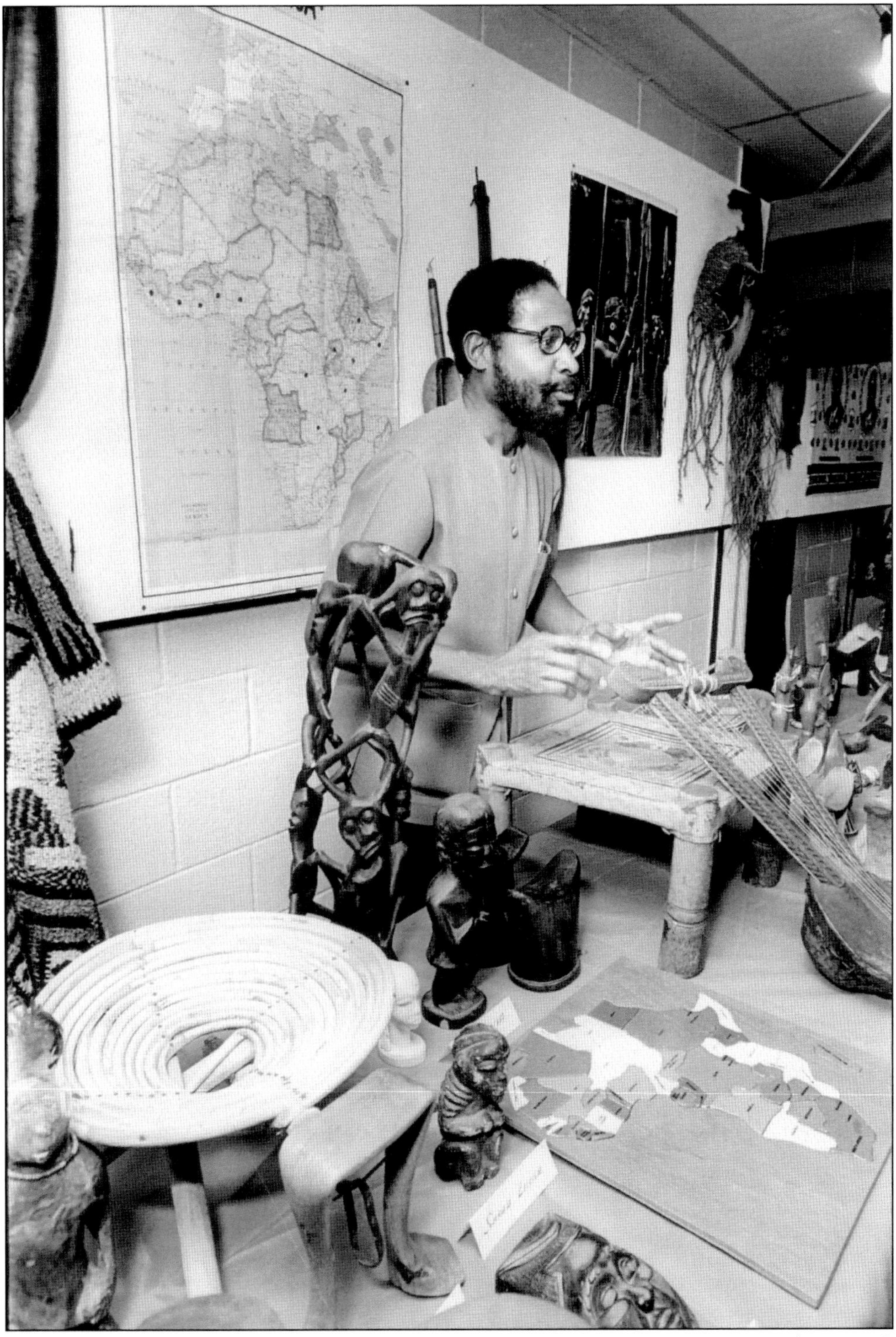

Over the years, Willingboro grew into an extremely diverse community. In 1971, the township initiated an annual international festival. In this 1978 photograph, local historian Giles Wright displays artifacts from Africa. (Courtesy Burlington County Times.)

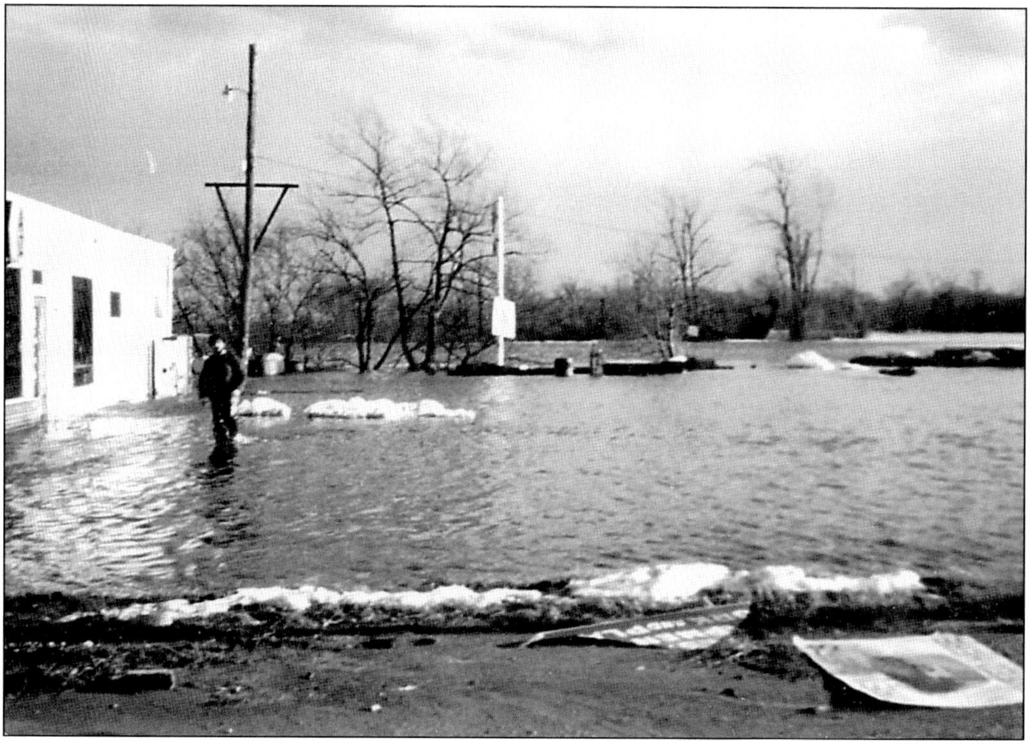

Heavy precipitation caused the Rancocas Creek to overflow its banks and flood part of the town in March 1978. This man stands in front of a flooded business along Route 130. (Courtesy Dave Retzko.)

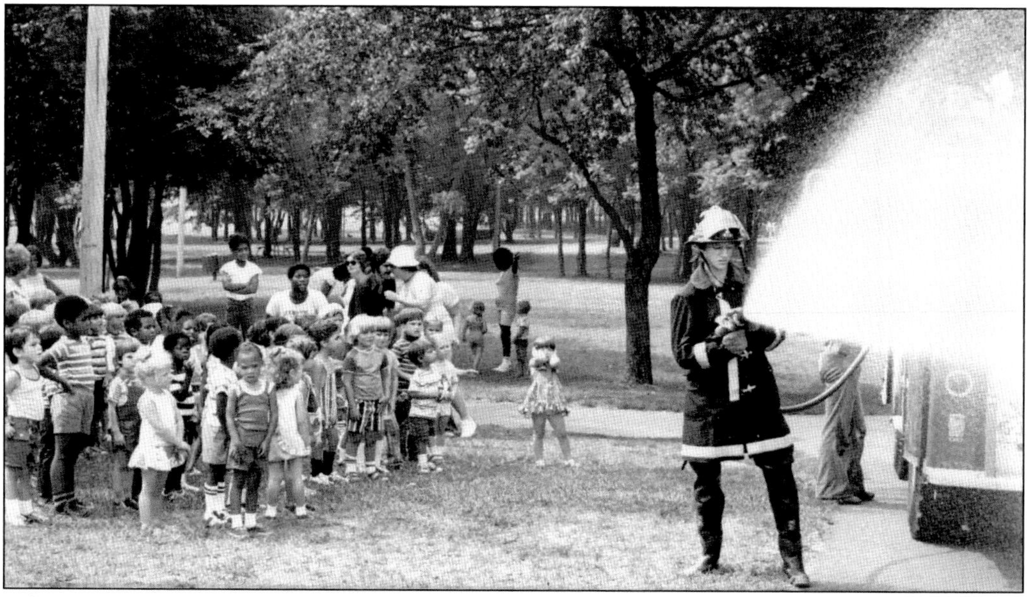

When not putting out actual blazes, the Willingboro Fire Department showed off its equipment and spread messages about fire safety. In this photograph from 1978, a fireman sprays a hose for a group of preschoolers at a playground. (Courtesy Willingboro Township Manager's Office.)

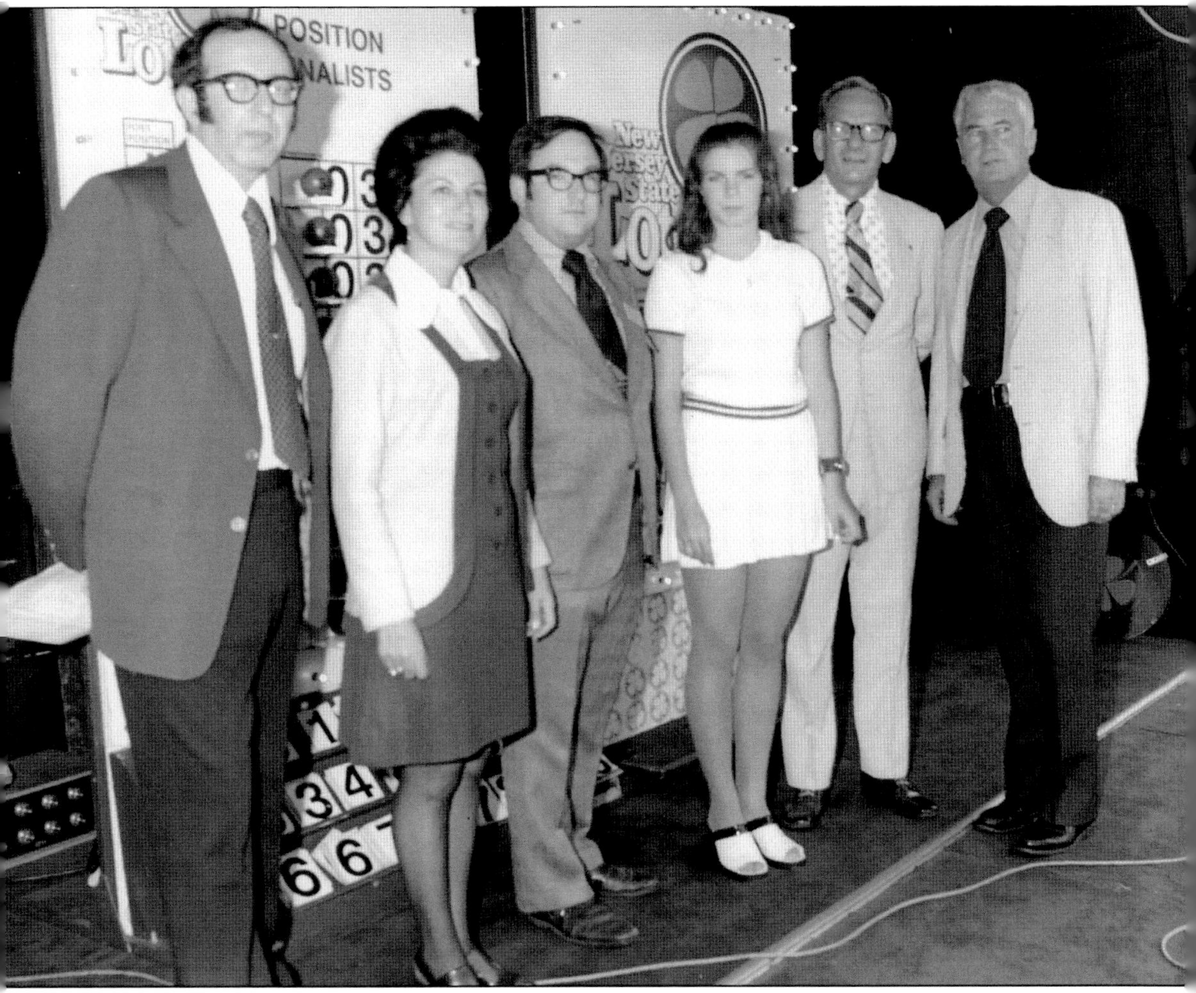

William Levitt took a gamble transforming Willingboro's farms into tracts of homes. The New Jersey lottery took no such chance in August 1973, when it enlisted township officials, business leaders, and residents to draw the winning numbers at the Willingboro Plaza shopping center. (Courtesy Willingboro Township Manager's Office.)

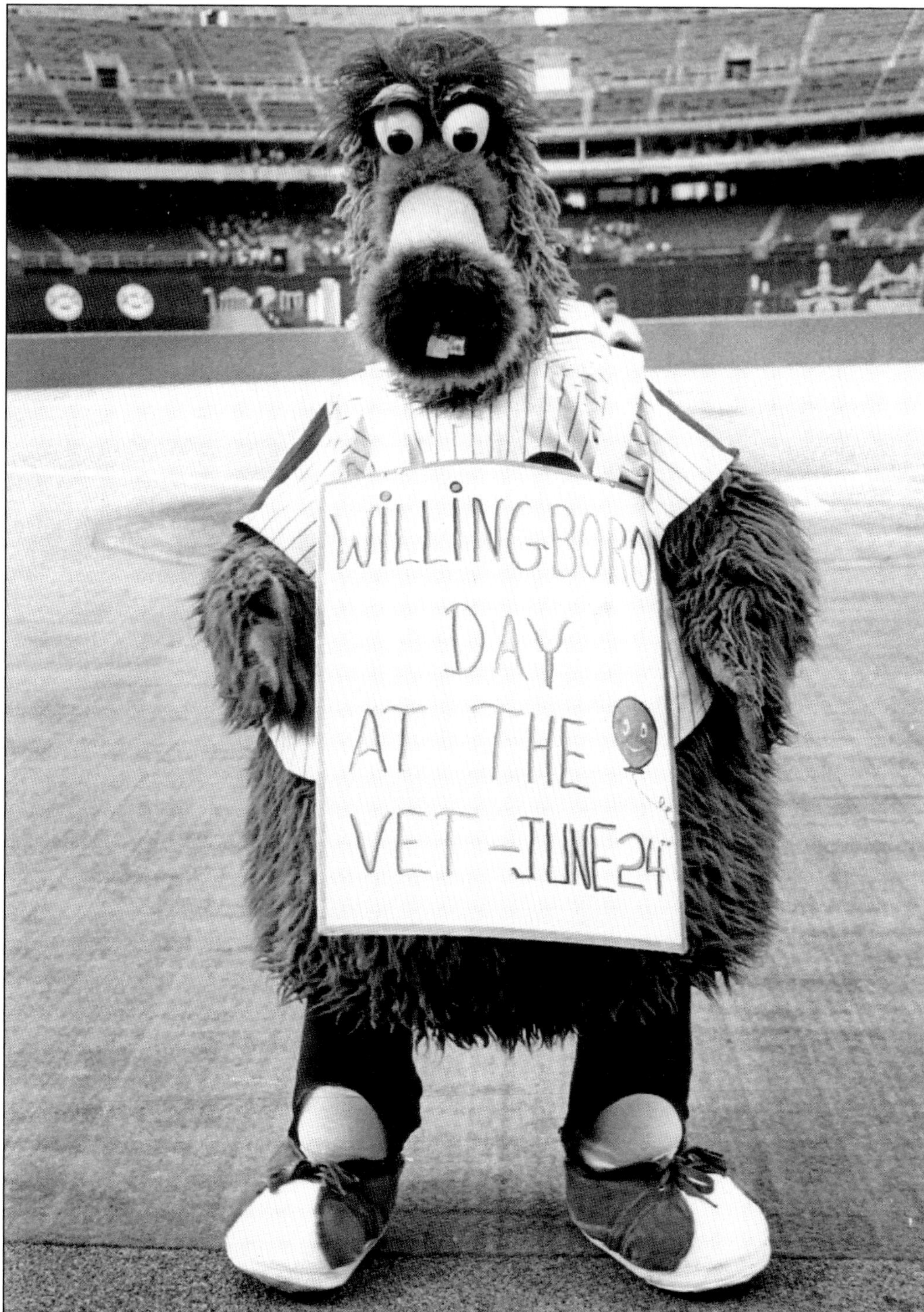

Every summer, the recreation department sponsored a trip to Veterans Stadium in Philadelphia to see a Phillies baseball game. The people who went to the games said these were times to view all the town's movers and shakers. (Courtesy Willingboro Township Manager's Office.)